Proactive Personality and Behavior for Individual and Organizational Productivity

NEW HORIZONS IN MANAGEMENT

Series Editor: Cary L. Cooper, CBE, *Distinguished Professor of Organizational Psychology and Health, Lancaster University, UK*

This important series makes a significant contribution to the development of management thought. This field has expanded dramatically in recent years and the series provides an invaluable forum for the publication of high quality work in management science, human resource management, organizational behaviour, marketing, management information systems, operations management, business ethics, strategic management and international management.

The main emphasis of the series is on the development and application of new original ideas. International in its approach, it will include some of the best theoretical and empirical work from both well-established researchers and the new generation of scholars.

Titles in the series include:

Proactive Personality and Behavior for Individual and Organizational Productivity

Andrew J. DuBrin

Professor Emeritus of Management, Saunders College of Business, Rochester Institute of Technology, USA

NEW HORIZONS IN MANAGEMENT

Edward Elgar
Cheltenham, UK • Northampton, MA, USA

Published by
Edward Elgar Publishing Limited
The Lypiatts
15 Lansdown Road
Cheltenham
Glos GL50 2JA
UK

Edward Elgar Publishing, Inc.
William Pratt House
9 Dewey Court
Northampton
Massachusetts 01060
USA

A catalogue record for this book
is available from the British Library

Library of Congress Control Number: 2013946817

This book is available electronically in the ElgarOnline.com
Business Subject Collection, E-ISBN 978 1 78254 935 2

ISBN 978 1 78254 934 5

Typeset by Servis Filmsetting Ltd, Stockport, Cheshire
Printed and bound in Great Britain by T.J. International Ltd, Padstow

Contents

Preface

A highly valued employee at any level in the modern workplace is one who goes beyond accomplishing his or her assigned responsibilities. Performance of this nature is often driven by a proactive personality which in turn leads to proactive behavior. Workers with a proactive personality are inclined to engage in proactive behaviors such as looking for opportunities to improve work processes, going beyond the job description, taking the initiative to engage in job-relevant learning, to prevent problems from happening, and going out to meet customers. The proactive worker is likely to have high job performance and at the same time contribute to organizational productivity.

PURPOSE AND GOALS OF THE BOOK

Although extensive research has been conducted about employee proactive behavior, and thousands of popular articles have been written on the topic, a book on this subject has not yet been published. The purpose of the book is to consolidate information about proactivity in the workplace that could be applied toward helping workers themselves become more proactive, and managers within organizations understand effective ways of fostering proactive thinking and behavior. The book provides a detailed description of how proactive behavior contributes to important aspects of organizations that contribute to their well-being and success. Proactivity underlies important aspects of organization success such as opportunity recognition, entrepreneurial thinking, business strategy and planning, problem prevention, and talent management.

Although much of the book is based on empirical research, it is written in a style accessible to people who are not researchers in the field of proactive personality and behavior. The book is designed to be of value to scholars, individuals within organizations, managers and leaders, and practitioners such as human resource professionals, industrial and organizational psychologists, and organization development specialists. Another audience for the book is students in organizational behavior, organizational psychology, and organizational and industrial psychology.

The book should appeal to practitioners and policy makers who seek information in a more scholarly format than a strictly trade book.

STRUCTURE OF THE BOOK

To achieve its purposes and goals, the book is divided into 11 chapters. Chapter 1 describes the nature of the proactive personality, including nine representative characteristics of the proactive worker, such as a desire for control, and taking charge at work. A description is also provided of situational and environmental factors that influence the extent to which proactive behavior will emerge. Chapter 2 digs further into the proactive personality by describing many of the traits and behaviors associated with this type of personality, including traits within the Big Five personality factors. Other traits and behaviors linked to the proactive personality described in this chapter include organizational citizenship behavior, goal setting, and proactive motivation. Chapter 3 describes worker initiative as part of the proactive personality, in recognizing that many of the productivity benefits of proactivity stem from initiative taking. The chapter presents some of the evidence and opinion that initiative enhances job performance. The potential disadvantages of initiative taking are also described, such as being resented or working on the wrong projects as perceived by the manager.

Chapter 4 explores the vital topic of how the proactive personality is linked to job performance and satisfaction. Several studies are described that show a positive relationship between proactivity and objective, or measurable, job performance as well as with supervisory judgments of performance. A section of the chapter also describes how good performance can prompt a worker to take more initiative. Chapter 5 is a logical extension of Chapter 4 because it describes how the proactive personality is associated with career success. A key topic explored is that proactivity often prompts individuals to engage in behaviors that facilitate effective career management including finding a mentor or mentors, developing job- and career-relevant skills, and staying in good health. Proactivity is also needed to acquire power, establish a good reputation, and develop a personal brand.

Chapter 6 examines the highly important topic of how proactivity is linked to opportunity recognition and innovation. Another key topic in the chapter is how proactivity leads to seeing and seizing opportunities after searching for them. A related topic presented is how innovation has a strong component of proactive thinking and behavior. Chapter 7 describes how proactivity is part of the entrepreneurial behavior and personality. A key theme of the chapter is that successful entrepreneurs tend to be proactive, particularly with respect to being creative and adventuresome. An analysis is also presented of how entrepreneurial leadership is linked to the proactive personality, with such personality types having a strong desire to become entrepreneurial leaders in order to create value for the firm. Social entrepreneurship is described as another manifestation of proactivity.

Chapter 8 presents the complex topic of how business strategy is facilitated by proactivity. A key point of the chapter is that the business strategist must be proactive about the future and point the firm in the right direction. The chapter looks at several ways in which proactive thinking facilitates effective strategy, including finding hidden assets within the firm and expanding its boundaries. Chapter 9 deals with another domain in which proactive thinking and behavior is essential – problem prevention. Among the areas touched upon in which proactivity helps prevent problems are identifying danger signals, making use of Murphy's Law, visualization of potential problems, crisis prevention, and disaster planning.

Chapter 10 describes how the proactive personality and behavior can contribute to productive talent management. Among the talent management activities where proactivity can be helpful are employer branding, talent management planning, initiatives for cultural and demographic diversity, employee retention, and enhancing employee wellness. Chapter 11 presents the cornerstone topic of how leaders influence or enhance the possibility of proactivity among subordinates. Among the topics described are the influence of charismatic and transformational leadership, how leader charisma can trigger initiative taking, creating a climate for creativity, creating a climate for initiative, and the encouragement of honest whistleblowing.

To help the reader focus on the personal relevance of proactive thinking and behavior, all chapters contain a self-quiz or checklist closely related to the topic at hand. A sampling of the titles of these quizzes and checklists is as follows: "My Tendencies toward Being a Proactive Personality," "The Locus of Control Self-Quiz," "A Checklist of Behaviors and Attitudes Reflecting Initiative," and "The Resiliency Quiz." Each chapter contains a section labeled "Suggestions for Application" which helps the reader apply key concepts about proactive behavior personally, or in some cases aiding others to become more proactive. Each chapter also contains a summary to help the reader integrate the chapter material.

Acknowledgments

A project as complicated as a scholarly and professional book requires the cooperation of a group of dedicated and talented people. First, I thank the many proactive people I have met in both work and personal life whose behavior has given me an opportunity to observe the positive effects of proactive personality and behavior. Secondly, I thank the manuscript reviewers including Cary Cooper who saw the merit in this project.

Thank you also to the editorial and production staff at Edward Elgar who helped make this book possible: Alan Sturmer, Madhubanti Bhattacharyya, Diane Wardle and Victoria Nicols.

My family members continue to be a source of encouragement for my research and writing. My many thanks therefore to: Drew and Heidi, Douglas and Gizella, Melanie and Will, Drake, Rosie, Clare, Camila, Sofia, Eliana, Carson, Julian, and Owen. Thanks also to Stefanie for her presence in my life.

1. The nature of the proactive personality

In today's challenging workplace, high-level performance often means more than accomplishing one's assigned responsibilities. Such performance also means being proactive about what needs to be accomplished beyond the job description, including spotting unanticipated problems and opportunities. A few years ago, Dan Akerson, the CEO of General Motors, was eager to keep the company on a sustained path of success. During a meeting with workers he urged them to be leaders and to fix problems rather than wait to be told what to do. "You shouldn't stand around waiting for somebody to tell you where we're going to go," said Akerson. "We've got to get this company and the culture into the 21st century."[1]

Workers with a proactive personality are inclined to engage in proactive behaviors such as seeking feedback, going beyond the job description, taking the initiative to engage in job-relevant learning, and going out to meet customers.[2] A starting point in our study of the proactive personality and its implications for individual and organizational performance is for you to take the personality quiz presented in Figure 1.1. Taking the quiz will facilitate your thinking about the traits and behaviors frequently exhibited by the proactive person.

DEFINITIONS OF THE PROACTIVE PERSONALITY

As already implied, the definition of a proactive personality follows closely most dictionary definitions of proactive. Especially applicable here is the definition of proactive found in *The Oxford Pocket Dictionary of Current English.* As an adjective, proactive in reference to a person, policy, or action refers to "creating or controlling a situation by causing something to happen rather than responding to it after it has happened." The opposite to proactive is to be reactive, such as reacting to flood damage by cleaning up rather than being proactive and preventing flood damage through reinforced basement walls.

The pioneering definition of the proactive personality offered by

Indicate on a 1 to 5 scale the extent of your agreement with the statements below: agree strongly (AS), agree (A), neutral (N), disagree (D), disagree strongly (DS)

No.		AS	A	N	D	DS
1.	I plan carefully for things that might go wrong.	5	4	3	2	1
2.	I don't worry about problems until after they have taken place.	1	2	3	4	5
3.	If I see something that is broken, I fix it.	5	4	3	2	1
4.	I have been told several times that I am good at taking the initiative.	5	4	3	2	1
5.	I often let things like a computer password expire without making the necessary changes.	1	2	3	4	5
6.	When something important needs doing, I wait for somebody else to take the initiative.	1	2	3	4	5
7.	I think that having a home security system is a good investment in money.	5	4	3	2	1
8.	I look around for good opportunities that would help me in my career or personal life.	5	4	3	2	1
9.	I don't give much thought to the future because there is not much I can do about it.	1	2	3	4	5
10.	It is a good idea to start saving or investing for retirement at the beginning of your career.	5	4	3	2	1
11.	I begin projects and tasks by myself, without requiring prompting from somebody else.	5	4	3	2	1
12.	The old saying, "The early bird gets the worm" doesn't make much sense in real life.	1	2	3	4	5
13.	I let the future take care of itself without giving it much thought.	1	2	3	4	5
14.	I set my own goals rather than have others set them for me.	5	4	3	2	1
15.	I create a lot of change both in work and personal life.	5	4	3	2	1
16.	I have often asked for feedback on my job performance.	5	4	3	2	1
17.	If your job is going well it is a bad idea to explore new job possibilities from time to time.	1	2	3	4	5
18.	Once you have chosen a satisfactory career it is a bad idea to explore the possibilities of another career from time to time.	1	2	3	4	5
19.	I readily express my opinion about the effectiveness of a work process.	5	4	3	2	1
20.	It is best to stick carefully to your job description rather than create responsibilities for yourself.	1	2	3	4	5
21.	I regularly take positive steps to increase the chances that I will stay healthy and physically fit.	5	4	3	2	1
22.	I am quite innovative both in work and personal life.	5	4	3	2	1

Notes: scoring and interpretation: total the numbers corresponding to your answers. *100–125* Scores in this range suggest that you have strong tendencies toward being a proactive personality. Such proactivity should be (or already is) an asset to you in your career and personal life. Yet scoring 115 points or more could suggest that you sometimes annoy people with your constant need for taking on new responsibility and creating change.

70–99 Scores in this range suggest that you have about average tendencies toward being proactive. To enhance your success and have more fun in life, you might attempt to become more proactive.

25–69 Scores in this range suggest that you have a problem with proactivity. Both your work and personal life would probably be enhanced if you became more proactive.

Source: The idea for this scale and several of its statements stem from Thomas S. Bateman and J. Michael Crant, "The Proactive Component of Organizational Behavior: A Measure and Correlates," *Journal of Organizational Behavior*, March 1993, p. 112.

Figure 1.1 My tendencies toward being a proactive personality

Thomas S. Bateman and J. Michael Grant fits well the purpose of this book: a person with a proactive personality has a relatively stable tendency to effect environmental change.[3] Proactive behavior usually stems from a proactive personality, and refers to self-initiated, anticipatory action with the intent of either changing the situation or one's own behavior or attitudes.[4]

Figure 1.2 presents five definitions of the proactive personality and proactive behavior, the first of which is used as the primary definition of the proactive personality in this book. The definitions presented suggest that the proactive personality who follows through with proactive behavior is self-starting, geared toward the future, and attempts to bring about change in himself or herself or change the situation. Many entrepreneurs demonstrate their proactive personality by scanning the environment for

---

1. The relatively stable tendency to effect environmental change.
2. One who is relatively unconstrained by situational forces, and who effects environmental change.
3. Taking initiative in improving current circumstances or creating new ones; it involves challenging the status quo rather than passively adapting to present conditions.
4. A person whose behavior is characterized as self-directive and future focused, and who brings about change to the situation and/or change within him- or herself.
5. Anticipatory action that employees take to impact themselves and/or their environment.

Sources: Thomas S. Bateman and J. Michael Crant, "The Proactive Component of Organizational Behavior: A Measure and Correlates," *Journal of Organizational Behavior*, March 1993, p. 103; Bateman and Crant, p. 105; J. Michael Crant, "Proactive Behavior in Organizations," *Journal of Management*, Volume 26, p. 436; Uta K. Bindle and Sharon K. Parker, "Proactive Work Behavior: Forward Thinking and Change-Oriented Action in Organizations," in Sheldon Zedeck (Editor), *APA Handbook of Industrial and Organizational Psychology* (Washington, D.C.: American Psychological Association, 2010); Adam M. Grant and Susan J. Ashford, "The Dynamics of Proactivity at Work," *Research in Organizational Behavior*, Volume 28, 2008, p. 8.

Figure 1.2 Five representative definitions of the proactive personality and proactive behavior

a potentially profitable opportunity – a theme that will be explored in Chapters 6 and 7.

CHARACTERISTICS OF THE PROACTIVE WORKER

The characteristics of the proactive worker are strongly influenced by the individual having a proactive personality. A person with a proactive personality has a predisposition to search for ways to manifest proactive behavior. An example is that a worker with a proactive personality might search for ways to help the company engage in practices that sustain the environment, or be sustainable. The worker in question might suggest, for example, that the company plant a large garden on the roof of the building because "green" roofs typically help reduce the amount of energy needed to heat and cool a building. In this section we describe nine representative characteristics of the proactive worker. However, the characteristics and behaviors of people with proactive personalities will be mentioned at various places in this book.

1.   Desire for Control

Susan J. Ashford and J. Stewart Black studied how the desire for control was related to proactive behavior during organizational entry among 69 managers who had obtained an MBA. The period of time studied was classified as organizational entry because it covered the first six months of the job. The independent variable of desire for control was measured by a questionnaire about how much control the respondent would like to have in a wide variety of work-related areas in their new jobs. Each item used a seven-point response format, ranging from 1 (*strongly disagree*) to 7 (*strongly agree*). The results indicated that the desire for control is related to the newcomer's proactivity level during the first six months of employment. It was also shown that compared with managers with a low desire for control, managers with a high desire for control engaged in the following socialization tactics: (a) sought more information, (b) socialized more, (c) networked to a greater extent with interdepartmental colleagues, (d) negotiated more job changes, and (e) tried to put a positive frame around their situations.

The study authors carefully point out that control seeking is not a complete explanation for proactivity during the period of organizational entry. Other factors may have contributed to proactivity. One example is that tolerance for ambiguity may prompt newcomer managers to be more proactive, with the goal of reducing the uncertainty and ambiguity associated with the new work setting.[5]

2. Taking Charge at Work

Related to the desire to control is the proactive behavior of taking charge, defined as discretionary behavior intended to bring about functional change. Taking charge is regarded as extrarole behavior critical for organizational effectiveness because managers cannot anticipate all the activities that employees need to perform to accomplish company objectives. Taking-charge behaviors are change oriented and aimed at improvement, such as suggesting a way to shorten waiting lines at sporting event refreshment stands in order to process more customers during half-time at the events.

Elizabeth Wolfe Morrison and Corey C. Phelps developed a scale to measure tendencies toward taking charge in order to investigate specific behaviors associated with this type of extrarole behavior. The scale was administered to 275 white-collar employees from different organizations.[6] A sample question is, "This person often tries to bring about improved procedures for the work unit or department." The results of the study indicated that employees were more likely to take charge when they perceived top management to be open to employee suggestions and to employee-initiated change. As will be described later in this chapter, situational factors can facilitate proactivity.

3. Above-Average Cognitive Skills

Being intelligent, or having good cognitive skills, is an obvious contributor to proactivity. With good cognitive skills, the worker has a better chance of recognizing what could be done to improve the present situation or prevent problems. A study conducted in East Germany found a stable positive relationship between cognitive ability and personal initiative (a key part of proactivity).[7] Ashford and Black interpreted several studies to suggest that generalized cognitive ability may be predictive of proactive behavior on the job.[8] A recommendation published in the *Harvard Business Review* for finding and grooming breakthrough innovators suggests that company leaders scour the ranks for raw talent. The raw talent in question, based somewhat on cognitive skills, has to do with workers who are not content with following yesterday's best practices but look for new, effective work methods.[9]

The type of cognitive skill particularly well suited for proactive behavior has been described by Douglas A. Ready, Jay A. Conger and Linda A. Hill as *catalytic learning capability.* People with this type of capability have the capacity to scan for new ideas, and the intelligence to absorb the new ideas. Furthermore, these workers have the common sense to translate the new learning into productive action for their customers and their employers.[10]

4.   High Self-Efficacy

The widely accepted concept of self-efficacy refers to feeling self-confident with respect to a given task. A belief that one can be successful in being proactive is important because there is the risk of appearing foolish if one fails at the proactive task. A review of many studies suggests that there is consistent and strong evidence that perceived capability is positively associated with proactivity on the job.[11] An example of the link between self-efficacy and proactivity might take this form: a sales representative at a motorcycle manufacturer is confident of her ability to spot trends in consumer preferences. She proactively searches out possible growth niches for one of the company's motorcycle models. She then has the courage to report back to higher-level management that she sees growth possibilities for three-wheel motorcycles for seniors. At first the CEO is amused at her suggestion but then recognizes that the sales rep has identified a consumer trend worth pursuing.

5.   Setting Challenging Goals

Self-efficacy relates closely to goal setting because self-confidence with respect to a specific task increases the probability that the person will establish goals to reach out and accomplish more. The proactive person will typically establish challenging, and sometimes risky, goals.[12] Although some proactive people set risky goals, these goals are likely to be realistic, meaning that although the goals are difficult, they are attainable. The typical proactive person is not a dreamer, but someone who focuses on attaining goals that others may not bother pursuing. The motorcycle sales representative mentioned above is a good example of establishing a stretch goal (using full capabilities but still attainable). She established the goal of spotting a consumer trend that could translate into a profitable new product for her company. Such a goal is challenging because most new product ideas never get to market, or fail after being introduced to the market.

6.   Opportunity Seeking and Breaking Things that Merit Breaking

The worker with a proactive personality by definition seeks out constructive opportunities. At a modest level, the proactive worker might seek out opportunities such as a way to reduce shipping costs on a particular product, or a method of recycling the cut hair that falls on the floor at a hair salon. On a grander scale, the proactive person seeks out opportunities such as providing medical services to people in remote geographic areas via telemedicine, or thinking of a way to enable civilians to travel to outer space for recreational purposes.

"Breaking things that merit breaking" refers to radically changing or even getting rid of a work process that is no longer of value, or even counterproductive. Many medical offices, for example, have discontinued the practice of telephoning patients to remind them of upcoming appointments. Instead, the patients who use e-mail are sent e-mail messages to remind them of the appointments. Leadership at Facebook has attempted to institutionalize the practice of breaking things worth breaking. Employees are encouraged to "move fast and break things," through the process of giving them considerable leeway to solve problems on their own.[13]

7. Independent Judgment Combined with Willingness to Speak Out

In the process of examining the characteristics of proactive employees Donald J. Campbell identified independent judgment and willingness to speak out as being significant enterprising qualities.[14] Independent judgment is part of proactivity because the worker will not automatically accept the judgment of a supervisor or manager. For example, the sales manager might insist that "every customer is critical to our success." The sales representative with independent judgment might point out politely that some of the current list of customers actually lose money for the company because of all the demands they make and the time required to meet those demands. Willingness to speak out is often companion behavior to independent judgment because the proactive worker must communicate his or her independent judgments to the right person.

8. Early Riser

A behavioral characteristic of proactive people is that they tend to wake earlier than their less proactive counterparts. A survey of 367 students conducted by Christoph Randler found a small but positive correlation between self-reporting as a morning person and proactivity, as measured by a research questionnaire. Sample questions included: "I spend time identifying long-range goals for myself" and "I feel responsible for my own life." Randler also found a negative correlation between proactivity and *social jetlag*. The latter is caused by the mismatch between a person's biological timekeeping and the demands of social time, as measured by the difference between a student's choice of rise times between weekdays and weekends.[15] A plausible interpretation of these findings is that proactive people are more eager to get on with the day's activities and therefore minimize sleeping late.

9.   Assessing the Probable Success of the Proactive Behavior

Another characteristic of the proactive personality is to size up the probability of the success of the proactive behavior, rather than impetuously engaging in unassigned tasks. Based on a rational model of motivation, taking charge involves a calculated decision process in which people assess the likelihood that they will be successful. Also, they weigh the consequences of their action, such as whether the risks of taking charge outweigh the benefits.[16] Assume that a ski enthusiast is a product development specialist at a manufacturer of smart phones. She gives some thought to suggesting that the company develop a smart phone that can be built into the chin strap of a ski helmet. The device would enable skiers who are smart-phone habituated to make and receive calls while skiing and on ski lifts. Before proposing her idea to her manager she carefully weighs such factors as the potential market for the device, and also whether any similar smart-phone applications have been a commercial success.

Another part of the rational decision process is that a person considers proactive behavior because he or she perceives this behavior as important for fulfilling responsibilities, goals, or aspirations. The person thinks, even at a pre-conscious level, "What are the potential payoffs of this behavior in terms of my own interests? If I take the initiative in this situation, will it move me one step closer to promotion?"

CONDITIONS THAT FOSTER PROACTIVE BEHAVIOR

Our focus in this book is the individual with a proactive personality who engages in proactive behavior. The situation or the environment, however, influences whether or not proactive behavior will surface. At the extreme, environmental forces such as a manager who resists change can suppress proactive behavior. As stated by Jessica Pryce-Jones, proactive behavior is affected by both trait (who you are) and state (your environment).[17]

Environmental Antecedents of Proactive Behavior

An analysis by Sharon K. Parker, Helen M. Williams, and Nick Turner provides insight into the environmental antecedents of proactive behavior at work.[18] Job autonomy and a supportive climate appear to be important triggers of proactive behavior. Job autonomy is particularly important because it fosters personal initiative, expressing voice (or opinion) and suggesting improvements. Autonomy is also helpful because the task becomes more controllable for the worker. The controllability factor often boosts self-efficacy.

Experiencing job autonomy also enhances proactivity because having the experience of autonomy leads to a more flexible role orientation, or a willingness to go beyond the job description. A basic example follows: The manager of a bottle and can recycling center is informed by the company owner, "This is not an easy way to make a living because the profit margins are so thin. Just do what you can to make your center profitable." Rather than only following standard procedures, the manager of the recycling center will look for new ways to squeeze some profit, perhaps by enhancing the volume of bottles and cans brought in for recycling. One proactive step the manager might take is to encourage local Boy Scout and Girl Scout troupes to bring bottles and cans to his center.

Parker, Williams, and Turner also suggest that coworker trust will facilitate proactive behavior. Cognitive-motivational states are the mechanisms through which trust affects proactivity. First, if workers believe that their relationship with coworkers is characterized by trust, as a consequence they are likely to gain confidence in their own abilities: "If my team members believe in me, I should believe in me." Trust also facilitates proactivity because coworkers will accept mistakes as learning experiences. When mistakes are perceived as learning experiences, workers are more likely to go beyond core tasks and become more confident to expand their role.

Another contribution of trust is that if individuals have trust in coworkers' abilities and believe they will receive the support of coworkers, they are likely to be more open to change and feel in control. (Part of being proactive is to welcome change.)

Using a sample of 282 wire makers in the U.K., Parker, Williams, and Turner tested a series of hypotheses about how personality factors combine with environmental factors to bring about proactive behavior. Proactive idea implementation was measured by questions about specific actions taken in the job setting. First, workers indicated how many new ideas they had had in the last 12 months (on a scale ranging from no new ideas, one or two new ideas, 3–10 new ideas, to more than 10 new ideas) in relation to five key goals. The goals were (a) saving money or reducing costs, (b) improving quality, (c) improving customer delivery times, (d) making a better product, and (e) working together effectively. Secondly, if workers had had at least one new idea they were asked whether they put the idea forward, and whether it was implemented.

Several of their findings support the analysis of environmental factors just mentioned, as well as the importance of a proactive personality for worker proactivity. Support was found for the idea that engaging in proactive behavior involves rational decision making about whether such actions will be successful. One critical self-assessment is whether the individual has the capability to engage in a range of relevant activities. For example, a wire worker might size up whether she had the technical knowledge to make suggestions about the conversion of a particular metal into wire of appropriate strength. Another key finding was that employees who define their role more flexibly, including long-term goal setting beyond their immediate job, are more likely to be proactive.

An implication of the study findings in terms of situational forces is that if management wants a proactive workforce, managers should build employee self-efficacy and promote flexible role orientations. Coaching and training are useful interventions for building employee self-efficacy and more flexible role orientations. The study also suggests that granting job autonomy can enhance proactivity, although the process is long and slow. Furthermore, coworker trust has a slight positive effect on workers being proactive.

Several Situational Factors Enhancing Proactivity in the Form of Creativity

Another perspective on how situational factors can foster proactive behavior is to examine how situational factors enhance creativity. This is because creativity is usually a form of proactivity, although not typically classified in this manner. A few of these situational factors are:

1. *Intellectual challenge.* Matching people with the right assignments enhances creativity and proactivity because it supports seeking new ideas worth pursuing, and capitalizes on the advantages of the task being self-motivating. The amount of stretch is consistent with goal theory: too little challenge leads to boredom, but too much challenge leads to feelings of being overwhelmed and loss of control. Intellectual challenge can also trigger proactive behavior because the worker feels mentally energized and in the mood to do some something proactive.

   The leader or manager must understand his or her group members well enough to offer them the right amount of challenge. Moderate time pressures can sometimes bring about the right amount of challenge.

2. *Empowerment including freedom to choose the method.* Research with information technology workers in the People's Republic of China supported the idea that an empowering style of leadership facilitates worker creativity, and therefore proactivity. Specifically, when workers are empowered they are more likely to go through the steps for creative problem solving. Going through these steps, such as searching for creative alternatives, requires a degree of proactivity because the worker must stay focused on doing something out of the ordinary. Part of the creativity was attributed to empowering workers to have a sense of self-determination which sparked their creative thinking.[19]

   Workers also tend to be more creative when they are granted the freedom to choose which method is best for attaining a work goal. Stable goals are important because it is difficult to work creatively toward a moving target. Proactivity enters the picture in choosing a method or methods to attain a goal because the worker might attempt methods that have not been tried before. For example, an operations manager at a scrap metal company was given the goal of increasing the amount of scrap brought in by 10 percent. His solution was to start a door-to-door campaign at rural homes asking residents if they wished to get rid of appliances and other metal items that had been discarded in the back yard. Teenagers were hired to do the canvassing. The haul of scrap metal was large enough to move the sales manager close to the goal of obtaining 10 percent more scrap metal.

3. *Supervisory encouragement and linking innovation to performance.* The most influential step a leader can take to bring about creative problem solving and proactive thinking is to develop a permissive atmosphere that encourages people to think freely. Praising creative work and proactive thinking is important because, for most people to sustain their passion, they must feel that their work matters to the organization. Creative ideas should be evaluated quickly rather than put through a painfully slow review process.

   In addition to encouraging innovation, supervisory leaders should promote the idea that innovative thinking improves job performance. A study conducted with 238 pairs of workers and supervisors in four U.S. companies in several different industries supported the importance of employee expectations. When employees believed that innovative thinking would lead to better job performance, they were more likely to solve problems creatively. The supervisor could help in the process by explaining how innovation improves job performance.[20] Similarly, the leader might encourage proactivity by encouraging workers to look for problems to fix rather than focusing mostly on problems that already exist.

4. *Effective design of workgroups.* Workgroups are the most likely to be creative when they are mutually supportive and when they have a diversity of backgrounds and perspectives. Blends of gender, race, and ethnicity are recognized today as contributing to creative thought, similar to cross-functional teams with their mix of perspectives from different disciplines. The various points of view often combine to achieve creative solutions to problems. The mix of viewpoints might also encourage group members to think proactively, such as searching for new ways to complete their tasks, and new tasks to pursue.

    Homogeneous teams argue less, but they are often less creative. Putting together a team with the right chemistry – just the right level of diversity and supportiveness – requires experience and intuition on the leader's part.

    A leadership and management practice related to workgroup design is encouraging face-to-face contact to facilitate innovative thinking. It is more difficult for geographically dispersed workers to think creatively. According to Eric Schmidt, a Google executive, the best programming team is two people programming together. The second-best programming team is everybody fitted into one room. All other variants work less well for innovation.[21]

5. *Have favorable exchanges with workers.* Another insight into encouraging a creative and proactive climate is for leaders to have favorable exchanges with group members, as defined by LMX (leader–member exchange model) theory. A study with 191 research and development specialists found a positive relationship between LMX ratings and creativity of workers as measured by supervisory ratings.[22] When group members have positive relationships with their manager, they may have a more relaxed mental attitude that allows the imagination to flow. A useful strategy for enhancing creativity and proactivity throughout the organization is to emphasize the importance of working with a sense of heightened awareness, of being alert to new possibilities.

6. *Give financial rewards for innovation.* Creativity and proactivity are self-rewarding to some extent because they are exciting. Nevertheless, financial rewards for contributions to innovation help sustain a climate of innovation. Jeffrey Wadsworth is the chief executive of the Battelle Memorial Institute, a think tank of 23,000 employees specializing in inventions for profit. He points out that financial rewards for

creativity are widespread in industry and universities. "If you publish a patent you get $1,000, or you get $1 in a frame. Or you get a piece of the action moving forward."[23] Another factor is that financial rewards have spurred useful inventions for hundreds of years. Furthermore, in 2010 three teams shared the Progressive Insurance Automotive award for the first production-ready automotive that can achieve a fuel efficiency of 100 miles per gallon or its energy equivalent.[24]

INDIVIDUAL AND ORGANIZATIONAL CONSEQUENCES OF THE PROACTIVE PERSONALITY

A major theme of this book is that proactivity has many positive consequences for the individual and the organization. This simple proposition explains why proactivity is widely viewed as an asset within an employee, and why many organizations seek to be proactive. Organizational proactivity is a function of key people within the organization being proactive, resulting in a collective proactive mentality. Here we take a preliminary look at some of the individual and organizational consequences of the proactive personality and behavior. All of these consequences will be explored in more detail at appropriate places in the book.

Individual Consequences

In the vast majority of work situations, employers value employees who display proactivity occasionally. We emphasize occasionally because an effective employee is reactive enough to take care of daily problems. Visualize a veterinarian assistant who provides basic care to cats and dogs such as nail clipping, removing mites from their ears, and dressing wounds. If she does not react to these daily problems, the veterinarian clinic will soon have no patients. Yet, some proactivity on the assistant's part is warranted, such as the clinic offering a program of preventive dental care.

Better job performance
A major individual consequence of being a proactive personality is that the worker performs better in a variety of ways. By such means as looking for problems to solve, preventing problems, and going beyond one's job description, the proactive worker attains above-average job performance. Thomas Bateman and J. M. Crant conducted a study demonstrating that real estate agents scoring high on a measure of proactive personality

performed better than agents who measured lower on the proactivity scale. Following the agents over a nine-month period of time, the study showed that the agents with a stronger proactive personality sold more houses, earned higher commissions, and generated more listings than their less proactive counterparts. A major contribution of the study was controlling for other factors that could have accounted for sales success, such as intelligence, years of experience, conscientiousness, and extraversion. Scores on the measure of proactivity predicted real estate sales success above and beyond the other factors.[25]

Another way in which proactive workers perform better is that they are frequently innovative. They scan their environment for the opportunity to provide new goods and services, as well as saving money for the organization and improving business processes. A representative idea is that it took an innovative thinker to urge McDonald's to have many stores (restaurants) in India with vegetarian-only menus to appeal to national and local tastes.

More effective job searching

Another positive consequence to the individual of having a high standing on proactivity is that he or she is more likely to conduct a successful job search. Examples of proactivity in a job search would be finding ways to expand one's network of contacts, and looking for unconventional job opportunities for a person with one's credentials. For example, a person with a degree in industrial design might seek an opportunity as a packaging design specialist in the pet food division of a food manufacturer.

Douglas J. Brown and his group of researchers tested a model of proactive personality with respect to job search with a sample of 180 graduating college students. All students were administered the Proactive Personality Scale among other measures. The study findings revealed that the proactive personality may be an important antecedent to a successful job search. Also, proactive personality was significantly related to job search self-efficacy. The relationship is important because job search self-efficacy was related to job search effort and positive outcomes to the job search.[26]

Retention of power

Focusing for a moment on the executive suite, being proactive can help a CEO retain power in struggles with boards of directors. Jeffrey Pfeffer writes that if a CEO moves first (is proactive) to rid the board of his or her opponents, the CEO can usually save his or her job. If board members organize to oust the CEO while he or she is occupied with other matters, they can often unseat the CEO before the latter can mount a counterattack. "Don't wait if you see a power struggle coming," advises Pfeffer. "While you hesitate, others are mobilizing the support to beat you."[27]

More favorable perception by others

A notable self-esteem advantage of displaying proactive behavior is the person is perceived more favorably by others, thereby enhancing his or her reputation. Bateman and Crant suggest that proactive behavior generally positively influences how people are perceived by others. In one of their studies, MBA students scoring high on a measure of proactive behavior were viewed by their peers as having a better chance of being transformational leaders in the future. In another study that involved a bank and a marketing services firm, managers with high standing on a proactive personality scale were described by their managers as being more charismatic, having other leadership qualities, and as having a penchant for being all round better organizational citizens.[28]

Another important way in which being proactive enhances how a person is perceived is that proactive people are more likely to receive *dispositional attributions*. This means that good deeds by the individual are more likely to be perceived as a product of good inner qualities rather than situational forces or good luck.[29] For example, assume that a sales representative who is known to be proactive facilitates the company winning a giant government contract. Many of her coworkers will think that her excellent inner qualities, rather than good luck, were responsible for winning the contract.

Organizational Consequences

The positive consequences to the organization stemming from proactivity follow the positive consequences to the individual, such as being more successful financially and developing a better reputation. Although we refer to a *proactive organization*, the initiative taking and opportunity seeking stem from the proactivity of key people within the organization.

When the term "proactive organization" is mentioned, it is usually associated with high-tech companies such as Apple Corporation, Samsung, and IBM. However, proactivity can also be a major contributor to the success of basic industries. A good example is Dollar General Corporation, self-defined as a small-box discount retailer. During the Great Recession, company executives proactively spotted major opportunities for expansion. With so many American consumers either in financial trouble, or worrying about being in financial trouble, the potential market increased for a store that offered brand name and house brands at prices much lower than those found in traditional stores. Even a few of the best-known discount stores had higher prices than Dollar General. Another result of proactive thinking by Dollar General leaders was to recognize that in addition to low prices, many consumers preferred to shop at small stores, much like the general stores of an earlier era. The proactive thinking paid big dividends as the company expanded from 5000 to over 10,000 stores in the period between 2008 and 2012.

Support for the idea that proactivity leads to positive consequences to the organization stems from an analysis of initiative by Michael Frese and Doris Fay. The researchers contend that personal initiative, a subset of proactivity on the job, is positively associated with performance not only at the individual and team level, but also at the organizational level.[30]

SUGGESTIONS FOR APPLICATION

1. A basic starting point in showing signs of having a proactive personality in the workplace is to perform well in areas outside your job description. The caution, however, is not to grab responsibility that belongs to a coworker, thereby creating conflict between you and that person.

2. Taking charge at work, or intending to bring about functional changes, is a particularly constructive way of demonstrating proactivity on the job. Taking charge facilitates organizational effectiveness, thereby enhancing the reputation of the person who has taken such initiative.

3. Establishing challenging goals feeds proactivity because in order to reach stretch goals, the person has to reach out and perform in ways not strictly suggested by a job role or description. In the pursuit of challenging goals, the proactive person does not waste effort in pursuit of goals that will most likely never be attained.

4. A way of expressing proactivity on a grand scale is to seek new opportunities, such as developing a new product or service, establishing a new company, or finding a new market for one's employer.

5. A key strategy for triggering proactivity among subordinates is to create a permissive atmosphere in which they are empowered, encouraged to take risks, and not penalized for stepping outside their job description within reason.

6. An advantage of being proactive on the job is that it may enhance your reputation because you are likely to be perceived favorably by others. This includes many people thinking that the good results you attain are the result of positive inner qualities.

SUMMARY

In today's challenging workplace, high-level performance often means accomplishing more than one's assigned job responsibilities, or being proactive. Workers with a proactive personality are inclined to engage in proactive behaviors such as seeking feedback, going beyond the job description, taking the initiative to engage in job-relevant learning, and going out to meet customers.

The characteristics of the proactive worker are strongly influenced by the individual having a proactive personality. Nine representative characteristics of the proactive worker are: (1) a desire for control, (2) taking charge at work, (3) above-average cognitive skills, (4) high self-efficacy, (5) setting challenging goals, (6) opportunity seeking and breaking things that merit breaking, (7) independent judgment combined with willingness to speak out, (8) being an early riser, and (9) assessing the probable success of the proactive behavior.

The situation or environment influences whether or not proactive behavior will surface. Job autonomy and a supportive climate appear to be important triggers of proactive behavior in the workplace. The experience of autonomy leads to a more flexible role orientation, or a willingness to go beyond the job description. Coworker trust often facilitates proactive behavior. An implication of a study in a manufacturing setting is that if management wants a proactive workforce, managers should build employee self-efficacy and promote flexible role orientations.

Several situational factors have been noted to enhance proactive behavior in the form of creativity, including (1) intellectual challenge, (2) empowerment including freedom to choose a method, (3) supervisory encouragement and linking innovation to performance, (4) effective design or workgroups, (5) having favorable exchanges with workers, and (6) giving financial rewards for innovation.

Individual consequences of being proactive include (1) better job performance, (2) more effective job searching, (3) retention of power, and (4) more favorable perception by others. The positive consequences to the organization stemming from proactivity follow the positive consequences to the individual, such as being more successful financially and developing a better reputation.

Suggestions for application of the information in this chapter include (a) performing well outside your job description, (b) taking charge at work, (c) establishing challenging goals, (d) seeking new opportunities, (e) creating a permissive atmosphere for subordinates, and (f) being proactive to enhance one's reputation.

REFERENCES

1. Tom Krisher, "GM Beset by Old Culture, CEO Says," Associated Press, August 10, 2012. Reprinted in *Democrat and Chronicle*, Rochester, New York, August 10, 2012, p. 5B.
2. Jessica Pryce-Jones, "How to Think Ahead of the Game," *Psychology Today* (www.psychologytoday.com), November 19, 2010, p. 1. Retrieved September 12, 2012.
3. Thomas S. Bateman and J. Michael Crant, "The Proactive Component of Organizational Behavior: A Measure and Correlates," *Journal of Organizational Behavior*, March 1993, p. 103.
4. Uta K. Bindle and Sharon K. Parker, "Proactive Work Behavior: Forward Thinking and Change-Oriented Action in Organizations." In Sheldon Zedeck (Editor), *APA Handbook of Industrial and Organizational Psychology* (Washington, D.C.: American Psychological Association, 2010).
5. Susan J. Ashford and J. Stewart Black, "Proactivity During Organizational Entry: The Role of Desire for Control," *Journal of Applied Psychology*, April 1996, pp. 199–214.
6. Elizabeth Wolfe Morrison and Correy C. Phelps, "Taking Charge at Work: Extrarole Efforts to Initiate Workplace Change," *Academy of Management Journal*, August 1999, p. 403.
7. Doris Fay and Michael Frese, "The Concept of Personal Initiative: An Overview of Validity Studies," *Human Performance*, Volume 14, Number 1, pp. 97–124. Cited in Bindle and Parker, "Proactive Work Behavior," p. 23.
8. Ashford and Black, "Proactivity During Organizational Entry," p. 210.
9. Jeffrey Cohn, Jon Katzenbach, and Gus Vlak, "Finding and Grooming Breakthrough Innovators," *Harvard Business Review*, December 2008, p. 65.
10. Douglas A. Ready, Jay A. Conger, and Linda A. Hill, "Are You a High Potential?" *Harvard Business Review*, June 2010, p. 82.
11. Bindle and Parker, "Proactive Work Behavior," p. 11.
12. Sharon K. Parker, "How Positive Affect Can Facilitate Proactive Behavior in the Work Place." Paper presented at the Academy of Management Conference, Philadelphia, PA, 2007. As cited in Bindle and Parker, "Proactive Work Behavior," p. 15.
13. Gretchen Spretizer and Christine Porath, "Creating Sustainable Performance," *Harvard Business Review*, January–February 2012, p. 95.
14. Donald J. Campbell, "The Proactive Employee: Managing Workplace Initiative," *Academy of Management Executive*, August 2000, p. 56.
15. Christoph Randler, "Proactive People are Morning People," *Journal of Applied Social Psychology*, Volume 39, pp. 2787–2797.
16. Sharon K. Parker, Helen M. Williams, and Nick Turner, "Modeling the Antecedents of Proactive Behavior at Work," *Journal of Applied Psychology*, May 2006, p. 638.
17. Pryce-Jones, "How to Think Ahead of the Game," p. 1.
18. Parker, Williams, and Turner, "Modeling the Antecedents of Proactive Behavior at Work," pp. 636–652.
19. Xiamomeng Zhang and Kathryn M. Bartol, "Linking Empowering Leadership and Employee Creativity: The Influence of Psychological

Empowerment, Intrinsic Motivation, and Creative Process Engagement," *Academy of Management Journal*, February 2010, pp. 107–128.

20. Feron Yuan and Richard W. Woodman, "Innovative Behavior in the Workplace: The Role of Performance and Image Outcome Expectations," *Academy of Management Journal*, April 2010, pp. 323–342.

21. Quoted in "How Google Fuels Its Idea Factory," *Business Week*, May 12, 2008, p. 58.

22. Pamela Tierney, Steven M. Farmer, and George B. Graen, "An Examination of Leadership and Employee Creativity: The Relevance of Traits and Relationships," *Personnel Psychology*, Autumn 1999, pp. 591–620.

23. Quoted in "The Profit Motive," *The Wall Street Journal*, September 27, 2010, p. R8.

24. Eric S. Hintz, "Creative Financing," *The Wall Street Journal*, September 27, 2010, p. R8.

25. Thomas Bateman and J. Michael Crant, "Proactive Behavior: Meaning, Impact, Recommendations," *Business Horizons*, May/June 1999, pp. 63–81; Crant, "The Proactive Personality Scale and Objective Job Performance among Real Estate Agents," *Journal of Applied Psychology*, August 1995, pp. 532–537.

26. Douglas J. Brown, Richard T. Cober, Kevin Kane, Paul E. Levy, and Jarrett Shalhoop, "Proactive Personality and the Successful Job Search: A Field Investigation with College Students," *Journal of Applied Psychology*, May 2006, pp. 717–726.

27. Jeffrey Pfeffer, "Power Play," *Harvard Business Review*, July–August 2010, p. 90.

28. Bateman and Crant, "Proactive Behavior: Meaning, Impact," p. 66.

29. Adam M. Grant and Susan J. Ashford, "The Dynamics of Productivity at Work," *Research in Organizational Behavior*, Volume 28, 2008, p. 18.

30. Michael Frese and Doris Fay, "Personal Initiative (P!): An Active Performance Concept for Work in the 21st Century," *Research in Organizational Behavior*, Volume 23, 2001, pp. 133–187.

2. Traits and behaviors associated with the proactive personality

Although proactivity is a personality trait of profound significance for the individual and the organization, it exists among other related traits and behaviors. For example, the proactive worker might also have a high standing on the trait of conscientiousness, and be motivated by an internal drive to perform meaningful and exciting work. A good example of the complexity of the proactive personality is legendary hedge fund manager, Ray Dalio, the founder of Bridgewater Associates. When asked about making investment decisions, he said, "I'm very big on having clarified principles. I don't believe in being reactive. You can't do that in the markets effectively. I can't. I need perspective. I need a game plan."[1] Dalio's comments could be interpreted to mean that he is proactive and also uses a series of goals to achieve the end results he wants.

In this chapter we explore several of the personality traits linked to the proactive personality as well as several of the major behaviors, including being a good organizational citizen, setting goals, and enhanced interpersonal relationships. Initiative, one of the major behaviors associated with proactivity, receives separate treatment in Chapter 3.

THE FIVE FACTOR MODEL AND PROACTIVITY

A logical starting point in understanding how the proactive personality is related to other personality traits is to examine its relationship with a commonly used measure of personality in organizations, the Big Five. These factors, which are said to account for much of the human personality, are also referred to as the "Five Factor Model." In review, the Big Five are as follows:

1. *Neuroticism* reflects emotional instability and identifies people prone to psychological distress and coping with problems in unproductive ways. Traits associated with this personality factor include being anxious, insecure, angry, embarrassed, emotional, and worried. A person of low neuroticism – or high emotional stability – is calm and confident, and usually in control.

2. *Extraversion* reflects the quantity or intensity of social interactions, the need for social stimulation, self-confidence, and competition. Traits associated with extraversion include being sociable, gregarious, assertive, talkative, and active. An outgoing person is often described as extraverted, whereas introverted persons are described as reserved, timid, and quiet.

3. *Openness* reflects the proactive seeking of experience for its own sake. Traits associated with openness include being creative, cultured, intellectually curious, broadminded, and artistically sensitive. People who score low on this personality factor are practical, with narrow interests.

4. *Agreeableness* reflects the quality of one's interpersonal orientation. Traits associated with the agreeableness factor include being courteous, flexible, trusting, good-natured, cooperative, forgiving, softhearted, and tolerant. The other end of the continuum includes disagreeable, cold, and antagonistic people.

5. *Conscientiousness* reflects organization, self-restraint, persistence, and motivation toward attaining goals. Traits associated with conscientiousness include being hardworking, dependable, well organized, and thorough. The person low in conscientiousness is lazy, disorganized, and unreliable.

The relationship between the proactive personality and the Big Five factors was explored by Debra A. Major, Jonathan E. Turner, and Thomas D. Fletcher in the context of a study about personal learning and development.[2] The results showed that the proactive personality accounted for about 26 percent of the Big Five factors, including the facets that make up the five factors. A standard measure of the proactive personality was administered to participants in the study. The Big Five factors and 30 facets of personality were measured with the NEO Personality Inventory. (Motivation to learn was also measured by a questionnaire.) The 183 participants were employees at a midsized financial services organization.

Table 2.1 presents the facets (or traits within) the five major factors that are significantly related to the proactive personality. Seven of the nine facets show a positive relationship to the proactive personality: assertiveness, activity, actions, ideas, values, altruism, and achievement striving. Two of the nine facets show a negative relationship with the proactive personality: vulnerability and dutifulness. The negative relationship with vulnerability suggests that the proactive person is able to cope with stress, is neither dependent nor hopeless, and does not panic in difficult situations. The negative relationship with dutifulness suggests that the proactive personality does not strictly adhere to his or her ethical principles, does not

Table 2.1   Definitions of the big five facets significantly related to the proactive personality

Big Five factor and facet	Definition of facet	Relationship direction
Neuroticism Vulnerability	Inability to cope with stress; dependent; hopeless; or panicked in difficult situations	Negative
Extraversion Assertiveness	Dominant, forceful; tendency to speak up; often a leader	Positive
Activity	Sense of urgency; need to keep busy, maintains a rapid tempo	Positive
Openness Actions	Willingness to try different activities; preference for novelty over the familiar or routine	Positive
Ideas	Intellectual curiosity; willingness to consider unconventional ideas	Positive
Values	Readiness to reexamine values (social, political, or religious)	Positive
Agreeableness Altruism	Concern for the welfare of others; tendency to show generosity and consideration and to provide help	Positive
Conscientiousness Dutifulness	Strict adherence to one's ethical principles; fulfills moral obligations; dependable and reliable	Negative
Achievement striving	Hardworking; high aspirations; diligent and purposeful; sense of direction in life	Positive

Source: Debra A. Major, Jonathan E. Turner, and Thomas D. Fletcher, "Linking Proactive Personality and the Big Five to Motivation to Learn and Development Activity," *Journal of Applied Psychology*, July 2006, p. 932.

always fill moral obligations, and is not always dependable and reliable. Although at first these negative relationships may seem surprising, they fit the pattern of proactive people who sometimes take risks rather than stick to their regular obligations.

The study also found that proactive personality, extraversion, openness, and conscientiousness were all significant predictors of motivation to learn. A link between the proactive personality and willingness to learn is not surprising because reaching out to acquire new, relevant knowledge is part of being proactive.

A large study of the relationship between the proactive personality and the Big Five model of personality was conducted by Kilian Werenfried Wawoe, using seven samples in the Netherlands, India, the United States, Romania, and Brazil.[3] A total of 1487 questionnaires were completed by a variety of office workers in such fields as banking, real estate, and business process outsourcing. Standard personality measures were used for both the proactive personality and the Big Five factors. The study author took into account cultural differences in the meaning of many of the facets contained in the Big Five, particularly with respect to conscientiousness. For example, the same facet is labeled "achievement setting" in the United States, "goal focused" in the Netherlands, and "competence" in India.

Across the several studies, the clearest relationship between proactive personality and Big Five factors was found with extraversion. The relationship between proactivity and conscientiousness was more complex. Proactive employees seem to be significantly more organized, but somewhat low on dutifulness (as in the study cited above). Proactivity showed a positive relationship with achievement focus. A positive relationship was also found between proactivity and openness. With respect to the factor of neuroticism, some evidence was found that proactive employees have a higher degree of self-confidence and are less vulnerable.

Taking the two comprehensive studies just cited into account, we can conclude that the proactive personality overlaps to a small extent with several of the factors and facets within the Big Five factors. Despite the overlap, the proactive personality has enough independence as a personality trait to be worthy of the attention of scientists and practitioners.

INTERNAL LOCUS OF CONTROL AND PROACTIVITY

A natural relationship exists between proactivity and the locus of control, the way in which people look at causation in their lives. Some people have an internal locus of control because they perceive their outcomes as being controlled internally. As a result, they generally feel in control of their lives. Some people have an external locus of control because they perceive much of what happens to them as being controlled by circumstances.[4] People with an internal locus of control feel they can create their own opportunities in life, whereas those with an external locus attribute much of their success and failure to luck. Workers with an internal locus of control are generally more mature, self-reliant, and responsible. They also tend to be more proactive because they create circumstances that will lead to positive outcomes. An example would be a sales representative who searches out new valuable business contacts while held over at an airport.

Viewed broadly, general locus of control refers to the extent to which one usually attributes rewards to one's own behavior, rather than to external causes, such as luck or the actions of other people. The person with an internal locus of control would therefore believe that he or she was promoted because of superior job performance, not favoritism. Work locus of control focuses on the extent to which people attribute rewards on the job to their own behavior, such as in the example just presented. A meta-analysis of 29 studies involving a total of over 40,000 respondents found that work locus of control consistently yielded stronger relationships with work-related criteria than general locus of control. Among these work criteria were job satisfaction, job performance, and affective commitment.[5]

Locus of control, similar to proactivity, has a positive relationship with well-being at work.

Paul E. Spector and a team of 29 other researchers investigated how locus of control is related to job satisfaction and physical well-being. The study participants were 5185 managers from 24 geopolitical entities from five different continents. Support was found for the hypothesis that the salutatory effects of perceived control (an internal locus) are universal. However, the relationship between locus of control and psychological well-being was stronger than that between locus of control and physical well-being. Having an internal locus of control helps the worker deal more effectively with job stress.

The researchers also took into account that the effects of a culture being individualistic or collectivistic did not influence the relationship between locus of control and well-being.[6] (In an individualistic culture people are more concerned about themselves and their careers than in the welfare of the group. In a collectivistic culture, workers are more concerned about the welfare of the group and group achievement.)

Similar to people with a proactive personality, research suggests that people with an internal locus of control are more likely to have greater intrinsic motivation, and be more achievement oriented.[7] Higher intrinsic motivation may come about because "internals" believe that they are mostly in control of factors that lead to rewards, and are therefore not dependent on the promise of an external reward to accomplish good work. With respect to achievement motivation, internals strive to achieve worthwhile objectives because they are confident in their ability to control outcomes.

The self-quiz presented in Figure 2.1 is a standard measure of locus of control. While taking the quiz you will observe that states from both work and personal life are included.

Instructions: Check the box next to the statement that best describes how you feel.

1. ☐ A. Many of the unhappy things in people's lives are partly due to bad luck.
   ☐ B. People's misfortunes result from the mistakes they make.
2. ☐ A. One of the major reasons why we have wars is because people don't take enough interest in politics.
   ☐ B. There will always be wars, no matter how hard people try to prevent them.
3. ☐ A. In the long run, people get the respect they deserve in this world.
   ☐ B. Unfortunately, an individual's worth often passes unrecognized no matter how hard he or she tries.
4. ☐ A. The idea that teachers are unfair to students is nonsense.
   ☐ B. Most students don't realize the extent to which their grades are influenced by accidental happenings.
5. ☐ A. Without the right breaks, one cannot be an effective leader.
   ☐ B. Capable people who fail to become leaders have not taken advantage of their opportunities.
6. ☐ A. No matter how hard you try, some people just don't like you.
   ☐ B. People who can't get others to like them don't understand how to get along with others.
7. ☐ A. I have often found that what is going to happen will happen.
   ☐ B. Trusting to fate has never turned out as well for me as making a decision to take a definite course of action.
8. ☐ A. In the case of the well-prepared student, there is rarely, if ever, such a thing as an unfair test.
   ☐ B. Many times exam questions tend to be so unrelated to course work that studying is really useless.
9. ☐ A. Becoming a success is a matter of hard work; luck has little or nothing to do with it.
   ☐ B. Getting a good job depends mainly on being in the right place at the right time.
10. ☐ A. The average citizen can have an influence in government decisions.
    ☐ B. This world is run by the few people in power, and there is not much the little guy can do about it.
11. ☐ A. When I make plans, I am almost certain that I can make them work.
    ☐ B. It is not always wise to plan too far ahead because many things turn out to be a matter of luck anyway.
12. ☐ A. In my case, getting what I want has little or nothing to do with luck.
    ☐ B. Many times we might just as well decide what to do by flipping a coin.
13. ☐ A. What happens to me is my own doing.
    ☐ B. Sometimes I feel that I don't have enough control over the direction my life is taking.

Note: scoring and interpretation: the answers in the direction of an internal control are as follows: 1, B; 2, A; 3, A; 4, A; 5, B; 6, B; 7, B; 8, A; 9, A; 10, A; 11, A; 12, A; 13, A. The higher your score, the more you have an internal locus of control.

Source: Adapted slightly in format from Julian B. Rotter, "Generalized Expectancies for Internal versus External Control of Reinforcement," *Psychological Monographs*, Volume 80 (1, Whole No. 609), 1966.

Figure 2.1   The locus of control self-quiz

ORGANIZATIONAL CITIZENSHIP BEHAVIOR AND THE PROACTIVE PERSONALITY

Organizational citizenship behavior is closely related to the proactive personality because both focus on actions that go beyond role require-ments and both contribute to organizational effectiveness. Organizational citizenship behavior is generally defined as a willingness to work for the good of the organization without the promise of a specific reward. A good organizational citizen would engage in such behaviors as helping a person with a foreign-language translation outside of his or her department, and picking up litter on the company parking lot.

Given that proactive employees are willing to actively seek opportuni-ties to help their organizations and engage in activities beyond their job descriptions, they are frequently perceived to be good organizational citi-zens. Proactive employees are motivated to take the initiative to contribute to the organization, making them more likely to be willing to make discre-tionary contributions in the form of organizational citizenship behavior.[8]

To elucidate the link between the proactive personality and organiza-tional citizenship behavior, in this section we describe five topics: (a) the dimensions of organizational citizenship behavior (OCB), (b) the link between proactivity and challenge-oriented organizational citizenship behavior, (c) proactivity, organizational citizenship behavior, and leader–member relations, (d) proactivity, organizational citizenship behavior, and harmony, and (e) role breadth self-efficacy and the proactive personality.

The Dimensions of Organizational Citizenship Behavior

Similarly to the proactive personality, organizational citizenship behavior has various components or dimensions, all centering on the idea of the employee going beyond the confines of his or her formal role to help the organization. Part of understanding the dimensions of citizenship behav-ior is the observation that OCB can deal with the context of work as well as task performance itself. Dennis W. Organ, who developed the concept of organizational citizenship behavior, explains that the context of perfor-mance refers to helping and supporting coworkers. Years after his initial formulation of OCB, Organ redefined it as behavior that contributes "to the maintenance and enhancement of the social and psychological context that supports task performance."[9]

Several different researchers, including Organ, have identified dimen-sions of organizational citizenship behavior. A few of these dimensions stem from asking managers to identify worker behavior that is helpful, but not absolutely required. A synthesis of the work of several researchers in identifying dimensions of organizational citizenship behavior, resulted in the following five dimensions:[10]

1. *Altruism.* This dimension of OCB relates to behavior directly intended to help a specific worker in face-to-face situations. Examples include helping others who have been absent or late for valid reasons, volunteering for activities not required such as organizing an office party, orienting a coworker although not required, and assisting others with a heavy workload. Proactivity is demonstrated in this dimension because the good organizational citizen looks around to see who might need help.
2. *Civic virtue.* A worker who is civically virtuous keeps up with matters that affect the organization, such as being attuned to developments in the outside environment that could represent threats or opportunities to the firm. Proactivity is involved because the individual takes the initiative to scan the environment.
3. *Conscientiousness.* As a dimension of organizational citizenship behavior, "conscientiousness" refers to much the same idea as the personality dimension of conscientiousness as defined in the Big Five model of personality (see above.) In its earlier version with respect to OCB, conscientiousness was part of *generalized compliance*, representing impersonal behaviors such as complying with norms describing a good worker. Such behaviors would include being punctual, not exceeding time limits for lunch breaks, and not spending too much time on personal business during the workday.
4. *Courtesy.* A courteous employee makes the effort to consult with others before taking action, such as asking coworkers if it is acceptable to bring a child to work on a specific day, or whether they would want to receive work-related e-mails during weekends. Proactivity is involved because the worker takes the initiative to learn whether a given action is acceptable.
5. *Sportsmanship.* "Sportsmanship" conforms to the general language meaning of being a good sport, and not complaining about trivial matters. For example, an information technologist who was a good sport would not complain about having to work on New Year's Eve to fix a system malfunction. Sportsmanship deals more with reactivity than proactivity because the worker reacts to an inconvenience in a positive manner.

A meta-analysis of many studies of the relationships among these five dimensions showed that they are strongly related to each other. An exception was that sportsmanship and civic virtue showed only a slight relationship to each other. Another important part of the meta-analysis analyzed the relationship of the five dimensions of OCB to commonly used predictors of organizational citizenship behavior. The five predictors were (a) job satisfaction, (b) commitment to the job and organization, (c) fairness by the organization, (d) leader support, and (e) conscientiousness. Why conscientiousness is both a dimension of OCB and a predictor can be explained by the fact that conscientiousness is often used as a dimension to evaluate employee performance. This is true because a conscientious employee is often productive. In recognition of the importance of conscientiousness to the organization, it is also an OCB dimension.

One of the conclusions of the meta-analysis is that the five dimensions of organizational citizenship behavior seem to be behavioral manifestations of positive cooperativeness at work. This would lead to a definition of organizational citizenship behavior as a general tendency to be cooperative and helpful in workplace settings.[11] Proactivity is involved because the worker often has to look around for ways in which to be cooperative.

Proactivity and Challenge-Oriented Organizational Citizenship Behavior

Another way to simplify the many different dimensions proposed of organizational citizenship behavior is to classify them as *affiliation-oriented* versus *challenge-oriented* behaviors. Affiliation-oriented behaviors tend to maintain or enhance relationships, and are interpersonal and cooperative, and tend to solidify or preserve relationships with others. The altruism and courtesy dimensions described above are affiliation oriented. An example of an affiliation-oriented organizational citizenship behavior would be to organize a luncheon for a coworker who had become a great-grandfather for the first time. Another example would be to take the initiative to congratulate a worker in another department who recently earned the designation of Project Manager Professional.

The challenge-oriented behaviors are change oriented and include the risk that they could damage relationships with others in the workplace because they challenge the status quo. The most frequently researched forms of challenge-oriented behaviors are those that are intended to encourage something to happen, rather than stop or prevent something from happening. Visualize a marketing specialist who works for an automobile and truck manufacturer. Going a little outside her job description, she studies owners' manuals for several models of company vehicles. She observes that with a few extra words of explanation, it would be easier for new owners to use their vehicles properly without getting in touch with the dealer or the manufacturer for assistance. For example, she finds the instruction "press button" for setting the trip odometer back to zero.

Simply pressing the button would leave the car owner baffled because nothing changes on the odometer. However, if the instructions were added – "Press button and hold in for about five seconds" – resetting the trip odometer would proceed smoothly.

Researchers Scott B. MacKenzie, Philip M. Podsakoff, and Nathan P. Podsakoff wanted to learn more about how challenge-oriented and affiliation-oriented organizational citizenship behaviors affect organizational effectiveness through their impact on task performance at the workgroup level.[12] Data for the study were gathered from managers, staff personnel, and company records at a sample of limited-menu restaurants in the United States. Limited-menu restaurants include but are not limited to fast-service restaurants. The data consisted of questionnaire results as well as performance assessments made by the company training staff. The measures were multidimensional. One area includes ratings about how well the customer-contact workers complied with company standards for service. Three such examples are as follows:

- Did employees acknowledge customers with a friendly greeting within one minute after their arrival?
- Did servers recommend specific menu items being promoted by the company?
- Did the cashier inquire about the customer's satisfaction with the meal, thank the customer, and invite him or her to return?

A second area of measurement was back-of-house maintenance, with two examples as follows:

- Did cooking staff clean and maintain the grills and keep deep fry machines to company standards?
- Did dish washers clean dirty dishes in a timely manner?

A third area of measurement was administration, with two examples as follows:

- Was the manager visiting tables or greeting guests near the entrance?
- Was the manager assisting staff in a professional manner?

A fourth area was exterior maintenance, with two examples as follows:

- Did the staff remove litter from the parking area and sweep the walkways?
- Did the staff keep the windows clean?

Although a few of the above items appear to follow a job description, several others might reflect looking around for problems to solve. The key conclusion to the study was that challenge-oriented organizational citizenship behaviors have a positive impact on workgroup task performance up to a point. Beyond this optimal point, however, OCB improves performance only when affiliation-oriented OCBs are present. Another finding of note was that challenge-oriented organizational citizenship behaviors enhance workgroup task performance up to a point, but then impair it after that point. (For example, it could create a problem if a server keeps looking for ways to change a menu that many customers like.) It therefore appears that both challenge-oriented and affiliation-oriented organizational citizenship behaviors can enhance workgroup performance in the restaurant business serving moderately priced food.

One link of this complicated study to the proactive personality is that proactivity works best when it focuses on both work processes and helping coworkers. For example, the researchers found that if workers do not help each other, engaging in challenge-oriented behavior will lower the workgroup's profitability.

Proactivity, Organizational Citizenship Behavior, and Leader–Member Relations

Proactive employees usually have positive relationships with their supervisors. A major reason for the relationship is that supervisors appreciate employees who engage in such behaviors as looking for work that needs doing without being asked. It is also possible that a person with a proactive personality will take the initiative to build a good relationship with the supervisor. For example, the proactive subordinate might reflect, "What information might my manager find useful in his presentation to upper management next week?" Arriving at a useful idea, the subordinate might gather that information without being told and send the supervisor a document containing the potentially useful information. Whatever the factor contributing to the high-quality leader–member exchange, the proactive employee now experiences higher job satisfaction that prompts him or her to engage in organizational citizenship behavior.

Ning Li, Jian Liang, and J. Michael Crant conducted a study that provides insight into how proactivity, leader–member relations, and organizational citizenship behavior are connected.[13] Participants in the study came from seven state-owned companies in three Chinese cities. The four industries represented were manufacturing, electronics, telecommunications, and hotel. A total of 200 workers from 54 workgroups participated in the study. Subordinates completed measures of proactive personality, leader–member exchanges, and procedural justice. The procedural justice questionnaire concentrated on employee perceptions of the fairness of pay and performance appraisals.

The results of the study showed that proactive personality was associated with establishing a high-quality relationship with the worker's supervisor. In turn, the quality of the leader–member exchange influenced how employees experienced greater job satisfaction and displayed more organizational citizenship behavior. A subtle finding in the study was that a proactive personality is associated with less organizational citizenship behavior when the worker perceives that the climate is unjust. In operational terms this means that a worker is less likely to be a good organizational citizen if he or she thinks that his or her pay and performance appraisals are not entirely fair.

The researchers also observed that, compared with reactive employees, proactive employees are likely to perceive an obligation to engage in organizational citizenship behavior in response to fair treatment. The presence of perceived justice provides a link between proactivity and organizational citizenship behavior.

Proactivity, Organizational Citizenship Behavior, and Harmony

Another explanation of a factor that facilitates (or moderates) the relationship between proactivity and organizational citizenship behavior also derives from a work setting in China. The study authors, Yiqun Gan and Fanny M. Cheung, explain that in Chinese work settings, the positive relationship between proactive personality and organizational citizenship behavior may not necessarily take place. They hypothesized that harmony in the workplace might moderate (explain) the link between proactivity and citizenship behavior.[14] Harmony is a personality trait related to one's inner peace of mind, contentment, and harmony with others. A person with a high standing on harmony assigns high priority to harmony, has high endurance, makes concessions to avoid trouble, usually agrees with others, is peaceful, even-tempered, satisfied, and careful about not offending others. Harmony is therefore close in meaning to conflict avoidance and is valued in Chinese cultures.

The 158 study participants were recruited from six state-owned companies in Beijing, China. A Chinese version of the Proactive Personality Scale was administered to participants as well as the Harmony scale from a Chinese personality inventory. A sample item is, "If someone offends me, I will try hard to forgive that person." Organizational citizenship behavior was measured by ratings from a participant's immediate supervisor.

The results of the study showed that in a Chinese work setting, the personality trait of harmony was found to be an important moderator of the relationship between proactivity and citizenship behavior. For workers having a high standing on harmony, high proactive personality is associated with high supervisor-rated organizational citizenship behavior. If a worker does not have harmonious interpersonal relationships, even if the person has a proactive personality, he or she will not be rated highly on organizational citizenship behavior. In short, in the Chinese culture harmony is a necessary quality for proactive personality to facilitate a person being perceived by the supervisor as having good organizational citizenship behavior.

Role Breadth Self-Efficacy and the Proactive Personality

A final explanation here about how the relationship between proactivity and organizational citizenship focuses on a worker's perceived capability of carrying out a broader and more proactive set of work tasks extending beyond the job description. A sensible worker will most likely want to take on a daring new task if it appears probable that he or she can pull it off.

As defined by Sharon K. Parker, role breadth self-efficacy (RBSE) is the extent to which people feel confident that they are able to carry out a broader and more proactive role, beyond formal requirements. RBSE is considered here within a discussion of organizational citizenship behavior because being a good organizational citizen involves role breadth. RBSE may underlie organizational citizenship behavior because it focuses on what workers feel (or think) they can do. It explicitly focuses on activities that require proactivity. In contrast, OCB can include dimensions that are more reactive in their orientation, such as compliance with procedures and punctuality requirements. Figure 2.2 provides 10 specific items that relate to role breadth self-efficacy.

Parker did not find a strong positive relationship between RBSE and proactive personality in two studies in work settings. Nevertheless, she believes hiring workers with a high standing on the proactivity trait can contribute to having more workers with role breadth self-efficacy.[15]

GOAL SETTING AND THE PROACTIVE PERSONALITY

A person with a proactive personality takes naturally to goal setting because he or she by nature enjoys the idea of looking into the future and making improvements. For example, a manufacturing engineer might look around the factory and think to himself, "I see enough wasted motion

"How confident would you feel?"
1. Analyzing a long-term problem to find a solution
2. Representing your work area in meetings with senior management
3. Designing new procedures for your work area
4. Making suggestions to management about ways to improve the working of your section
5. Contributing to discussions about the company's strategy
6. Writing a proposal to spend money in your work area
7. Helping to set targets/goals in your work area
8. Contacting people outside the company (e.g., suppliers, customers) to discuss problems
9. Presenting information to a group of colleagues
10. Visiting people from other departments to suggest doing things differently

Source: Sharon K. Parker, "Enhancing Role Breadth Self-efficacy: The Roles of Job Enrichment and Other Organizational Interventions," *Journal of Applied Psychology*, December 1998, p. 839.

Figure 2.2   Items reflecting role breadth self-efficacy behavior

around here to look for ways to increase production by 5 percent." His goal is implicitly to reduce waste in work processes by 5 percent. Here we look at two aspects of goal setting that are linked closely to goal setting: self-concordant goals and a model of proactive motivation.

Proactivity and Self-Concordant Goals

According to the self-concordant model of motivation, the reasons why individuals establish and pursue goals critically determine their motivation and self-regulation of behavior. The self-concordance model assumes that people have innate growth tendencies and psychological needs that guide their regulation of behavior. Self-concordant (autonomously regulated) goals are consistent with one's values, interests, and needs. For example, the manufacturing engineer just mentioned might regard a goal of reducing factory inefficiencies as being consistent with his professional values and need for personal development.

Gary J. Greguras and James M. Diefendorff conducted a study that included testing the hypothesis that more proactive individuals are more likely to set self-concordant goals than less proactive individuals. Data were collected from 165 full-time employees in Singapore, in a variety of managerial and individual contributor positions in several industries. The participants completed a test of the proactive personality, a measure of goal self-concordance, and also reported the extent of their goal attainment. Self-measures were also taken of need satisfaction and life satisfaction, whereas supervisors rated in-role (expected) job performance and organizational citizenship behavior.

The results of the study suggested that more proactive individuals were more likely to set self-concordant goals as well as attain them, which in turn led to psychological need satisfaction. When psychological need satisfaction was high, employees were more likely to experience life satisfaction, in-role performance, and organizational citizenship behavior. The researchers concluded that proactive employees in contrast to less proactive employees are more likely to (a) pursue goals for autonomous reasons, (b) attain their goals, and (c) experience greater psychological need satisfaction.

An implication drawn from the study is that managers might consider using proactive personality as a predictor in personnel selection, especially when employees experience a good person–organization fit. (The latter refers to a good fit between the needs and values of both the individual and the organization.)[16]

Proactive Motivation and Goal Setting

A model of proactive motivation has been developed that reinforces the importance of goal setting to proactive personalities. According to the theorizing of Sharon K. Parker, Uta K. Bindl, and Karoline Strauss, proactivity is seen as a goal-driven process involving both the setting of a proactive goal, and striving to achieve that goal.[17] (Many dreamers set goals but do not put much effort into their pursuit.)

According to the model in question, individuals can pursue a range of proactive goals. The goals vary on two dimensions. The first dimension is the future the goals aim to bring about (achieving a better fit with one's work environment, improving the organization's internal functioning, or enhancing the organization's strategic fit with the environment). Respectively, three examples could be (a) taking the initiative to learn a second language to better fit the demographics of customers and coworkers, (b) finding a way to ship products at lower cost, and (c) suggesting a new product line to appeal to the growing number of low-budget consumers. The second dimension is whether the self or situation is being changed. One way of changing oneself would be to seek out feedback from the supervisor to enhance performance.

Another aspect of the model suggests that three motivational states prompt goal generation and goal striving. The three states are "can do," "reason to," and "energized to." "Can do" motivation stems from perceptions of self-efficacy, control appraisals and attributions, and whether the cost of the pursuit is sufficiently low. "Can do" questions of this type would include, "Can I do it?" "How feasible is it?" and "How risky is it?"

"Reason to" motivation refers to why someone is proactive, including intrinsic motivation. The concern of the potentially proactive individual often focuses on the payoff from being proactive, wondering if anybody cares. Assume that a food technician in a yogurt factory thinks he knows of a good way to get more milk from cows owned by the farmers from whom the company purchases the milk. He would be more likely to present his plan to management if he believed that management really cared about increasing the milk yield from cows.

"Energized motivation" refers to activated positive affective states that trigger proactive goal setting. The basic idea is that when a person is experiencing a positive mood state, the person is more likely to establish challenging goals and anticipate problems worth tackling. If our food technician is in a good mood this week because of factors internal or external to the job, he is more likely to think of ways to squeeze more milk from cows. In a somber mood, he is less likely to worry about enhancing cow productivity to help the yogurt company be more profitable.

As suggested in relation to "reason to" motivation, people with a proactive personality are usually intrinsically motivated – the joy they find within the task is a major motive for being proactive. Intrinsic motivation arises from the individual's positive reaction to the task itself. The reaction can be expressed as interest, involvement, curiosity, or positive challenge.[18] A person with strong intrinsic motivation might also be interested in external rewards. An example would be an engineer who develops a patent. Although she enjoys the exciting work that goes into developing a product worthy of a patent, she is also motivated by the prestige and financial reward accompanying the patent.

As part of a larger study conducted in four Fortune Global 500 companies, Baek-Kyoo (Brian) Joo and Taejo Lim tested the hypothesis that proactive personality will be related to intrinsic motivation.[19] A sample item from the questionnaire about intrinsic motivation was "I enjoy coming up with new ideas for products." Analysis of the data revealed that proactive personality was significantly related to intrinsic motivation. An implication of this study is that to trigger the proactivity of workers, it is helpful to provide them with challenging and stimulating work. One example would be to ask an industrial design specialist if he could come up with an idea for a beer bottle that was more fun for a beer drinker to hold.

EFFECTIVE INTERPERSONAL RELATIONSHIPS AND PROACTIVITY

Another benefit to proactivity for workers is that they are likely to develop positive interpersonal relationships by reaching out to please work associates. For example, the improved leader–member relations already mentioned are a byproduct of taking the initiative to please the manager. Here we describe briefly three of the many ways in which proactivity can enhance interpersonal relationships.

1.   Improved Socialization into the Organization

"Socialization" refers to the newcomer learning the customs and culture of an organization. Although the efforts of managers and human resource professionals are important in helping workers become socialized, employee proactivity can facilitate the socialization process. The proactive employee makes the effort to learn how things are done and to gain entrance into in-groups. As many workers are employed by a series of organizations, proactivity in the socialization process becomes more important for individuals and the organization.

Connie R. Wanberg and John D. Kammeyer-Mueller studied three proactive socialization behaviors: sensemaking, relationship building, and positive framing.[20] Sensemaking, or figuring out what certain behaviors and statements mean, involves information seeking. Relationship building in the study in question referred to behaviors engaged in by the newcomer directed toward initiating social interaction in the workplace. Positive framing refers to a cognitive self-management mechanism new employees rely on to alter their understanding of a situation by controlling the positive frame they put on a situation. Positive framing would include an employee explicitly attempting to put a positive spin on a situation and perceive it to be an opportunity rather than a threat. A proactive newcomer in learning about a planned layoff might think to herself, "With a thinned-down company, I will have more opportunity to broaden my job responsibilities and get noticed."

Based on surveys and observations of individuals who went from being unemployed to being employed, the researchers found several results related to proactivity and socialization. Sensemaking and relationship building showed a positive association with role clarity and social integration. This finding suggests that if workers engage in the proactive behaviors of sensemaking and building relationships, they will develop a better understanding of their job role and integrate themselves better into the workgroup.

2. Flattering Others to Gain Career Advantage

An appropriate degree of flattery can be an effective approach to building relationships in the workplace. Flattering others is proactive because the flatterer must be alert to opportunities to flatter a target, and then develop effective flattering statements. An example of flattering a marketing executive might be, "Your strategy of introducing our high-end products to India has been a breakthrough in terms of sales." Flattery is likely to be effective because most people want to receive accolades, even if they are not completely warranted.[21]

A study indicated that even at the highest positions in business organizations, flattery helps a person gain advantage. Specifically, ingratiating oneself with the CEO, including flattery, was a major factor in receiving an appointment as a board of director at a major company. Not carefully monitoring (carefully scrutinizing) the CEO's activities also worked in a person's favor for receiving a board appointment.[22] Not finding fault with a CEO might be interpreted as a form of flattery.

3. Enhanced Customer Service Performance

Proactivity on the part of customer-contact workers can pay big dividends to the organization because customers are more satisfied, resulting in higher sales, improved customer retention, and fewer complaints. According to Steffen Raub and Hui Liao, standard customer service and proactive customer service are qualitatively different. *General service performance* refers to service that follows formalized job descriptions and service scripts. The customer-contact worker completes core service tasks using standard service procedures. General service performance still plays an important role in influencing customer satisfaction because customer expectations are met.

Proactive customer service performance provides unexpected service extras that are neither prescribed by service standards nor responses to service delivery failures. Proactive service has a strong positive impact on customers' perceptions of service quality. Proactive customer service employees take the initiative to anticipate customer needs or problems, establish partnerships with other service employees that could help customers in the future, and proactively solicit feedback from customers. An example of proactive customer service would be a new car sales representative observing that a customer was quite confused about the complex instrumentation in the vehicle. The representative then takes the initiative to recommend that the new owner return to the dealer a few days later to help answer questions about using the electronic commands in the vehicle.

(The rep senses that the customer is somewhat overwhelmed with all the new learning on the day of purchase.)

A large study by Raub and Liao of frontline service employees of a multinational hotel chain found that employee self-efficacy is positively associated with individual-level proactive customer service performance. It was also found that proactive customer service contributed to customer satisfaction beyond general service performance.[23]

SUGGESTIONS FOR APPLICATION

1. Developing your willingness to learn will help enhance your status as a proactive personality, even if you are not already a proactive personality. New learning is proactive because it often relates to knowledge and skill that you not already using or have no immediate need to use. Emphasizing the extraverted aspects of your personality can also enhance your image as a proactive personality.

2. Developing an internal locus of control, or attributing rewards and punishments received to be a result of one's own behaviors, is helpful in becoming more proactive. The explanation is that if you think you can control external events you are more likely to attempt to change them in your favor.

3. The proactive personality and organizational citizenship behavior are closely linked. Displaying organizational citizenship behavior in its many forms would help you be proactive in the workplace. Challenge-oriented organizational citizenship behaviors (those aimed at encouraging something to happen) are particularly helpful for displaying proactivity.

4. A useful application of proactivity is to look for ways to develop effective exchanges with your immediate manager (leader–member exchanges). One of the many outcomes of a positive leader–member exchange is that it will facilitate your engaging in organizational citizenship behavior, further enhancing your status. Proactivity is also important for enhancing relationships with work associates in addition to an immediate manager.

5. Self-concordant goals are the most closely associated with the proactive personality. Such goals fit one's values, interests, and needs. It is possible that setting self-concordant goals will foster a person engaging in proactive behavior.

SUMMARY

The proactive personality is related to other traits and behaviors, with considerable research relating proactivity to the Big Five personality factors and their facets. One study showed that proactivity accounted for about 26 percent of the Big Five factors, with seven facets of these factors showing a positive relationship to proactivity: assertiveness, activity, actions, ideas, values, altruism, and achievement. The facets of vulnerability and dutifulness were found to be negatively related to proactivity. A large, cross-cultural study found that the clearest relationship with proactive personality was found with extraversion.

A natural relationship exists between proactivity and internal locus of control because people with an internal locus of control feel that they can create their own opportunities in life. Locus of control, similar to proactivity, has a positive relationship with well-being at work. Similarly to people with a proactive personality, research suggests that people with an internal locus of control are more likely to have greater intrinsic motivation, and be more achievement oriented.

Organizational citizenship behavior is closely related to the proactive personality because both focus on actions that go beyond role requirements and both contribute to organizational effectiveness. Five key dimensions of organizational citizenship behavior are altruism, civic virtue, conscientiousness, courtesy, and sportsmanship. The dimensional analysis suggests that organizational citizenship behaviors are behavioral manifestations of cooperativeness at work.

A study showed that challenge-oriented (change-oriented) organizational citizenship behaviors have a positive impact on workgroup performance up to a point. Beyond this optimal point, OCB improves performance only when affiliation-oriented (helping people) OCBs are present.

Proactive employees usually have positive relationships with their supervisors. A study showed that proactive personality was associated with establishing a high-quality relationship with the worker's supervisor. In turn, the quality of the leader–member exchange influenced how employees experience greater job satisfaction and display more organizational citizenship behavior. A study conducted in China showed that for workers with a high standing on harmony, proactive personality is positively associated with organizational citizenship behavior as rated by supervisors.

Role breadth self-efficacy (feeling confident about an expanded role) may underlie organizational citizenship behavior because it focuses on what workers feel they can do. RBSE explicitly focuses on activities that require proactivity.

A person with a proactive personality takes naturally to goal setting because he or she by nature enjoys the idea of looking into the future and making improvements. A study showed that more proactive individuals are more likely to set self-concordant (fitting one's values and interests) goals and attain them than less proactive individuals. Attaining these goals was associated with higher psychological need satisfaction.

A model of proactive motivation suggests that individuals can pursue a range of proactive goals that vary on two dimensions: (a) the future the goals aim to bring about, and (b) whether the self or the situation is changed. The model also suggests that three motivational states prompt goal generation and goal striving. The three states are "can do," "reason to," and "energized to." An idea related to this model is that research indicates that proactive personality is significantly related to intrinsic motivation.

Another benefit to proactivity for workers is that they are more likely to develop positive interpersonal relationships by reaching out to pleas of work associates. Proactivity also leads to improved socialization into the organization for newcomers. Proactivity also helps in knowing when to flatter work associates, and for providing enhanced customer service.

The association between proactivity and other traits and behaviors has practical application. Examples include the following: showing a willingness to learn demonstrates proactivity; developing an internal locus of control enhances proactivity; challenge-oriented organizational citizenship behaviors show proactivity; proactivity leads to better leader–member exchanges; and self-concordant goals fit proactivity.

REFERENCES

1. Brian O'Keefe, "Inside the World's Biggest Hedge Fund," *Fortune*, March 30, 2009, p. 81; "Bridgewater's Dalio: U.S. Economy Out of 'Intensive Care'," *Business & Financial News Reuters.com*, www.reuters.com, September 12, 2012, p. 1. Retrieved December 3, 2012.
2. Debra A. Major, Jonathan E. Turner, and Thomas D. Fletcher, "Linking Proactive Personality and the Big Five to Motivation to Learn and Development Activity," *Journal of Applied Psychology*, July 2006, pp. 927–935.
3. Kilian Werenfried Wawoe, "Proactive Personality: The Advantages and Disadvantages of an Entrepreneurial Disposition in the Financial Industry," Doctoral Dissertation, Amsterdam, Holland: Vrije Universiteit, 2010.
4. Julian P. Rotter, "Generalized Expectancies for Internal vs. External Control of Reinforcement," *Psychological Monographs*, Volume 80, 1966, pp. 1–28.
5. Qiang Wang, Nathan A. Bowling, and Kevin J. Eschleman, "A Meta-Analytic Examination of Work and General Locus of Control," *Journal of Applied Psychology*, July 2010, pp. 761–768.

6. Paul E. Spector and 29 other researchers, "Locus of Control and Well-Being at Work: How Generalizable Are Western Findings?" *Academy of Management Journal*, April 2002, pp. 453–466.

7. Robert W. Renn and Robert J. Vandenberg, "Differences in Employee Attitudes and Behaviors Based on Rotter's (1966) Internal–External Locus of Control: Are they All Still Valid?" *Human Relations*, Volume 44, 1991, pp. 1161–1178; Paul E. Spector, "Behavior in Organizations as a Function of Employee Locus of Control," *Psychological Bulletin*, Volume 91, 1982, pp. 482–497.

8. Ning Li, Jian Lang, and J. Michael Crant, "The Role of Proactive Personality in Job Satisfaction and Organizational Citizenship Behavior: A Relational Perspective," *Journal of Applied Psychology*, March 2010, p. 396.

9. Dennis W. Organ, "Organizational Citizenship Behavior: It's Construct Clean-Up Time," *Human Performance*, Volume 10, 1997, p. 91.

10. Jeffrey A. LePine, Amir Erez, and Diane E. Johnson, "The Nature and Dimensionality of Organizational Citizenship Behavior: A Critical Review and Meta-Analysis," *Journal of Applied Psychology*, February 2002, pp. 52–65.

11. LePine, Erez, and Johnson, "The Nature and Dimensionality of Organizational Citizenship Behavior," p. 61.

12. Scott B. MacKenzie, Philip M. Podsakoff, and Nathan P. Podsakoff, "Challenge-Oriented Organizational Citizenship Behaviors and Organizational Effectiveness: Do Challenge-Oriented Behaviors Really Have an Impact on the Organization's Bottom Line?" *Personnel Psychology*, Number 3, 2011, pp. 559–592.

13. Ning Li, Jian Liang, and Crant, "The Role of Proactive Personality in Job Satisfaction and Organizational Citizenship Behavior," p. 396.

14. Yiqun Gan and Fanny M. Cheung, "From Proactive Personality to Organizational Citizenship Behavior: Mediating Role of Harmony," *Psychological Reports*, Volume 106, Number 3, pp. 755–765.

15. Sharon K. Parker, "Enhancing Role Breadth Self-Efficacy: The Roles of Job Enrichment and Other Organizational Interventions," *Journal of Applied Psychology*, December 1998, pp. 835–852.

16. Gary J. Greguras and James M. Diefendorff, "Why Does Proactive Personality Predict Employee Life Satisfaction and Work Behaviors? A Field Investigation of the Mediating Role of the Self-Concordance Model," *Personnel Psychology*, Autumn 2010, pp. 539–560.

17. Sharon K. Parker, Uta K. Bindl, and Karoline Strauss, "Making Things Happen: A Model of Proactive Motivation," *Journal of Management*, July 2010, pp. 1–30.

18. Therese M. Amabile, *Creativity in Context: Update to the Social Psychology of Creativity* (Boulder, CO: Westview Press, 1996), p. 115.

19. Baek-Kyoo (Brian) Joo and Taejo Lim, "The Impacts of Organizational Learning Culture and Proactive Personality on Organizational Commitment and Intrinsic Motivation: The Mediating Role of Job Complexity." Paper presented at 2008 Midwest Academy of Management Conference, October 2–4, St. Louis, MO.

20. Connie R. Wanberg and John D. Kammeyer-Mueller, "Predictors and Outcomes of Proactivity in the Socialization Process," *Journal of Applied Psychology*, June 2000, pp. 373–385.

21.   Marshall Goldsmith, "All of Us Are Stuck on Suck-Ups," *Fast Company*, December 2003, p. 117.
22.   James D. Westphal and Ithai Stern, "Flattery Will Get You Everywhere (Especially If You Are a Male Caucasian): How Ingratiation, Boardroom Behavior, and Demographic Minority Status Affect Additional Board Appointments at U. S. Companies," *Academy of Management Journal*, April 2007, pp. 267–288.
23.   Steffen Raub and Hui Liao, "Doing the Right Thing Without Being Told: Joint Effects of Initiative Climate and General Self-Efficacy on Employee Customer Service Performance," *Journal of Applied Psychology*, May 2012, pp. 651–667.

3. Initiative as part of the proactive personality

Workplace initiative is intertwined with proactivity. One could argue that a person with a proactive personality frequently takes the initiative, or that a person who takes the initiative is being proactive. A useful definition of workplace initiative based on a composite of viewpoints is that personal initiative refers to a behavioral pattern of individuals who take an active, self-starting approach to work.[1] Ronald Bledow and Michael Frese explain similarly that personal initiative is an active performance concept emphasizing that workers self-start to accomplish positive individual and organizational outcomes.[2]

Given that initiative and proactivity are close to being the same thing, it follows that initiative is perceived to be a sought-after employee quality. As one example, interviews were conducted with several Pittsburgh executives to uncover the key traits they seek in potential hires as well as internal candidates for promotion. The critical success factor most often mentioned was initiative.[3] Furthermore, Robert E. Kelley writes that demonstrating initiative is the most powerful work skill for bridging the chasm between the average worker and the super-productive worker. Newcomers to an organization are quickly judged on whether they go beyond their specific responsibilities and take the initiative.[4]

At the leadership level, initiative taking often begins with the attitude, "It starts with me." A cohort of senior leaders at Lockheed Martin on many nights looked for opportunities to seek out other managers and employees to talk with and strengthen relationships. They also took the initiative to organize a dinner in order to interact with new managers from around the corporation. The act of investing the time to meet with the new managers and getting to know them was seen as having a positive impact on building morale and strengthening relationships among the different levels of management.[5]

In this chapter we examine workplace initiative from several perspectives: behaviors and attitudes reflecting initiative; how initiative relates to job performance; the link between initiative, well-being, and stress; situational influences on initiative; and the potential disadvantages of taking the initiative.

WORK BEHAVIORS AND ATTITUDES REFLECTING INITIATIVE

It is common knowledge that managers and human resource specialists believe that initiative, or self-starting ability, contributes to individual and organizational effectiveness. In this section we describe many of the specific attitudes and behaviors that reflect initiative. The checklist presented in Figure 3.1 points to a sampling of attitudes and behaviors that reflect taking the initiative.

Three Key Aspects of Personal Initiative: Self-Starting, Proactivity, and Persistence

As emphasized in the research of Michael Frese and Doris Fay, initiative is multi-faceted consisting of a variety of behaviors related to self-starting, proactivity, and persistence. All of these facets reflect active behavior.[6] Despite the emphasis on behavior, attitudes may be antecedents to the behavior. For example, a worker might harbor the attitude that environmental sustainability is very important. She then takes the initiative to send a report to management touting the potential energy savings from planting a garden on the office building roof.

Self-starting behavior points to the basic idea that a person engages in constructive activity without being told, without receiving explicit instruction, or without being part of his or her formal role. The implication is that the person with personal initiative pursues self-set goals in contrast to assigned goals. A quality technician at a company that manufactures dehumidifiers might set the goal of contacting friends and relatives to encourage them to purchase his company's brand of dehumidifier even though such action is not part of the technician's job description.

Initiative in higher-level jobs is more difficult to define because taking the initiative is part of the job, such as the CEO developing ideas for expanding the company's market for its goods and services. For example, the last several CEOs at IBM have vastly expanded the company's offerings as a provider of information technology services in addition to selling hardware and software. Expanding the impact of IBM is part of the job of these executives, rather than acting outside their role requirements.

Proactivity in the present context refers to having a long-term focus and not waiting until one is faced with a demand. Problems and opportunities are anticipated, and the worker conjures up methods and procedures to meet these problems. Assume that a sales representative at an automobile service center reads several forecasts about a severe winter, loaded with

The list below provides examples of attitudes and behaviors reflective of personal initiative taken in the workplace. The reader might relate these attitudes and behaviors to himself or herself, or to a work associate. "Yes" indicates that the attitude or behavior was observed. "No" indicates that the attitude or behavior was not observed.

Number	Attitude or behavior reflecting initiative	Yes	No
1.	When something goes wrong, I attempt to solve the problem.	❏	❏
2.	When I run out of assigned work to perform, I search for something constructive to do.	❏	❏
3.	I sometimes create useful work for myself on the job.	❏	❏
4.	I have contributed several or more new ideas to my present or past employers.	❏	❏
5.	I do the research necessary to back up suggestions for improvement that I might have.	❏	❏
6.	If nothing constructive is happening during a group meeting, I will suggest that we focus on something that can be converted into action.	❏	❏
7.	I am often on the lookout to improve my company's products, services, or work processes.	❏	❏
8.	I typically keep pushing for a job-related idea in which I believe.	❏	❏
9.	I like to ask "what if" questions on the job.	❏	❏
10.	I often take constructive action on the job without being told.	❏	❏
11.	I believe that it is part of my job to do such things as picking up trash from the floor or tightening a loose screw on a doorknob.	❏	❏
12.	If there is something I do not understand about my job, I will ask my supervisor, a coworker, or a tech support specialist.	❏	❏
13.	I teach myself new skills that can improve my job performance.	❏	❏
14.	I will ask questions to get to the root of a problem.		
15.	If I am having a problem with my boss I will ask to discuss the problem in person, by phone, or through messages.	❏	❏
16.	I will often start working on a small problem before it grows into a big one.	❏	❏
17.	I quite often will work on a problem without being told.	❏	❏
18.	Many of the goals I pursue on the job are those that I set for myself.	❏	❏
19.	I frequently undertake self-improvement activities related to my job or career.	❏	❏
20.	I regularly take steps to build a network of influential people.	❏	❏

Note: scoring and interpretation: the more of these behaviors and attitudes that are true for a person, the more he or she can be classified as having initiative or self-starting ability. A score of 16 or greater would suggest high initiative, whereas a score of 6 or below would suggest low initiative.

Figure 3.1   A checklist of behaviors and attitudes reflecting initiative

snow and ice. She then decides to get permission to clear up some storage space to make room for the many snow tires the service center will most likely need to order. Her proactivity facilitates the center being able to meet customer demand easily. If she only reacted to the problem of limited storage space at a later date, the service center might not have had enough room to meet customer demand.

Persistence in overcoming barriers is often needed to reach one's goal while taking the initiative. Sometimes even the most logical and straightforward plans meet with resistance. For example, our service center sales representative might find that a warehouse supervisor thinks that all the obsolete and damaged goods in the warehouse are too valuable to be discarded, such as tires for trucks that have not been manufactured in 10 years. She is also told that the stockpile of old boxes might be needed for shipping defective parts back to the manufacturer. The sales representative may have to patiently explain several times that the company owner has authorized her to create some storage space.

Frese and Fay reason that the three aspects of personal initiative – self-starting, proactivity, and persistence – reinforce each other. A proactive attitude leads to the establishment of self-started goals because these goals are needed to accomplish activities outside the job description. The self-started goals lead in turn to the need to be persistent to overcome barriers to goal attainment. Upon finding barriers to goal attainment, more self-started goals may be required. For example, our sales representative, upon meeting resistance to clearing out the warehouse, may need to establish goals for overcoming the resistance. She might establish the goal of getting top management at the service center to accompany her on a visit to the warehouse to legitimate her plan. Another point of reinforcement is that self-starting implies the person visualizes potential future issues. As a result, the worker has to be proactive.

In addition to the three aspects of personal initiative reinforcing each other they may occur virtually at the same time. After self-starting takes place, the individual has to proactively look at the future, and be persistent in pursuit of the self-started goals.

Facets of the three aspects of personal initiative

To take a more in-depth look at the three aspects of personal initiative, each aspect has its own four facets. According to Frese and Fay, the three aspects of personal initiative are covered by an action sequence that works its way into the four facets of each aspect.[7] The action sequence is (1) goals or redefinition of tasks, (2) information collection and prognosis, (3) planning and execution, and (4) monitoring and feedback. The four facets for the three aspects (self-starting, proactivity, and persistence) all relate to the action sequence.

Self-starting facets   The first facet is active goals, including redefinition of the goals. The goals are determined by the nature of the task, such as setting a goal for creating more available space in the warehouse. The goal is subject to redefinition or refinement, such as the goal of selling obsolete inventory to a salvage dealer.

The second facet is active search, such as exploration and active scanning. The self-starter will often need to collect information to accomplish the goal, such as the warehouse worker investigating the best way to discard excess inventory, including environmental regulations.

The third facet is active planning, such as establishing dates for accomplishing a task as well as figuring out which other workers would be available to help accomplish the initiative. Contingency planning is an important part of formulating plans to accomplish the initiative. For example, "What do I do if the company will not fund my idea?"

The fourth facet is self-developed feedback and active search for feedback. The self-starter will often develop his or her own sources of feedback. Part of being a proactive personality is to want to know if the course chosen is constructive. The technician cited earlier who is attempting to get people to purchase his company's brand of dehumidifier might inquire at the sales department to see if his efforts have resulted in any additional orders for the company.

Proactive facets The first facet of the proactive aspect is anticipating future problems and opportunities, and conversion into a goal. Proactive goals imply that the person takes a long-term approach to work, such as the auto service center worker thinking that creating more warehouse space to meet seasonal demand is an idea that will serve the company well for many years. The second facet of the proactive aspect involves information collection and making prognoses. The person considers potential problem areas and opportunities before they happen. To be safe, the worker develops knowledge on alternative routes to getting the initiative accomplished. The service center worker might think, "Suppose the surge in demand for snow tires does not materialize? Should I make suggestions for another effective use of the extra warehouse space?"

The third facet stems from the second. The person develops backup plans, as indicated by suggesting an alternative use for the additional warehouse space. The fourth facet is the development of early signals for potential problems and opportunities. An office manager might have taken the initiative to plan a large office party to help build relationships with members of a just-acquired sister company. If only a couple of staff members signed up for the party after two weeks, does she recommend that the party be cancelled?

Persistence (overcoming barriers) facets   Persistence, or overcoming barriers, involves the person protecting goals, information collection, plans, and feedback against disturbances. The first facet is protecting goals when frustrated or stressed by complexity. It is necessary for the initiative taker to keep moving forward even when not much progress is being made in terms of goal attainment. The office manager who planned the party for helping integrate the cultures of the two companies might attempt a follow-up e-mail campaign to get people to sign up. The persistent person keeps trying rather than blaming others for his or her goals being blocked.

The second facet of persistence is to collect information and make prognoses. The office manager might get in touch with a couple of people to help figure out why enrollment for the party has been slow. If she develops a good understanding of why enrollment is slow, she can better forecast how many workers are likely to attend the party. Instead of being discouraged when a barrier arises, the persistent person keeps going with the belief that the initiative will eventually pay off.

The third facet to persistence and overcoming barriers is returning to the plan quickly when the plan is disrupted or disturbed. Suppose that the office manager soon finds that not enough people have signed up for the party to bother with the idea. Part of her persistence might be to develop a backup or contingency plan. Instead of an evening party, she makes plans for a Saturday afternoon picnic to which family members are invited. The picnic concept is widely accepted, and the contingency planning is vindicated. The fourth facet of persistence is protecting the feedback search. Because feedback is not always spontaneous, the initiative taker might be forced to ask key people questions, "What do you think of my plan so far? How well is it working?"

Job Crafting and Initiative

The process of workers taking the initiative to make their jobs more interesting and productive has been studied systematically. The traditional view of a job is that a competent worker carefully follows a job description, and good performance means that the person accomplishes what is specified in the job description. A contemporary view is that a job description is only a general guideline: the competent worker is not confined by the constraints of a job description. He or she takes on many constructive activities not mentioned in the job description, thereby demonstrating initiative and proactivity.

One way workers frequently deviate from their job descriptions is to modify their job to fit their personal preferences and capabilities.

According to the research of Amy Wrzesniewski and Jane E. Dutton, employees craft their jobs by changing the tasks they perform, and their contacts with others, to make their jobs more meaningful.[8] To add variety to his job, for example, a team leader might make nutritional recommendations to team members. The team leader has altered his task of coaching about strictly work-related issues to also coaching about personal health. He has also broadened his role in terms of his impact on the lives of work associates.

Job crafting refers to the physical and mental changes workers make in the task or relationship aspects of their job. Three common types of job crafting involve changing (1) the number and type of job tasks, (2) the interactions with others on the job, and (3) one's view of the job. The most frequent purpose of crafting is to make the job more meaningful or enriched. A baker, for example, might take the initiative to offer figurines of same-sex couples on wedding cakes to broaden the customer base. Examples of the three most frequent forms of job crafting follow, with each one requiring worker initiative.

1. *Changing number, scope, and type of job tasks.* A product development engineer might change the quality or amount of interactions with people as a way of gaining acceptance for her ideas and moving the project to completion.
2. *Changing quality and/or amount of interaction with others encountered on the job.* Custodial workers in an office might interact with office workers to better understand their needs for office cleanliness.
3. *Changing the view of the job.* A customer-care worker in a call center might decide to perceive every customer demand for help or complaint as an important problem to be resolved, even one as mundane as having forgotten to plug the computer into an electric outlet.

JOB PERFORMANCE AND INITIATIVE

An axiom of impressing superiors as well as attaining tangible good performance is to take the initiative, or not wait until you are told to perform a constructive task. People who take the initiative are also perceived to be more likely candidates for promotion. Here we look at some of the evidence and opinion about the relationship between job performance and initiative.

Empirical Research about the Link between Performance and Initiative

A study of 126 employee–supervisor dyads conducted by Jeffery A. Thompson demonstrated that initiative taking helps explain the link between proactivity and job performance.[9] The study participants were college alumni working in a variety of job types and industries. Self-questionnaire measures were taken of proactive personality and human network building. Supervisors rated the employees on initiative taking and job performance. Supervisors indicated the number of times in the last six months this employee took *initiative* in each of the following ways: (a) "implemented a solution to a departmental or organizational problem," and (b) "spearheaded a new program or effort of his or her own design." The average number of initiative-taking behaviors was 3.3, with a range from 0 to 14.

The results indicated that proactive personality was linked to subjective evaluations of performance by supervisors. The link was interpreted to mean that proactivity has a measurable impact on supervisory percep-tions. Another interpretation of the results was that initiative taking mediates the relationship between proactive personality and performance. Proactive personality appears to predict the extent to which an employee takes the initiative to go beyond his or her immediate job tasks. In turn, the initiative taking appears to have a direct positive relationship with job performance. (Again, we see how proactivity and initiative taking are closely intertwined.)

Network building enters the picture because the results suggested that proactive employees gain performance benefits by building social networks that provide them the resources to pursue high-level initiatives. Proactive employees often search for allies and advocates to support their initiatives. In addition, proactive employees seek out network members of power and influence. An example of how a network member might help a proactive employee would be to provide specific advice about how to implement a creative suggestion.

Additional evidence of the link between initiative and job performance stems from the development of a written test that measures initiative by having people indicate how they would respond to specific situations. As developed by Ronald Bledow and Michael Frese, the test presents a series of situations followed by courses of action. Each course of action is answered "most likely" or "least likely." One such scenario is the problem of a supervisor dealing with new trainees in the department who need help, yet the supervisor is facing heavy work pressures. One course of action is "I tell the trainees that I am available after work to answer their questions."

A study conducted with employees in six regional German banks found that the situational judgment test of initiative was valid in terms of predicting job behavior. Relevant to the present discussion, personal initiative as measured by the test was related to supervisors' ratings of overall performance. Apparently the supervisors acknowledge the positive contribution of personal initiative to general performance.[10]

A review by Frese and Fay of several empirical studies suggests that personal initiative benefits the organization when such behavior is widespread in the company. In a sample of medium-sized German companies, a climate that welcomed initiative showed a substantial positive relationship to profitability. The interpretation of these results is that widespread personal initiative in organizations improves the ability to deal with challenges. A specific challenge is the introduction of process innovations. Climate for initiative proved to have a moderator effect with respect to the link between process innovation and profitability. The introduction of process innovation resulted in higher profitability only for those companies that showed a strong climate for innovation. One reason is that actions and ideas that improve production need to be self-started because the supervisor cannot be present all the time to provide direction.[11]

Representative Opinion about the Link between Initiative and Job Performance

As implied above, initiative taking has long been offered as a bromide for one's manager, and therefore obtaining a favorable performance evaluation. A representative approach is to assume responsibility for free-floating (non-assigned) problems. The person who picks up the free-floating responsibility will often gain the edge by being perceived as responsible. Assuming responsibility for even a minor task, such as ordering lunch for a meeting that is running late, can enhance the impression one makes on an immediate manager. A case history of how initiative taking can enhance a person's stature in the organization follows:

> Ben is a human resources specialist at a meat-packing company. His company was being pressured by the local and federal governments to take more drastic steps to reduce workplace hazards. A task force was appointed by the CEO to study the problem. Ben was not assigned as one of the taskforce members. Nevertheless, he thought he could make a contribution to the study of the problem. Without being given the assignment, Ben prepared a 25-page report on current trends in workplace accidents in the food-processing industry.
>
> Ben submitted his report to the taskforce, simply stating that his findings might be of some use to the group. The report therefore made the job of the taskforce much easier, and Ben's efforts were widely praised. In recognition of his hard work and interest, the CEO then appointed Ben to the taskforce. Ben's

boss, the vice-president of human resources, also received praise for having such a helpful professional on the staff.[12]

A standard approach to taking the initiative that can facilitate being regarded positively by the organization is to volunteer for leadership assignments related to company activities. Such assignments include taskforces, special projects, committees, and important community projects. Accepting leadership responsibility helps a person gain advantage in two meaningful ways. First, the person is perceived as a self-starter who is motivated to serve the needs of the organization. Secondly, assuming leadership responsibility is a direct way of demonstrating leadership. By demonstrating leadership skill on a temporary assignment, the person becomes a stronger candidate for occupying a formal leadership position within the organization.

Based on observations in many organizations, Stephen Bucaro makes the following observations about the advantages of taking the initiative on the job: taking the initiative can lead to skill development because the new task might require some new learning. With more skill, the employee becomes more valuable to the organization. The individual will achieve more independence by demonstrating a concern for the organization, and that his or her judgment can be trusted.[13]

Another perspective on the relationship between initiative and job performance is that initiative taking is part of a leader's role. However, a philosophical issue arises in this argument. If part of a leader's role is to take the initiative, when a leader takes the initiative is he or she going beyond the normal role requirements of the position? Similarly if a smart-phone designer conjures up an elegant design for a smart phone, is she displaying initiative? Yet if the department administrative assistant suggested the new design, he would be displaying initiative.

Initiative is such an integral part of leadership that many dictionaries list *leadership* as a synonym for *initiative*. Geno A. Bulzomi writes that an effective leader understands the meaning of initiative, takes the initiative, and possesses the stamina to fully execute his or her initiative.[14] Making an inference from studies conducted in the World War II era, Bernard M. Bass concluded that initiative contributes to leadership effectiveness.[15] Chapter 8 in this book about business strategy, planning, and proactivity could be interpreted to explain further the link between initiative and leadership.

INITIATIVE, WELL-BEING, AND STRESS

Initiative taking has many positive consequences for the individual so it is not surprising that the high-initiative individual is more likely to feel a sense of well-being, as well as minimize the potential negative effects of job stress. Visualize a web designer working for a company that is headed toward bankruptcy. He needs the revenue from a job to pay his living expenses, and he also needs to work as a web designer to preserve his self-esteem. Instead of agonizing about the prospects of being laid off when his employer declares bankruptcy, he takes the initiative to calmly search for a new position in a crowded field. He steps up his network building by being more active on LinkedIn, as well as making telephone and in-person contacts with other web designers in his community. Within 30 days he finds a new position at slightly higher pay, thereby avoiding the overwhelming stress of being unemployed. Experiencing a minimum of stress, he also preserves his sense of well-being.

A Study of the Relationship between Personal Initiative and Well-Being

A study conducted by Toon W. Taris and Etty G. A. Wielenga-Meijer with 834 Dutch blue-collar telecommunication workers examined whether personal initiative contributed to worker well-being.[16] The study participants were responsible for the groundwork for telecommunication services, such as trenching for cable networks – a job with heavy physical demands. The researchers reasoned that people high on initiative would be likely to utilize the resources offered by their jobs to maximize outcomes, including those related to well-being. In addition, they should be capable of minimizing the adverse effects of harmful conditions which might endanger their well-being.

The specific aspects of well-being studied were emotional exhaustion and learning motivation. Personal initiative was measured by a seven-item scale, a representative item being, "When something goes wrong, I look immediately for a solution." Emotional exhaustion was measured by a five-item scale, with a typical item being, "I feel empty at the end of the work day."

The results of the study most relevant to the link between personal initiative and well-being are reported here. High ratings on personal initiative were associated with low scores on emotional exhaustion, as well as high scores on learning motivation. An important implication the authors draw from their results is that workers with high initiative are not only more productive and successful than others (as in the research cited above), but also more motivated to learn and less emotionally exhausted than others. As a result, they have a higher sense of well-being. (We recognize that motivation to learn and low emotional exhaustion are but two contributors to well-being. Among the many other work-related contributors to a sense of well-being are low job stress, physical fitness, and having a network of social support.)

An Analysis of the Link between Stressors and Personal Initiative

The complex relationship between job stressors and personal initiative has been analyzed by Doris Fay, Sabine Sonnentag, and Michael Frese. Stressors, and the stress they create, can impair initiative taking. The reverse is also true because taking the initiative can cause stress. A third possibility is that job stressors can encourage initiative to modify the stressors.[17] We look at the three observations separately.

Stress impedes initiative

Initiative and innovation are aimed at improving work processes and procedures or preparing for future problems or demands. Spotting the opportunity for initiative requires long-term planning and environmental scanning, such as looking for changes in government regulations that could affect the business. When stress becomes too heavy, attention is diverted away from the mental processes required for taking the initiative. For example, when highly stressed a person might not be so observant of business trends.

The stressor of role overload can create a situation in which the worker does not have enough slack time to think about ways of taking the initiative. As many busy professionals and managers say, "My job leaves me no time to plan." Similarly, the sales representative who is so overloaded serving current customers might not take the time to cultivate new customers. Being overloaded with work, the worker may have reduced opportunities to identify areas for taking the initiative.

Personal initiative creates stress

The action of taking the initiative consumes mental effort and time, leaving less time to handle regular chores. As a result the initiative taker may experience stress related to not having enough time to take care of regular responsibilities. If the worker does not expand the amount of time devoted to the job, he or she is forced to make a decision between the pursuit of the initiated action and the regular tasks. Role conflict leading to stress results because the worker must choose between pursuing two incompatible goals (executing the regular task versus the initiated task).

Stressors create the need for initiative

Faced with a stressor, the person typically perceives the need to cope with the problem creating the stress. This is most likely true when the stressor is an external threat because the person might believe that he or she can take appropriate action to deal with the threat. When the stress is an irrational fear, such as thinking that the office building will soon be invaded by terrorists, it is more difficult to cope with the stressor. Perhaps with the assistance of a counselor, the person can learn to modify his or her irrational fears.

To illustrate how initiative taking can help modify or eliminate a stressor, think of a commuter who lives in a congested area such as a suburb of Washington, D.C. She finds that by the third day of the week, she develops stress symptoms such as chest pains and headaches when faced with another long commute back and forth to the office. She then takes the initiative to propose of her manager that one day per week she will change her office hours from 10:30 a.m. until 6:30 p.m. In addition she proposes that she will work from home every other Friday. Taking into account that the commuter is an above-average performer, her manager accepts her modified work schedule. The woman has now modified her stressful commute enough to make it manageable. Knowing that the rigors of her commuting have been reduced, she experiences less job stress.

EXTERNAL AND SITUATIONAL INFLUENCES ON INITIATIVE

As with proactivity, the extent of initiative taking can be influenced by factors external to the individual. For example, initiative can be encouraged or discouraged by a manager. Frese and Day use the term *environmental supports* for factors that facilitate the display of initiative.[18] A key support is the amount of control the worker has with respect to the operations of the job. An example of high control would be when a worker can choose when to concentrate on analytical work. The opposite would be a worker who has no control over interruptions. On occasion a worker will exert initiative in an attempt to gain control, but in general lack of control can lead to a learned helplessness. The person lives with the low-control situation and no longer cares about exercising initiative. Job enrichment can also lead to a higher degree of worker initiative because the enriched job gives a person more opportunity for spontaneity, such as figuring out a way to better please a customer.

Quite similar to job control, a perception of job autonomy has a positive influence on initiative taking. Autonomy implies a freedom to make decisions, thereby leading to more personal initiative on the job.[19] Visualize a customer engineer working for a Chicago firm sent on an assignment to repair a commercial printer in Anchorage, Alaska. The engineer is likely to believe he has considerable job autonomy, and therefore is likely to exercise initiative in such matters as doing preventive maintenance on the printer.

A major factor that enhances initiative is the general climate or culture of an organization. A climate that encourages risk taking and going beyond one's job description is likely to result in widespread employee initiative taking. The travel agency Kayak, is one such firm. The technical staff are encouraged to conduct experiments about different versions of Kayak that would be most useful to customers. At the same time, the company founder, Paul English, purposely recruits staff members with a capacity for taking the initiative.[20]

As will be described in Chapter 11, leadership style can enhance or inhibit proactivity and initiative. A participative style leader who encourages group members to contribute to decision making is likely to foster initiative. In contrast, an authoritarian leader who discourages group member input on decision making is less likely to foster initiative.

DISADVANTAGES OF INITIATIVE TAKING

Although taking the initiative in the workplace can help the individual and the organization, several potential disadvantages of initiative have been observed and researched. A starting point is that taking responsibility for a problem outside of one's assigned tasks might be perceived as trespassing on someone else's turf, leading to resentment. For example, a manufacturing engineer who takes the initiative to advise the customer service manager on how to improve tech support of a company machine might be resented. The initiative taker may be perceived as bringing about unwelcome changes, or even as being rebellious and annoying. An example here is that a worker might suggest one more quality check which results in more work for colleagues.[21]

Another problem with taking the initiative to assume additional responsibilities is that the initiative taker may be perceived as not having enough work to do in his or her assigned role. The extra task for which the initiative taker assumes responsibility might become a permanent part of the job, leading to role overload.[22]

A subtle disadvantage to the organization from workers taking the initiative has been referred to by Donald J. Campbell as the *initiative paradox*. Managers may want employees to display initiative and judgment. At the same time, because managers desire predictable outcomes, they also expect initiative takers to take similar action to what the manager might have taken. The proactive employee might choose a course of action not compatible with the manager's thinking.[23] An example might be an employee who takes the initiative to resolve a customer problem by granting the customer a much larger concession than the manager would have thought reasonable.

Another potential problem with initiative is that it can be directed toward self-serving ends rather than improving group or organizational effectiveness.[24] The initiative taker benefits, whereas the organization suffers. An example of self-serving initiative would be a manager who takes the initiative to visit the factories of several suppliers in another country. She justifies the trip because she wants to investigate first hand whether human rights abuses are taking place in the factories. Yet, the manager's real intent is to voyage to a faraway land, with no serious intent of investigating potential human rights abuses.

A study conducted by Mark C. Bolino and William H. Turnley investigated the negative impact of the individual initiative aspect of organizational citizenship behavior on three outcomes: role overload, job stress, and work–family conflict. Ninety-eight couples were included in the study, with the partner completing a survey about the worker's initiative. Two sample personal initiative items were (a) "Works on his/her days off (e.g., weekends)," and (b) "Takes work-related calls at home." The results revealed that higher levels of employee initiative were associated with higher levels of role overload, job stress, and work–family conflict. Women tended to experience more work–family conflict based on initiative than did men. One straightforward interpretation of the results was that going the extra mile (personal initiative) is associated with overload, stress, and work–family conflict.[25]

SUGGESTIONS FOR APPLICATION

1. A major aspect of initiative from the standpoint of the individual is that initiative involves enhancing organizational effectiveness, not wasting time tackling unimportant matters. Before taking the initiative, attempt to gauge what impact a certain action will have on the group's performance, the company's profitability, or the long-term effectiveness of the organization. If your answers are positive investigate why the initiative you have in mind has not already been taken. Perhaps there is not enough time or resources. Perhaps the magnitude of the problem has not been recognized. It is also possible that action is not required because of political reasons.[26] For example, you recommend that the company stop doing business with an ineffective vendor. The company might be retaining the vendor because the CEO is a personal friend of a key executive at that company.

2. If you think you have uncovered a valid initiative, obtain approval from your immediate manager. It is not worthwhile pursuing an unsanctioned project that will never gain approval from your superiors. After you have attained approval, develop a plan for the implementation of your

initiative. Explain what your plan is intended to accomplish, and clearly identify the resources that will be needed to fully implement your idea.

3. Explain clearly how the success of your plan will be measured. Suppose, for example, a human resource specialist has taken the initiative to make apps (computer applications for smart phones) available for employees to process health insurance claims. How will she know if her plan has made claims processing more efficient, saved the company money, and improved employee morale?

4. As implied in Suggestion 1, carefully think through whether the initiative you recommend has unintentional negative consequences. For example, a staff member of the athletic department of a major university took the initiative to suggest that a pre-season activity should be open to the public without a fee. Thousands of community members stormed the facility, resulting in a rowdy crowd that led to fights among the fans, including hospitalization for a fan who was stabbed during the event.

SUMMARY

Workplace initiative and proactivity are closely related. It is common knowledge that managers and human resource specialists believe that initiative, or self-starting ability, contributes to individual and organizational effectiveness.

Initiative has been proposed as consisting of three aspects: self-starting, proactive, and persisting. Self-starting behavior means that a person engages in constructive activity without being told, without receiving explicit instructions, or without it being part of his or her formal role. "Proactive" in this context refers to having a long-term focus and not waiting until one is faced with a demand. "Persistence" refers to overcoming barriers to reach one's goals while taking the initiative. These three aspects of personal initiative reinforce each other.

Each aspect (self-starting, proactive, and persisting) has its own four facets, with an action sequence built into the facets: (1) goals or redefinition of tasks, (2) information collection and prognosis, (3) plan and execution, and (4) monitoring and feedback.

Job crafting is a form of initiative in which workers deviate from their job descriptions to modify their job to fit their personal preferences and capabilities. Three common types of job crafting involve changing (1) the number and type of job tasks, (2) the interactions with others on the job, and (3) one's view of the job. A frequent purpose of crafting is to make the job more meaningful or enriched.

Evidence and opinion exist that initiative enhances job performance.

One study showed that proactive personality was linked to subjective evaluations of performance by supervisors. The study also suggested that proactive personality appears to predict the extent to which an employee takes the initiative to go beyond his or her job tasks. Also, proactive employees gain performance benefits by building social networks that provide them the resources to pursue high-level initiatives.

The development of a situational judgment test of initiative revealed that situational judgment as measured by the test was related to supervisors' ratings of overall performance. A review of several empirical studies suggests that personal initiative benefits the organization when such behavior is widespread within the company. A climate that welcomed initiative showed a substantial positive relationship to profitability.

Assuming responsibility for free-floating problems can be a positively perceived type of initiative. Another useful form of initiative is volunteering for leadership responsibilities related to company activities. Taking the initiative can lead to skill development because the new task might require some new learning. Another perspective on the relationship between initiative and job performance is that initiative taking is part of the leader's job.

The high-initiative individual is more likely to feel a sense of well-being, as well as minimize the potential negative effects of stress. A study with Dutch workers found that high ratings on personal initiative were associated with low emotional exhaustion as well as high learning motivation (both aspects of well-being). The complex relationship between job stress and initiative includes the observations that (a) stress impedes initiative, (b) personal initiative creates stress, and (c) stressors create the need for initiative.

The extent of initiative can be influenced by factors external to the individual. Environmental supports for initiative include worker job control and a perception of job autonomy. A climate that encourages risk taking and going beyond one's job description is likely to result in widespread employee initiative taking. Leadership style can enhance or inhibit proactivity.

Although taking the initiative can help the individual and the organization, several potential disadvantages of initiative have been observed and researched. The initiative taker might be resented, or the additional responsibilities the worker assumes might become permanent. The initiative paradox is that managers may want employees to take the initiative, yet the employee might take actions different from what the manager wants. A study showed that the initiative aspect of proactivity can be associated with higher role overload, job stress, and work–family conflict.

Before taking the initiative, the person might gauge what impact a certain action might have on the group's performance, profitability, and long-term organizational effectiveness. Seeking approval from the manager before taking an initiative is helpful. Explain how the success of your plan will be measured. Carefully think through whether the initiative you recommended has unintentional negative consequences.

REFERENCES

1. Toon W. Taris and Etty G. A. Wielenga-Meijer, "Workers' Personal Initiative as a Moderator of the Relations Between Job Characteristics and Well-Being," *Psychological Reports*, Volume 107, Number 1, 2010, p. 255.
2. Ronald Bledow and Michael Frese, "A Situational Judgment Test of Personal Initiative and Its Relationship to Performance," *Personnel Psychology*, Summer 2009, p. 230.
3. Joyce Bender, "Initiative – The Key to Becoming a Star Employee," www.benderconsult.com/article9.html, p.1. Retrieved March 15, 2012.
4. Cited in Bender, "Initiative," p. 1.
5. Joyce E. A. Russell, "Career Coach: As a Leader – Your Legacy Begins Today," *The Washington Post* (www.washingtonpost.com). September 4, 2011, pp. 1–3. Retrieved April 3, 2012.
6. Michael Frese and Doris Fay, "Personal Initiative: An Active Performance Concept for Work in the 21st Century," *Research in Organizational Behavior*, Volume 23, 2001, pp. 139–153.
7. Frese and Fay, "Personal Initiative," pp. 143–151.
8. Amy Wrzesniewski and Jane E. Dutton, "Crafting Job: Revisioning Employees as Active Crafters of Their Work," *Academy of Management Review*, April 2001, pp. 179–201.
9. Jeffery A. Thompson, "Proactivity and Job Performance: A Social Capital Perspective," *Journal of Applied Psychology*, September 2005, pp. 1011–1017.
10. Bledow and Frese, "A Situational Judgment Test of Personal Initiative," pp. 229–238.
11. Frese and Fay, "Personal Initiative," p. 165.
12. Andrew J. DuBrin, *Stand Out! 330 Ways for Gaining the Edge with Bosses, Co-workers, Subordinates, and Customers* (Englewood Cliffs, N.J.: Prentice Hall, 1993), pp. 62–63.
13. Stephen Bucaro, "Success at Work: Techniques: Taking Initiative," *streetdirectory.com* (http://www.streetdirectory/com), Copyright© 2005. Accessed September 18, 2011, pp. 1–2.
14. Geno A. Bulzomi, "Leadership and Initiative Are Synonyms," *Ezine@rticles* (http://ExineArticles.com), © 2001. Retrieved February 15, 2012.
15. Bernard M. Bass with Ruth Bass, *The Bass Handbook of Leadership: Theory, Research & Managerial Applications*, fourth edition (New York: The Free Press, 2008), p. 87.
16. Taris and Wielenga-Meijer, "Workers' Personal Initiative," pp. 255–256.
17. Doris Fay, Sabine Sonnentag, and Michael Frese, "Stressors, Innovation, and Personal Initiative: Are Stressors Always Detrimental?" In Cary L. Cooper

(Editor), *Theories of Organizational Stress* (London: Oxford University Press, 1998), pp. 169–189.

18. Frese and Fay, "Personal Initiative," pp. 159–161.
19. Uta K. Bindl and Sharon K. Parker, "Proactive Work Behavior: Forward-Thinking and Change-Oriented Action in Organizations," In Sheldon Zedeck (Editor), *APA Handbook of Industrial and Organizational Psychology* (Washington, D.C.: American Psychological Association, 2010), p. 28.
20. Geoff Colvin, "Kayak Takes On the Big Dogs," *Fortune*, October 8, 2012, pp. 78–82.
21. Bucaro, "Success at Work," pp. 1–2.
22. Frese and Fay, "Personal Initiative," p. 141.
23. Donald J. Campbell, "The Proactive Employee: Managing Workplace Initiative," *Academy of Management Executive*, August 2000, pp. 57–58.
24. Adam M. Grant and Susan J. Ashford, "The Dynamics of Proactivity at Work," *Research in Organizational Behavior*, Volume 28, 2008, p. 8.
25. Mark C. Bolino and William H. Turnley, "The Personal Costs of Citizenship Behavior: The Relationship Between Individual Initiative and Role Overload, Job Stress, and Work–Family Conflict," *Journal of Applied Psychology*, July 2005, pp. 740–748.
26. The first three suggestions follow closely Sam Hull, "How to Show Initiative at Work," www.AskMen.com, 2006, pp. 1–3. Accessed September 18, 2012.

4. The proactive personality, job performance, and satisfaction

A key justification for studying proactivity in the workplace is that it contributes to important outcomes such as job performance and satisfaction. As described in the previous chapter, initiative as a major component of proactivity shows a positive relationship with job performance. A positive perspective on the contribution of proactivity to performance is that top performers frequently create circumstances that facilitate personal and organizational success in the quest of their goals.[1]

The situation of Ginni Rometty, the CEO of IBM, illustrates how proactive behavior can facilitate individual and organizational success. During her first customer conference at IBM she deviated from tradition by hosting a sales meeting in a loft. The purpose of the loft venue was to attract the attention of the chief marketing officers who were invited to accompany their chief information officers to the event. Earlier in her IBM career when Rometty was the general manager of the company's global services division, she pushed for the acquisition of PricewaterhouseCoopers' IT consulting business. Immediately after the acquisition, Rometty proactively left two-minute voice-mail messages on the phones of all 30,000 PwC consultants. Each consultant was welcomed personally to IBM, and assured that IBM would retain the best elements of the PwC culture. The initiative was very well received, and helped facilitate the vast majority of the acquired consultants staying with IBM.[2]

In this chapter we review some of the evidence and opinion about the relationship between proactivity and the outcomes of productivity and job satisfaction. We will also look at factors that moderate the relationship between proactivity and performance, and explore the idea that proactive work behavior can be taught.

The checklist presented in Figure 4.1 gives you an opportunity reflect on your proactive behaviors and attitudes that might be contributing to good job performance.

PROACTIVITY AND OBJECTIVE PERFORMANCE MEASURES

The standard meaning of an objective measure of performance is one that relates to a tangible, quantifiable way of measuring performance, such as sales volume, units produced, patents granted, or cost savings. A pioneering study of this type conducted about 20 years ago was mentioned in Chapter 1. J. Michael Crant used a sample of 131 real estate agents to investigate how well the Proactive Personality Scale related to an objective criterion. A job performance index was calculated for each agent from company records of houses sold, number of listings obtained, and income derived from commissions over a nine-month period. The study also took into account other factors that could be related to performance including experience, general mental ability, social desirability, and the personality traits of conscientiousness and extraversion. (Social desirability refers to the tendency to respond to test items in positive ways that might be expected by others, such as responding "yes" to the statement, "I think that all potential customers deserve my full and courteous attention.") Proactivity contributed an additional 8 percent of the variance in sales performance beyond the other measures.[3] The results of this study are not surprising because it is common knowledge that succeeding at real estate sales requires initiative and persistence.

As part of a broader study, Jeffrey P. Thomas, Daniel S. Whitman, and Chockalingam Viswesvaran conducted a meta-analysis of 25 independent studies, including 5045 participants, to investigate the relationship between proactivity and job performance. Although the relationship between the two variables was not strong, it was statistically significant. Proactive employees tend to perform better on their core tasks, such as a sales representative obtaining more sales or an administrative assistant making better arrangements for a business meeting at a convention center. Proactive personality was more strongly correlated with subjective measures of performance than with objective measures.[4] Many workers with a proactive personality are skilled at behaving in ways favored by the immediate manager.

In a review of the evidence provided by his own research and that of others, Michael Frese found some evidence of a positive relationship between both proactive personality and personal initiative, and organizational performance. Much of this evidence is based on business owners in small companies. The personality traits of small-business owners are more likely linked to organizational effectiveness than would be the traits of executives and organizational performance in a large organization.[5]

Directions: Below is a list of proactive behavior and initiative taking often linked to attaining good objective job performance or being perceived favorably by a supervisor. To the right of each statement, check whether you have engaged in this behavior, or have not yet done so.

Number	Proactive behavior	Yes	No
1.	I have worked on and fixed problems not already assigned to me.	❏	❏
2.	I take it on my own initiative to study information that will help me be more effective in my job.	❏	❏
3.	I have changed a work procedure that resulted in saving money for my employer.	❏	❏
4.	I have asked a supervisor for feedback in order to improve my performance.	❏	❏
5.	Without being asked, I have found at least two different ways to reduce costs.	❏	❏
6.	I have alerted my present (or past) manager to a problem he or she had not anticipated.	❏	❏
7.	I have learned at least two job-related skills on my own without being asked by a supervisor.	❏	❏
8.	I have alerted management to one or more ethical or legal problems in my workplace.	❏	❏
9.	I have taken the initiative to share useful job knowledge with a coworker.	❏	❏
10.	When I am given some leeway for doing my job, I quickly take the opportunity to develop a more efficient method for getting my work done.	❏	❏
11.	I voice my concerns about things in the workplace that I find disturbing.	❏	❏
12.	If a work procedure needs modifying, I will take it on my own to do it.	❏	❏
13.	When faced with a difficult problem, I will keep coming back to attempt to solve the problem.	❏	❏
14.	I have contributed constructive ideas related to my job several times.	❏	❏
15.	I can think of several times when I have brought about useful change in relation to my job.	❏	❏
16.	I am pretty good at anticipating problems that might arise.	❏	❏
17.	If I encounter something in relation to my job that bothers me, I will try to adjust the problem.	❏	❏
18.	I have taken steps to make a present or past job more enjoyable.	❏	❏
19.	In order to make me feel better about a present or former job, I have taken steps to add more tasks than I was assigned.	❏	❏
20.	I have often felt committed to my teammates and/or the entire organization.	❏	❏
21.	I seek out network members who can help me perform my job better.	❏	❏
22.	I have often challenged the status quo on the job.	❏	❏
23.	I actively look for ways to please my supervisor or immediate manager.	❏	❏
24.	I have a strong interest in helping coworkers.	❏	❏

| 25. | Before taking on a workplace initiative, I will size up the situation to figure out if the initiative would be welcome. | ❏ | ❏ |

Note: scoring and interpretation: the more of these behaviors and attitudes you have exhibited or experienced, the higher the probability that your proactivity enhances your job performance. If you responded "yes" to 10 statements or fewer, you have plenty of room for improvement in terms of developing more proactive behaviors and attitudes.

Sources: Many of the items in this list are based on information in the following: Frank Belschak and Deanne Den Hartog, "Being Proactive at Work – Blessing or Bane?" *Archive – 2010* (http://www.thepsychologist.org.uk), Volume 23, Part 11 (November 2010), pp. 1–7; Jeffrey P. Thomas, Daniel S. Whitman, and Chockalingam Viswesvaran, "Employee Proactivity in Organizations: A Comparative Meta-Analysis of Emergent Proactive Constructs," *Journal of Occupational and Organizational Psychology*, Volume 83, pp. 275–300; David Chan, "Interactive Effects of Situational Judgment Effectiveness and Proactive Personality on Work Perceptions and Work Outcomes," *Journal of Applied Psychology*, March 2006, pp. 475–481.

Figure 4.1   Proactive behaviors and attitudes often linked to positive job performance

PROACTIVITY AND SUBJECTIVE PERFORMANCE MEASURES

As mentioned above, proactive personality correlates positively with subjective measures of performance, particularly evaluations by a supervisor. As part of a larger study, David Chan investigated the relationship between proactive personality and job performance. Proactive personality was measured by the Proactive Personality Scale. The supervisors of 139 employees in a rehabilitation agency rated the participating subordinates on a three-item measure, including "This officer is good at meeting performance standards." A major finding was that employees with a high standing on proactive personality who also had good judgment about sizing up the situation (described later in a discussion of moderator variables) received positive supervisory ratings.[6]

A study conducted by Kilian Werenfried Wawoe in the Netherlands and India, involving approximately 600 bank employees, investigated the relationship between proactive personality and the manager's opinion about performance. (The opinion question was the same format as with the Chan study.) Three other subjective performance measures were included in the study. The appraisal score was based on the achievement of goals which were set at the beginning of the year. A bonus score was the manager's judgment of how large a bonus the employee should receive. A self-opinion score was an employee rating of his or her performance, such as "In my job, I function effectively." The first two performance measures were used by the company to allocate rewards.

In the Dutch sample, proactive personality correlated positively with bonus, appraisal, and self-opinion, although it was not correlated with the manager's opinion (the performance measure used in the research). In the Indian sample, proactive personality correlated with all measures of performance. Because measures were also taken of extraversion and conscientiousness, the author concluded that proactivity correlates positively with performance beyond two other relevant personality characteristics.[7]

The two preceding discussions have implied that employee proactivity often leads to enhanced performance. The relationship between these two factors might also work in reverse – that good performance can foster proactivity. For example, a hair stylist might receive a compliment from her boss for having done a fine job in trimming the hair traces on several intentionally bald customers. She is so encouraged by her good performance that she spreads the word among her social network friends and followers that she is now an avid "hair stylist for people with shaven heads."

Another possible link between performance and proactivity is that skillful demonstrations of performance may prompt organizational stakeholders to provide effective employees with political, financial, or social support that fosters proactivity. For example, a corporate professional who performs well in a series of assigned projects might be given seed money to explore any project he thinks might have long-range commercial potential for the company. Skillful performances might also serve as firsthand learning opportunities that build employees to anticipate, plan, and execute constructive changes. For instance, a worker who has to troubleshoot and adapt while performing a required task might develop the skill to proactively anticipate likely problems in future situations.

Effective performance may also provide insights about details that enhance employees' ability to proactively envision future environmental changes. An example of this complicated idea is that a purchasing agent might perform well in compensating for a supplier who fails to deliver because of being shut down by a hurricane. The purchasing agent then proactively develops a plan to have more backup suppliers to deal with problems at one key supplier.[8]

POTENTIAL DISADVANTAGES OF EMPLOYEE PROACTIVITY

Although proactivity may be linked to both subjective and objective performance measures, at times being proactive may lead to negative outcomes for the worker. (The same argument was presented in Chapter 3 about worker initiative.) Potential disadvantages of employee proactivity are presented in the following five points.

1. *Expressing concerns may backfire.* One of the first arguments regarding problems with proactivity was advanced by the research of Scott E. Seibert and his colleagues, who found that one type of proactivity – expressing one's concern at work – had negative consequences for an employee's career. Workers who voiced many concerns received fewer promotions and lower salaries than those who voiced fewer concerns. The same study also suggested that employees who challenge the status quo on the job without offering innovative solutions to the problems they have identified may experience negative career repercussions.[9]

2. *Developing a poor reputation.* Proactive workers face the potential problem of harming their reputation among coworkers because proactivity can take the form of bringing about unwanted change. The suggestions for change will sometimes lead to criticism and retaliation, including efforts to sabotage the proactive employee's work or remove the proactive employee from the workgroup. An example of a proactive suggestion that could lead to strong negative reaction from the group would be to advise upper management that travel allowances for the group could be reduced without damaging productivity. Coworkers who are not proactive may feel threatened by proactive employees who frequently push for change. Expecting and encouraging employees to be proactive may therefore trigger tension and conflict within the workgroup if it is not managed effectively.[10]

3. *Whistleblowing problems.* Whistleblowing, or alerting higher authorities about wrongdoing within the organization, is a form of proactivity that can backfire for the individual worker. Whistleblowers are often ostracized and humiliated by the organizations they hope to improve. They may be given poor performance evaluations and denied further promotions. Also, many whistleblowers are fired or demoted, even for high-profile tips that proved true.[11] More than half the time, the pleas of whistleblowers are ignored.

4. *The initiation of detrimental work activities.* Another negative performance consequence of proactivity is that the proactive worker may take it on his or her own shoulders to engage in practices that are detrimental to the task at hand, the workgroup, or the organization. Visualize a health-conscious baker at an upscale restaurant who decides that the bread and desserts served by his restaurant contain too much fat to be healthy. So the baker starts a program of baking

with almost no fat in bread and desserts. Suddenly, many customers complain that the bread and desserts taste terrible, and do not return to the restaurant. As a consequence of the baker's proactivity, the restaurant loses some valuable customers. Furthermore, they badmouth the restaurant on social media.

5. *Too much organizational dependence on employee proactivity.* In some cases proactive behavior can damage an organization's competitiveness and effectiveness. A possibility of this type might happen if the organization depends too strongly on employee proactivity, and uses proactivity as a substitute for institutionalized organizational practices. For example, proactive employees tend to seek out the advice and counsel of other employees about non-formal ways of getting things done instead of consulting a formal procedures manual. The organization then risks having too many activities carried out in nonstandard ways, such as granting customer discounts as well as deciding whether to work from a remote location.[12]

FACTORS INFLUENCING THE LINK BETWEEN PROACTIVITY AND PERFORMANCE

Following the path of most research in organizational behavior, organizational and industrial psychology, and related disciplines, many studies of the link between proactivity and performance have explored moderator variables. Moderator variables refer to factors that influence the relationship between two other variables such as tact influencing the relationship between influence tactics and goal attainment: it helps to be tactful when using influence tactics. Here we describe a group of key factors that moderate the relationship between the proactive personality and performance.

1. The Extent of Proactivity

As with most personality factors, proactivity should be at an optimum level to be fully effective. A team of researchers noted that the relationship between personality traits and performance is often thought to be linear. The researchers conducted two studies that generally supported the idea that a curvilinear (optimum) relationship exists between personality traits and job performance. The specific traits studied were conscientiousness and emotional stability, and the dependent (outcome) variables were task performance, organizational citizenship behavior, and counterproductive work behaviors. Another key finding of the study was that conscientiousness and emotional stability were more strongly associated with performance in jobs of high complexity than low complexity.[13]

The notion of curvilinearity and performance appears to fit proactivity. A worker with too low a standing on proactive personality would not seek out enough opportunities to perform beyond expectation. However, a person with too high a standing on proactive personality might become too bothersome to others. Furthermore, proactivity has more relevance for complex jobs. For example, proactivity might not have much of a performance impact in a cashier's position but could have a bigger impact on the performance of a technical support specialist. The organizational culture often influences the amount of proactivity that is welcome and tolerated. In an organization such as Google Inc., where idea generation is a strong cultural value, proactivity is quite welcome.

2.   Situational Judgment Skills

According to the research of David Chan, individual differences in *situational judgment effectiveness* (SJE) play a critical role in whether proactivity will lead to positive outcomes. Situational judgment effectiveness refers to the general ability of an individual to make an accurate judgment of the surrounding situation and to respond positively to the practical situational demands. The interaction between SJE and proactive personality determines whether the individual will have positive or negative work perceptions and positive or negative work outcomes. Chan measured the perceptions of procedural justice, supervisor support, and social integration. ("Social integration" refers to personal relationships with coworkers.) The work outcomes measured were job performance, job satisfaction, and organizational commitment. The major conclusion from the study was that strong proactivity leads to positive work perceptions and work outcomes only when SJE is high. Negative perceptions and work outcomes result when SJE is low.

An implication Chan draws from his research is that highly proactive workers who are low in situational judgment are unable to accurately identify, understand, and effectively respond to the practical demands and constraints of the workplace. As a result, these individuals are more likely to develop unrealistic expectations and demands about the working environment that are unlikely to be met.[14]

3.   Work Engagement

In the context used here, *work engagement* refers to high levels of personal investment in the work tasks performed in a job.[15] As a result, the self is injected into the job. Engaged workers would therefore feel personally responsible for good and poor performance and would take pride in accomplishment. When a worker is engaged in the job (or committed to the organization), proactivity is more likely to be directed toward attaining high performance. A person has to be committed enough to the organization to want to change something and to trust that the initiative will not backfire. Work engagement, in turn, requires that self-efficacy is high enough for the individual to believe his or her proactive efforts will actually result in positive change.[16]

4.   Prosocial Motivation and Low Negative Affect

According to a study with two different samples conducted by Adam M. Grant, Sharon Parker, and Catherine Collins, the combination of prosocial motivation and low negative affect influences how well proactive behavior correlates with supervisors' performance evaluations. ("Prosocial motivation" refers to the desire to help others in the workplace, or being other oriented and altruistic. "Negative affect" refers to the display of negative emotions.) The two samples studied were 103 managers and their direct supervisors, and 55 firefighters and their platoon supervisors. The study authors reasoned that when employees express prosocial values, supervisors tend to attribute their proactive behaviors to benevolent intentions. The argument was also presented that employees with high negative affect may be more sensitive to problems and injustice. As a result, supervisors tend to attribute their proactive behaviors to "bad attitudes."

The results of the study indicated that supervisors' ratings of proactive behavior were more positively related to their evaluations of employees' performance when employees expressed more prosocial values or low negative affect. The authors concluded that they found support for the moderating roles of prosocial values and negative affect with the two samples studied.[17]

5.   Job Autonomy

As with the initiative component of proactivity described in Chapter 2, the degree of autonomy granted to the worker can influence the extent of his or her proactive behavior. Furthermore, when workers are granted more autonomy the relationship between proactivity and job performance is likely to be stronger. This is true because when the worker is performing his or her tasks more independently, there is greater room for taking the initiative and seeking out opportunities that have a payoff in good performance. Visualize a marketing manager for several senior residences. The CEO wants to attract more guests (customers) to the homes, so he tells the marketing manager to do whatever she thinks is feasible to attract more business to the residences. The marketing manager can now be as inventive as possible without having to gain approval from the CEO for her initiatives. As a result she develops several outreach programs that have a big payoff in increased sales, thereby enhancing her job performance.

A study conducted by Jerry Bryan Fuller, Jr., Kim Hester, and Susie S. Cox with 120 utility company workers explored the moderating effect of job autonomy on the relationship between proactive personality and job performance. Performance data were collected from company records, and questionnaires were used to measure proactive personality and perceived job autonomy. An example of a job autonomy question was, "I have considerable opportunity for independence and freedom in how I do my job." The study hypothesis was that proactive personality is positively related to the results of performance appraisal and, furthermore, that the relationship between proactivity and performance was moderated by job autonomy. The relationship between proactivity and job performance was stronger when workers perceived themselves to have high job autonomy. An implication of the results for management is that elevating performance is not just a function of selecting job candidates with proactive personalities, but also a matter of assigning these people freedom to determine how to perform their job.[18]

PROACTIVITY AND JOB SATISFACTION

Proactive personality and job satisfaction show a positive relationship, as confirmed by a meta-analysis of over 100 independent samples.[19] A logical connection exists between proactivity and job satisfaction for several reasons. Proactive individuals will often remove obstacles to their job satisfaction, such as the five-day-per-week commuter in a crowded metropolitan area taking the initiative to suggest that he work remotely one day per week. Workers who behave proactively are likely to experience more intrinsic motivation in their jobs because they have created several features of their job. Intrinsic motivation, in turn, has long been associated with job satisfaction. Part of the intrinsic motivation stems from experiencing task significance, such as the physical therapist who gives nutritional advice to patients feeling that he or she is making a bigger impact on their lives. Proactive workers may also create conditions that give them a feeling of job success, which brings them personal satisfaction.

One analysis suggests that the proactivity–satisfaction relationship may also be bidirectional. Satisfied employees may have higher motivation to seek out the opportunity to expand their work roles because they have positive work-related attitudes. In contrast, a dissatisfied worker might not have much incentive to move beyond his or her job description. Furthermore, employees who are low in satisfaction may develop a sense of learned helplessness that blocks proactivity.[20]

One component of a broader study supports the relationship between the proactive personality and job satisfaction. Ning Li, Jian Liang, and J. Michael Crant surveyed 200 Chinese employees within 54 workgroups and found that proactive personality was associated with employees establishing a high-quality exchange relationship with their supervisors. In turn, the high-quality relationship was associated with higher job satisfaction and organizational citizenship behavior.[21] (This finding supports the idea that a positive relationship with one's immediate manager enhances job satisfaction.)

In the study under consideration, the participants were chosen from seven state-owned companies in the manufacturing, electronics, telecommunications, and hotel industries in three Chinese cities. (Other aspects of this study were also described in Chapter 2 in the context of the link between proactivity and organizational citizenship behavior.) Questionnaires were used to measure proactive personality, leader–member exchange, and organizational citizenship behavior. Proactive personality was shown to have a positive effect on job satisfaction, even after taking into account age and the individual's perception of justice. The point here is that age could influence job satisfaction and so could the feeling that one is part of a fair work environment. (Younger people often feel a surge of job satisfaction as they launch their career, and older people often become more content with what opportunities they have in the workplace.)

Another important study finding in relation to the present discussion was that the leader–member exchange served as a linking mechanism helping to explain how proactive workers experience higher job satisfaction. Proactive employees actively manage their relationships with their supervisors, and as a result experience greater job satisfaction than do their less proactive coworkers.

ENHANCING PERFORMANCE THROUGH TRAINING IN PROACTIVE THINKING

If we accept the widely held belief and well-researched finding that worker proactivity is associated with good job performance, the question arises whether proactive thinking can be taught and learned. If 10 percent of a large company's workforce could become more proactive the impact on generating revenue and decreasing costs would be enormous. Or, if a potential entrepreneur could learn to think proactively, he or she might be better able to spot an opportunity for a new business concept. The idea of training to become more proactive is similar to assertiveness training, so popular in the 1960s and 1970s, designed to enhance and develop the trait of assertiveness – closely related to extraversion.

A study was conducted by Eric G. Kirby, Susan L. Kirby, and Melanie A. Lewis to determine if proactivity can be increased through training. The performance measured was classroom performance, with subject matter closely aligned to workplace activities and strategic thinking. A sample of 184 undergraduate students from a large southwestern university was recruited to participate in the study. Data were gathered by using a pretest/posttest field experiment. The students in strategic management were used as an experimental group, receiving a semester's worth of training in "the art of strategic thinking."

The training was designed to develop proactive thinking in the form of facilitating a student's ability to recognize critical events, analyze the impact and implications of these events, develop strategies for dealing with these events, and generating recommendations for courses of action to implement the strategies chosen by the student. The topics included recognizing and capitalizing on opportunities, observing and defending against threats, capitalizing on core competencies for competitive advantage, and generally outwitting the competition.

In contrast to the experimental group, the production and operations students served as the control group and received no training in proactive thinking. The training in the production and operations management classroom concentrated exclusively on the development of quantitative and theoretical skills linked to the design and management of manufacturing systems.

The dependent variable of performance was measured through course exams as well as peer evaluation of performance in group assignments. The control measures included general mental ability, experience in terms of previous credit hours attained, socially desirable responses, and prior performance as measured by GPA (grade point average). A final control measure was self-directed learning readiness, or willingness to learn. The latter measure relates to proactivity because self-directed learners show initiative, independence, and persistence in learning.

The results of the study strongly suggested that proactivity did account for a significant amount of variance for both exam scores and peer evaluations, even when controlling for other variables such as general mental ability and learning readiness. Also of interest for the study of proactivity, it also showed a significant relationship with experience, general mental ability, extraversion, and prior performance.

An important implication of the study is that a proactive behavior can be increased through training. From the individual's standpoint, increased proactivity can lead to improvements in conditions and rewards associated with work, possibly leading to increased satisfaction. From an organization's standpoint, an increase in proactive thinking and behavior can lead to improvements in productivity, profitability, and competitive advantage. The study also suggested that proactivity can be improved with training because the experimental group demonstrated an average increase of nearly three points on the Proactive Personality Test.[22]

SUGGESTIONS FOR APPLICATION

Considering that proactivity often leads to improved job performance and satisfaction, and that proactivity can be enhanced, the person wanting to become more proactive might consider the following eight suggestions.

1. Self-reflect to answer such questions as, "What kinds of tasks require immediate attention when they arrive?"

2. Examine critically how you might perform these tasks more efficiently. For example, search for steps in the process to eliminate, consolidate, or shorten.

3. Try to prevent problems from taking place. Tackle possible breakdowns in advance to prevent them from becoming a reality, in the same manner as checking the oil level in a vehicle before taking a trip.

4. Develop a mental set that looks to solve problems instead of complaining about or agonizing over the problems. Decide what needs to take place to overcome the problem and how this process can be implemented.

5. Take care of less urgent, ordinary tasks so you can be prepared to take on a new, major task that comes your way. Prioritize your tasks so you know which of these can be set aside temporarily so you can tackle a task out of the ordinary. Eliminate tasks that are unnecessary and take time from work that adds value to the team or the organization.

6. Evaluate your work processes as you go along. Make note of what works and what does not. Make notes for improvement and look for an opening to implement the improvements.

7. Attempt to anticipate needs. Look ahead to estimate when you will be busiest and when your peak energy will be required. At the same time, attempt to anticipate knowledge and skills you will need.

8. If you seem to be fighting fires continually, investigate what can be done to prevent some of these problems so you will free up some energy to be proactive.[23]

SUMMARY

A key justification for studying proactivity in the workplace is that it contributes to important outcomes such as job performance and satisfaction. Several studies have shown a positive relationship between proactivity and objective, or quantifiably measurable, job performance. Proactive employees tend to perform better on their core tasks, such as a sales representative obtaining more sales. Some evidence suggests that a positive relationship exists between both proactive personality and personal initiative and organizational performance, particularly in small firms.

Proactive personality correlates positively with subjective measures of performance, particularly supervisory evaluations. One study showed that employees with a high standing on proactive personality who also had good judgment about sizing up the situation received positive supervisory ratings. Proactive personality contributes to high performance evaluations beyond the effects of extraversion and conscientiousness.

The relationship between proactivity and performance can also work in reverse: good performance can foster proactivity. Another possible link between performance and proactivity is that skillful demonstrations of performance may prompt organizational stakeholders to provide effective employees with political, financial, or social support that fosters proactivity.

Potential disadvantages of employee proactivity are as follows: (1) expressing concerns may backfire; (2) the proactive employee may develop a poor reputation; (3) whistleblowing problems; (4) the initiation of detrimental work activities; and (5) too much organizational dependence on employee proactivity.

A group of key factors that moderate the relationship between the proactive personality and job performance are as follows: (1) the extent of proactivity; (2) situational judgment skills; (3) work engagement; (4) prosocial motivation and low negative affect; and (5) job autonomy.

Proactive personality and job satisfaction show a positive relationship, as confirmed by a meta-analysis of over 100 independent samples. Proactive individuals will often remove obstacles to their satisfaction and are likely to have more intrinsic motivation, leading to job satisfaction. Proactive workers may also create conditions of job success, leading to satisfaction. The proactivity–satisfaction relationship may also be bidirectional: satisfied employees may have higher motivation to seek out the opportunity to expand their work roles because they have positive work-related attitudes. One study suggested that proactive employees establish a good relationship with their immediate manager, which leads to job satisfaction.

A study with undergraduate students suggests that proactive thinking can be taught and learned. The performance studied was course grades and peer ratings on group performance. The training dealt with learning how to think strategically. Control variables in the study included general mental ability, previous credit hours earned, and GPA. Proactivity did account for a significant amount of variance for both exam scores and peer evaluations.

Suggestions for becoming more proactive include self-reflection on how to perform tasks more efficiently; preventing problems; developing a mental set for solving problems instead of complaining; and attempting to anticipate needs.

REFERENCES

1. Jeffrey P. Thomas, Daniel S. Whitman, and Chockalingam Viswesvaran, "Employee Proactivity in Organizations: A Comparative Meta-Analysis of Emergent Proactive Constructs," *Journal of Occupational and Organizational Psychology*, Volume 83, 2010, p. 276.
2. Jessi Hempel, "IBM's New CEO Looks Ahead," *Fortune*, October 8, 2012, pp. 116–123.
3. J. Michael Crant, "The Proactive Personality Scale and Objective Job Performance Among Real Estate Agents," *Journal of Applied Psychology*, August 1995, pp. 532–537.
4. Thomas, Whitman, and Viswesvaran, "Employee Proactivity in Organizations," p. 285.
5. Michael Frese, "The Word Is Out: We Need an Active Performance Concept for Modern Work Places," *Industrial and Organizational Psychology: Perspectives on Science and Practice* (http://www.siop.org/journal/siopjour nal.aspex). Accessed September 12, 2012.
6. David Chan, "Interactive Effects of Situational Judgment Effectiveness and Proactive Personality on Work Perceptions and Work Outcomes," *Journal of Applied Psychology*, March 2006, pp. 475–481.
7. Kilian Werenfried Wawoe, "Proactive Personality: The Advantages and Disadvantages of an Entrepreneurial Disposition in the Financial Industry," Doctoral dissertation, Vrue University, 2010, pp. 35–43.
8. Most of the ideas, but not the examples, in this paragraph are from Thomas, Whitman, and Viswesvaran, "Employee Proactivity in Organizations," p. 278.
9. Scott E. Seibert, Maria L. Kraimer, and J. Michael Crant, "What Do Proactive People Do? A Longitudinal Model Linking Proactive Personality and Career Success," *Personnel Psychology*, Winter 2001, pp. 864–868.
10. Frank Belschak and Deanne Den Hartog, "Being Proactive at Work – Blessing or Bane?" *Archive – 2010* (http://www.thepsychologist.org.uk), Volume 23, Part 11 (November 2010), p. 4. Retrieved May 3, 2012.
11. "A Tip for Whistleblowers: Don't," *Mother Jones*, June 2007, reprinted in *The Wall Street Journal*, May 31, 2007, p. B6.

12. Belschak and Den Hartog, "Being Proactive at Work," p. 5.
13. Huy Le, In-Sue Oh, Steven B. Robbins, Remus Isles, Ed Holland, and Paul Westrick, "Too Much of a Good Thing: Curvilinear Relationships Between Personality Traits and Job Performance," *Journal of Applied Psychology*, January 2011, pp. 113–133.
14. Chan, "Interactive Effects of Situational Judgment Effectiveness and Proactive Personality on Work Perceptions and Work Outcomes," pp. 475–481. Chan, "What Good Is It to Have a Proactive Personality If You Do Not Have Effective Situational Judgment Skills?" *SMU Knowledge Hub*, October 2005, pp. 1–2.
15. Michael S. W. Christian, Adela S. Garza, and Jerel E. Slaughter, "Work Engagement: A Quantitative Review and Test of Its Relations with Task and Contextual Performance," *Personnel Psychology*, Number 1, 2011, p. 89.
16. Frese, "The Word Is Out," p. 6.
17. Adam M. Grant, Sharon Parker, and Catherine Collins, "Getting Credit for Proactive Behavior: Supervisor Reactions Depend on What You Value and How You Feel," *Personnel Psychology*, Spring 2009, pp. 31–55.
18. Jerry Bryan Fuller, Jr., Kim Hester, and Susie S. Cox, "Proactive Personality and Job Performance: Exploring Job Autonomy as a Moderator," *Journal of Managerial Issues*, Spring 2010, pp. 1–4.
19. Thomas, Whitman, and Viswesvaran, "Employee Proactivity in Organizations," p. 289.
20. Thomas, Whitman, and Viswesvaran, "Employee Proactivity in Organizations," p. 279.
21. Ning Li, Jian Liang, and J. Michael Crant, "The Role of Proactive Personality in Job Satisfaction and Organizational Citizenship Behavior: A Relational Perspective," *Journal of Applied Psychology*, March 2010, pp. 395–404.
22. Eric G. Kirby, Susan L. Kirby, and Melanie A. Lewis, "A Study of the Effectiveness of Training Proactive Thinking," *Journal of Applied Social Psychology*, Volume 32, Number 7, pp. 1538–1549.
23. Adapted from "How to Be Proactive," *wikiHow* (www.wikihow.com/Be-Proactive), pp. 1–2. Retrieved September 23, 2011.

5. The proactive personality and career success

Proactive personality contributes to high job performance and satisfaction, and organizational success. The focus of this chapter is how being proactive also contributes to an individual's career success, as illustrated by the story of Los Angeles attorney Darrell D. Miller. After graduating in 1985 from a conservatory of music, and performing around the world in various music productions, Miller decided to study law. He said he had an epiphany thinking about the information superhighway because for him it represented an entirely new paradigm. "Where most Americans had grown up with three primary distribution channels of broadcast television content, we were now going to have a lot of choices," he explains. "I thought either I can be part of the distribution platform or I can be part of the content creation mechanism for that platform. And I chose to go where the content is being created and to build a reputation of representing content creators."

After graduating from the Georgetown University Law Center in 1990, Miller moved to Los Angeles and worked at a law firm focusing on civil litigation and corporate law. Six years later Miller opened his own law firm serving as a counsel for a variety of film and entertainment projects. His reputation as a strategic entertainment attorney grew. Miller then became a partner in another law firm and co-chair of the Entertainment and Sports lawyer practice. His responsibilities include management of many areas, from new media and licensing agreements to merchandising, intellectual property, and distribution agreements.[1]

The proactive thinking of the attorney just described included sensing the opportunities developing for distributing entertainment content beyond the traditional channels of broadcasting entertainment. Miller was also proactive in developing a plan for how he could contribute legal counsel to the then evolving world of entertainment. In this chapter we explore proactivity and career success from several perspectives: empirical research on the topic, career management, acquiring power, reputation enhancement, personal branding, career resilience, and career satisfaction.

EMPIRICAL RESEARCH ABOUT PROACTIVE PERSONALITY AND CAREER SUCCESS

A pioneering study about the relationship between the proactive personality and career success was conducted by Scott E. Seibert, J. Michael Crant, and Maria L. Kraimer. Participants in the study were alumni of a private Midwestern University who were graduates of the business or engineering schools. The final sample consisted of 496 alumni who completed a standard self-report measure of proactive personality, along with 408 for analyses of the significant-other measure of proactive personality.

The "significant-other" measure of proactive personality consisted of ratings by a spouse, friend, or coworker of the participant's tendency toward proactivity. Statistical analysis revealed that the test measure of proactive personality and the ratings by the significant other had a strong positive relationship to each other. Subjective career success was measured with a self-report five-item career satisfaction scale, from very dissatisfied to very satisfied. A representative item to be rated was, "The progress I have made toward meeting my goals for advancement." Objective career success was measured with self-reported ratings on number of promotions received so far during the subject's career, and current annual salary.

A key result of the study was that scores on the proactive personality questionnaire were positively associated with the objective measures of career success – salary and promotions. Proactive personality test scores were also positively associated with career satisfaction. Ratings of proactive personality by a significant other also showed positive relationships with salary, promotions, and career success measured in terms of satisfaction. The relationship between significant-other ratings of proactive personality and the self-rating of career satisfaction was not as strong as the relationship with promotions and salary.

The authors of the study explained that prior to their study proactivity had been linked to leadership, sales performance, personal achievement, and entrepreneurship. Proactive personality was now shown to also be related to objective and subjective career success.[2] (Later in this chapter we have a separate section on the link between proactivity and career satisfaction, yet one could argue that if you are satisfied with your career you are successful.)

A couple of years later, Seibert, Kraimer, and Crant conducted a two-year longitudinal study of the relationship between proactive personality and career success.[3] The purpose of the study was to develop and test an integrated model relating proactive personality to career success as influenced through four intervening variables. The variables were voice (expressing one's opinion), innovation, knowledge of organizational politics, and taking the initiative in one's career. The subjects for the Time 1 phase of the study were the same as those reported in the study reported above. The final sample consisted of 180 respondents who had complete data including supervisor ratings at Time 1 and Time 2.

Proactive personality was assessed at Time 1. Four proactive behaviors were measured at Time 2. The data included self-reports of two proactive behaviors – political knowledge and career initiative. Voice was rated by supervisors using a six-item scale, with ratings from 1 (*strongly agree*) to 7 (*strongly disagree*). An example of an item measuring voice is, "This particular employee speaks up and encourages others in this group to get involved in issues that affect the group."

Innovation behavior was also rated by the alumnus's supervisor on a four-item measure of role performance. An example item is "coming up with new ideas." Knowledge of organizational politics was measured by a 1-to-7 scale of agreement about topics such as, "I know who the most influential people are in my organization." Career initiative was also measured by a 1-to-7 scale, with statements such as, "I have updated my skills in order to be more competitive for promotions."

Data were also collected for the career outcomes of current salary, number of promotions during the two years, and career satisfaction (as with the earlier study reported above). Proactive personality was shown to be positively related to innovation, political knowledge, and career initiative. In contrast, in this study proactive personality did not show a statistically significant relationship to voice. (It has been argued that just because people express their opinion frequently, they may not necessarily do something proactive about their thoughts or concerns.) The indirect result of the study with respect to proactive personality was that the correlates of proactivity – innovation, political knowledge, and career initiative – had a positive relationship with salary growth and number of promotions during the previous two years, as well as career satisfaction.

An interpretation offered of the results was that workers with a proactive personality tend to engage in behaviors that have a positive effect on their careers. The authors also note that proactive personality manifests itself in specific behaviors and thinking patterns (such as innovation) which in turn account for differences in career-related outcomes. Furthermore, specific proactive behaviors, such as learning the political landscape, can create conditions leading to extrinsic (e.g., more promotions) and intrinsic (e.g., career satisfaction) career success. Based on the results, the authors offer this advice:

Being an innovator rather than a status quo-oriented employee, engaging in behaviors to become more politically astute than ill-versed, and actively engaging in career planning and career-related feedback are specific actions one can take to enhance the likelihood of an extrinsically rewarding and intrinsically satisfying career.[4]

PROACTIVITY AND CAREER MANAGEMENT

Thinking and behaving proactively relates to career success in terms of outcomes such as earnings and promotions. At the same time, proactivity prompts career-minded people to engage in career-management behaviors that contribute to positive career outcomes. In this section we describe a list of proactive behaviors that contribute to effective career management. Most of these behaviors have been observed rather than researched systematically yet still contribute to a comprehensive understanding of how proactivity contributes to individual and organizational productivity. For example, if a proactive worker takes the initiative to develop an advanced job-related skill, he or she might become more productive.

1. Finding a Mentor or Mentors

Being mentored is widely regarded as an effective tactic for career management. In some companies, corporate professionals are assigned a mentor, which makes proactivity unnecessary in finding a mentor. In most career settings, however, proactivity facilitates finding a mentor. Pinney Allen had a distinguished career an attorney, and then became the head of the Atlanta Girls' School, a college preparatory institution whose mission is to develop the full potential of girls and young women. She advises her students to actively seek mentors throughout their careers, and to search in unexpected places. Allen says, "We think that someone who doesn't share our experience or look like us couldn't possibly relate to us, but the person who seems different, who offers a unique opportunity for learning, might be your gold mine."[5]

A considerable amount of mentoring now takes place using company-sponsored software or social media to match people who want to be mentored with potential mentors.[6] Proactivity is still helpful in taking the initiative to make effective use of an automated system. For example, the proactive person seeking a mentor might establish criteria for a preferred mentor, and the search for a potential mentor or mentors who meet these criteria.

2.   Securing a Suitable New Position

As mentioned in Chapter 1, a personal benefit of proactivity is that such thinking and behavior facilitates a successful outcome in the job search, as demonstrated in a study with recent college graduates.[7] A similar study with 875 students found that proactive personality made a modest incremental contribution to predicting job search behavior.[8] (*Prediction* in this sense means that a positive relationship was found between scores on the proactive personality test and job search behaviors.)

   Specific aspects of the job search are also likely to be facilitated by proactivity. For example, many job seekers are concerned that they will be discriminated against because they are considerably older than others seeking a similar position. Stu Coleman, a staffing specialist, recommends that the job seeker concerned about being relatively old, pre-empt employers' concerns. "Anticipate the objections someone might have with an older employee and make sure you address them proactively. You need to get past the preconceived notions and biases from the beginning." One such initiative is for the concerned job applicant to reassure the employer in a covering letter of the benefits to be gained from hiring an experienced worker.[9]

3.   Attracting the Attention of an Executive Placement Specialist

For people already employed who are seeking an executive or other high-level position, a major challenge is how to attract the attention of executive placement specialists – often referred to as *headhunters*. Proactively contacting these placement specialists directly, such as sending them a job résumé or telephoning, is usually a waste of time. The executive placement specialists are paid by recruiters to find key recruits, and they believe that they should find the candidate, not the reverse.[10] The antidote to this problem is for job seekers to proactively find a way for the headhunter to find them.

   Executive recruiter Les Berglas recommends that the job seeker take several proactive steps to get noticed by him or other recruiters. First, the attention should be sought of people in a person's network who might know a recruiter. The network member might then recommend the job seeker to the recruiter because being recommended carries some weight. Secondly, have a favorable posting on LinkedIn that includes accomplishments and awards because recruiters scan LinkedIn looking for talented people. Thirdly, getting quoted in a relevant trade publication carries considerable weight with executive recruiters.[11]

4. Developing a Job and Career-Relevant Skill

Based on years of practice in leadership development, John H. Zenger, Joseph R. Folkman, and Scott K. Edinger believe that a career can be advanced by developing skills that complement what the worker already does best. Proactivity is required to identify what skills would be complementary, and to take the initiative to develop those skills. Feedback from others is particularly useful in developing leadership skills because effective leadership depends heavily on the perception of others. Proactivity is often essential for receiving feedback from coworkers and subordinates.

Developing the new skills is regarded as the business equivalent of cross training, or enhancing complementary skills that will enable a manager or professional to make full use of existing strengths. A basic example is that technical skills can be enhanced when communication skills improve, making a leader's skills more apparent and useful. Examples of companion behaviors for a given leadership skill include connecting emotionally with others, collaborating and fostering teamwork, taking the initiative, and championing change.[12]

5. Avoiding Being Laid Off Including Being Indispensable

Yet another practical application of proactivity is for the corporate worker to take steps to decrease the possibility that he or she will be laid off as part of downsizing. When the employer is suffering financially it is time to proactively prepare for the possibility of one's position collapsing. Dee Soder, a managing partner at an executive advisory firm, recommends that when layoffs seem likely, the person potentially affected should prepare an updated résumé focused on his or her most marketable skills. The person should upload his or her latest performance reviews, summary of accomplishments, work samples, and letters of appreciation from customers to a computer file that he or she can access outside of the company system.[13] Another key proactive step to help avoid being part of a downsizing event is to make sure company executives are aware of and appreciate one's recent accomplishments. For example, it can be helpful to send a detailed progress report of one's activities to key people in the organization.[14]

In addition to being aware of general signs that layoffs are possible, the career-minded worker should proactively look for subtle signs that the immediate manager is distancing himself or herself from the individual. One signal that a person's job may be in jeopardy is the supervisor's lack of casual interaction with him or her, including friendly e-mail messages. Changes in the way the person is treated by the manager can also suggest that a person's job is in danger. Examples include the boss taking a few days to respond to e-mail or voice-mail messages, and one's suggestions being ignored during group meetings.[15]

Another strategy for avoiding being part of a layoff list is to take proactive steps to be indispensable (or at least important to the purposes of the organization). As recommended by Steven Covey, several suggestions for being perceived as indispensable by the employer are as follows: First, find solutions to pressing organizational unit, or organizational, problems instead of panicking under pressure. Secondly, build a constituency of support by such means as offering help to coworkers when they feel overloaded with work. Thirdly, expand your role by stepping outside your job description (as in being a good organizational citizen).[16]

6.   Developing a Protean Career

During the past two decades the career environment has shifted away substantially from one in which most corporate professionals and managers confined their career to advancement within one or a few organizations. Careers today are viewed as without boundaries, and in which the psychological contract between employer and employee no longer usually includes a promise of long-term employment and steady career advancement. A *protean career* attitude reflects the extent to which an individual manages his or her career in a proactive, self-directed way. Such a career is driven by personal values, and career success is based on subjective, personal criteria of success.[17]

An empirical test of the effectiveness of a protean career attitude in managing one's career was provided in a survey conducted by Ans De Vos and Nele Soens. The subjects were 289 Belgian employees who had participated in career counseling. Protean career attitude was measured by an inventory, with a sample item being, "I am in charge of my own career." Inventory measures were also taken of career insight, career self-management behaviors, career satisfaction, and perceived employability. Career insight focused on how well career counseling had given the respondents better insight into their career aspirations. The results showed that protean career attitude related significantly to career self-insight, career self-management behaviors, career satisfaction, and perceived employability. One interpretation of the results was that having a protean career attitude (which includes a heavy element of proactivity) is important for individuals in the current career landscape.[18]

7. Staying in Good Health

Another way in which proactivity contributes to career management is for the employee to take a proactive stance about physical health. The reason is that many employers want employees to stay healthy in order to reduce health insurance costs, as well as for humanitarian reasons. Employees at some companies are encouraged to take an annual online assessment, and work on the goals identified by the assessment. Employers in a variety of for-profit, not-for-profit, and governmental organizations offer health insurance policies that reward or penalize employees for progress on personal health goals. If the employee feels forced into taking strides to improve health, such as through exercise and diet, he or she is being reactive.[19] In contrast, employees who take the initiative to stay in good health so they will be better accepted by their employers are being proactive.

PROACTIVITY FOR ACQUIRING POWER

Acquiring power is an important part of career management for upwardly mobile people, and acquiring power often requires substantial proactive thinking and behavior. The subject of power acquisition is almost as broad as the study of organizational politics. It will serve our purposes to illustrate several ways in which being proactive is linked to acquiring power within the organization. In his analysis of power in different domains, Jeffrey Pfeffer suggests that a key tactic for acquiring and retaining power is to make the first move. A surprise move can catch opponents off guard before they understand what is taking place. For example, if a CEO moves first to get his or her opponents removed from the board of directors the CEO can usually retain his or her position. If a power struggle is brewing, it pays to take the offensive. Pfeffer also recommends co-opting antagonists as a way of making them part of your team or giving them a stake in the system.[20]

Co-optation is proactive because one side takes the initiative to enlist the cooperation of an existing or potential adversary. Assume that the head of an employee wellness program is receiving considerable opposition to some of her initiatives from the chief financial officer, particularly her plan to have an onsite physical exercise program during working hours. To soften the opposition, the wellness director invites the CFO to become a member of the "employee wellness advisory board" composed of company executives and distinguished citizens from the community.

Another way that proactivity can be employed to acquire power, is for a worker create a new position for him- or herself within an organization.[21]

For example, a worker in the customer service department of a public utility might spend a good chunk of time responding to e-mails and social media postings from customers who have comments and complaints. The customer service representative then proposes to her manager that responding to these messages could easily be a full-time responsibility. She also argues that promptly responding to complaints and comments would enhance the reputation of the utility within the community. Her suggestion is approved, and the woman becomes a full-time specialist in responding to online inquiries.

Gathering powerful people into one's network is yet another way that proactivity contributes to power acquisition. Developing power contacts is a focused type of social networking. These contacts can benefit a person by supporting his or her ideas in meetings and other public forums. One proactive approach to developing these contacts is to be more social, such as throwing parties and inviting powerful people and their guests.

Considerable networking for the development of power contacts now takes place through social networking geared toward professionals, such as LinkedIn. Specialty sites such as those geared toward specific industry groups including sales and marketing, and information technology are also well suited to networking. Business writer Denise Campbell notes that social media websites have become to business professionals and entrepreneurs what golf is to C-suite occupants – an opportunity to strategically network and execute business transactions.[22]

PROACTIVITY FOR ESTABLISHING A POSITIVE REPUTATION

Proactivity can be important for establishing a positive reputation, and a positive reputation in turn facilitates attaining career success. A positive reputation contributes to career success in such ways as being recommended for promotions both outside and inside the company, increasing a base of clients or customers, avoiding being placed on a layoff list, and attracting the attention of investors if one is a business owner.

A modest proactive maneuver for reputation enhancement is to ask for one's fair share of the credit for contribution to a project. For example, if a person has made a valuable contribution to the project, yet the effort goes unrecognized, the proactive person might say, "I was thrilled to contribute to such a successful project. It would mean a lot to me if you mentioned my contribution when you discuss the project with the CEO." A related initiative for receiving credit is to keep a journal of the activities that one does well. Details of specific accomplishments should be noted, including contributions and notes of thanks from colleagues and customers.[23]

The traditional approach to proactively establishing a good reputation is to perform in an outstanding manner, both within one's own organizational unit and in cross-functional assignments. Searching out ways to perform exceptionally well for customers and clients also fits the traditional approach to reputation enhancement. In the modern era, reputation management often refers to developing a positive online reputation. Taking the offense to develop a positive online reputation includes such steps as making posts that are thoughtful, objective, rational, and that provide useful information. Positive mentions of an individual by a second party, particularly on LinkedIn, can contribute to reputation enhancement. Proactivity can influence this process in another way: the individual might ask others to consider writing an endorsement of his or her capabilities and skills.

At an organizational level proactivity is important to help cope with large numbers of negative messages posted online about an organization. Two examples of this negativity are as follows: (1) In 2012, the National Organization for Marriage initiated a "Dump Starbucks" campaign in protest of the café chain's support of gay marriage rights. (2) In 2012, a social media drive by activists proposed a boycott of restaurant chain Chick-Fil-A after the company president publicly opposed the rights of gays and lesbians to marry people of the same sex.

According to Rob Norman, CEO of a large advertising firm, business executives should craft their corporate images during tranquil times and then aggressively amplify these reputation-enhancing self-portraits during moments of peak public interest, such as a proposed boycott. Norman explains in these words: "The idea of producing a bank of preemptive content – about how we produce our food, how we pay our employees, how we run our diversity policies – and then activating them with paid media at the moment that the controversy arrives is almost a prerequisite strategy for everyone now."[24] Proactivity is involved in this tactic because company leadership prepares in advance to cope with an online (and perhaps offline) attack.

PERSONAL BRANDING AND PROACTIVITY

A popular approach to enhancing career success is to build a *personal brand*, the qualities based on an individual's collection of strengths that make him or her unique, thereby distinguishing the person from the competition. The personal brand becomes a person's external identity as perceived by others. According to Peter Montoya and Tim Vandehey, the personal brand is what a person stands for, including the values, abilities, and actions that others associate with that person. At the same time, the personal brand is a professional alter-ego designed to influence how others perceive the person, and turning the perception into opportunity. The personal brand tells the audience three things: (1) who the person is, (2) what the person does, and (3) what makes the person different, or how he or she creates value for the target market.[25]

Establishing the ingredients to one's brand requires considerable proactivity, such as in developing a strength (high level of skill) of potential value in a competitive workplace. Illustrative strengths include an American or English person becoming fluent in Mandarin Chinese, or the ability to find valuable information on the Internet not readily found on the typical search engines. (Reactivity would be developing a skill only when required by a job responsibility.) Promoting the basket of strengths that constitute the brand also requires considerable proactivity. Examples include developing an electronic business card summarizing one's uniqueness that could be flashed at networking events, or creating a social media profile containing the same information. A personal brand could also be demonstrated by displaying key strengths and values while working collaboratively with others such as serving on a taskforce.

Suzanne Bates, an executive coach, provides useful details about how job seekers can take the initiative to capitalize on their personal brands. She advises that job seekers can build their brand awareness by communicating their brand values during job interviews and by raising their visibility in their industry. Visibility is enhanced by networking, developing strong relationships and getting to know people who share one's values. Connections are not only a representation of a personal brand, but these people can be a source for recommending the person for job openings.[26]

PROACTIVITY FOR ATTAINING CAREER RESILIENCE

Personal resilience, or bouncing back from setbacks, usually requires proactive thinking and behaving. A resilient person can withstand pressure and emerge stronger because of the experience. The resilient person profits from a setback by taking a proactive stance on what to do better next time, such as a negotiator losing out because of taking a rigid stance instead of being more flexible. People with a resilient disposition are better able to stay calm, and have a healthy level of physical and psychological wellness in the face of challenges. They accept the reality that a problem exists, so

From 1 to 5, rate how much each of the following applies to you (1 = very little, 5 = very much).

1	2	3	4	5	If I have a bad day at work or school, it does not ruin my day. I make plans to do better the next time.
1	2	3	4	5	After a vacation, I can usually get right back into work at my regular work pace.
1	2	3	4	5	Every "no" I encounter is one step closer to a "yes."
1	2	3	4	5	The popular saying "Get over it" has a lot of merit in guiding my life.
1	2	3	4	5	The last time I was rejected for a job (or assignment) I wanted, I looked for another suitable opportunity.
1	2	3	4	5	I enjoy being the underdog once in a while because it means I have to figure out how to win.
1	2	3	4	5	I enjoy taking risks because I believe that the biggest rewards stem from risk taking.
1	2	3	4	5	I rarely worry about, or keep thinking about, mistakes I have made in the past. Instead, I look to improve.
1	2	3	4	5	If I ran for political office and lost, I would be willing to run again.
1	2	3	4	5	When I encounter a major problem or setback, I will talk over the situation with a friend or confidant, and make plans for doing better.
1	2	3	4	5	I am physically sick much less frequently than most people I know, including friends, coworkers, and other students.
1	2	3	4	5	The last time I lost my keys (or wallet or handbag or smart phone), I took care of the problem within a few days and was not particularly upset.
1	2	3	4	5	I get more than my share of good breaks.

Notes: scoring and interpretation: add the numbers you have circled to get your total score.
60–70 You are highly resilient with an ability to bounce back from setbacks.
45–59 You have an average degree of resiliency when faced with problems.
30–44 Setbacks and disappointments are a struggle for you.
1–29 You may need help in dealing with setbacks.

Figure 5.1   The resiliency quiz

they are likely to develop a plan (be proactive) to work their way out of the problem.[27] The personal resiliency quiz presented in Figure 5.1 gives the reader an opportunity to think through his or her tendencies toward resiliency as well as reflect on the link between proactivity and resilience.

Attaining resilience is often linked to recovery, or sufficient rest time in a non-work setting, to overcome the work pressures. Sabine Sonnentag conducted a study with 147 public service employees and suggested that those who had sufficient recovery from work during leisure time tended to be more proactive. Data for the study were collected on five different days.

Proactivity in this study was defined operationally as taking personal initiative and pursuing job-related learning. Trait personal initiative and trait pursuit of learning were both measured by a questionnaire. A sample item measuring trait personal initiative was, "I actively attack problems." A sample item measuring trait pursuit of learning was, "I often look for opportunities to develop new skills and knowledge." Feelings of recovery were linked to leisure-time activities, with a sample item being, "Because of leisure activities pursued yesterday, I feel relaxed." Work engagement as a trait was also measured in the study, with a sample item being, "I am enthusiastic about my job."

A conclusion reached in the study was that recovery has a positive effect on work engagement and proactive behavior, with work engagement mediating the effects of recovery on proactive behavior. Workers who feel that they sufficiently recover from work pressures during leisure time experience a higher level of work engagement the next day. This high level of work engagement in turn helps the workers be more proactive in terms of taking the initiative and pursuing learning goals.[28]

PROACTIVITY AND CAREER SATISFACTION

Proactivity can be related to career satisfaction in several ways. The proactive person may receive more career rewards, such as higher income, more promotions, and more prestige, all of which contribute to satisfaction. Proactivity can also lead to solving a higher number of difficult problems, which can enhance job satisfaction. Being proactive can also lead to a feeling of control over one's career outcomes, which tends to be more satisfying than a lack of control. The research described next supports the idea that proactivity can enhance career satisfaction, although the evidence is indirect.

Two studies conducted by Berrin Erdogan and Talya N. Bauer framed intrinsic career success as job and career satisfaction, reinforcing again the argument that you are successful if you are satisfied. One study setting was 15 elementary and high schools in Turkey, and the subjects were 434 school teachers. The second study involved university professors in the United States. A slightly positive finding was that proactive personality was more positively related to job and career satisfaction when there was a good fit between the values of the person and organization (P–O fit). The interpretation given to this finding was that when workers find a congruence between their values and those of the organization, they engage in more proactive efforts that fit the needs of the organization. As a result, these workers have greater success in furthering their job and career objectives.

The two studies also found that proactive personality was related to career satisfaction and objective career success only when employees possessed skills and abilities that met the demands of their job. An interpretation given for this finding is that when workers have a good fit with their jobs, they attain more success with their job-related initiatives. As a result they further their career, leading to more satisfaction and objective career success.[29]

SUGGESTIONS FOR APPLICATION

1. Making a concentrated effort to develop your proactive tendencies will often increase the probability of attaining the career outcomes of objective success and career satisfaction.

2. A key step in developing your personal brand is to evaluate your strengths and weaknesses, much like a SWOT (strengths, weaknesses, opportunities, and threats in the marketplace) analysis. If you are job hunting, prepare an objective assessment of your strengths, weaknesses, opportunities and threats in the marketplace for hiring.[30]

3. To identify your brand, it is also helpful to think about the unique qualities that set you apart from others in your field. Review what influential people have said about you over the years, and look for repeated compliments.[31] Think through which of these strengths might be marketable, such as having received several compliments about your ability to manage a crisis.

4. Although a personal brand highlights an individual's strengths, it should not be too promotional to the point of self-adoration and narcissism. Your personal brand should suggest that you are a team player who adds value to the company based on individual play and working cooperatively with others.[32]

5. For employers to capitalize on the advantages of hiring workers with a proactive personality, it may also be important to look for a good fit between those workers and their environment. In particular, there should be a good fit between the person and the organization, as well as between the person and the job.[33]

SUMMARY

Proactivity contributes to individual career success. A pioneering study on the topic found that proactive personality was positively associated with two objective measures of career success – salary and promotions – and also with career satisfaction. Ratings by significant others also showed positive relationships with the same outcomes. A follow-up, longitudinal study found that proactive personality was positively related to innovation, political knowledge, and career initiative. It was also found that several correlates of proactivity – innovation, political knowledge, and career initiative – had a positive relationship with salary growth and number of promotions during the previous two years, as well as career satisfaction.

Proactivity often prompts individuals to engage in behaviors that facilitate effective career management, such as the following: (1) finding a mentor or mentors, (2) securing a suitable new position, (3) developing a job- and career-relevant skill, (4) avoiding being laid off including being indispensable, (5) developing a protean career, and (6) staying in good health.

Acquiring power is an important part of career management for upwardly mobile people, and acquiring power often requires substantial proactive thinking and behavior, as illustrated by the following approaches. A key tactic for acquiring and retaining power is to make the first move. Co-optation is proactive because one side takes the initiative to enlist the cooperation of an existing or potential adversary. Creating a new position for oneself is a method of acquiring power. Gathering powerful people into one's network requires proactivity.

Proactivity can be important for establishing a positive reputation, and a positive reputation facilitates career success. A modest proactive maneuver for reputation enhancement is to ask for one's fair share of credit for contribution to a project. The traditional approach to proactively establishing a good reputation is to perform outstandingly in and outside one's organizational unit. Taking the offense to develop a positive online reputation is helpful. Organizations can also be proactive about reputation enhancement, such as taking the initiative to produce a bank of preemptive content to deal with potential future negative social media posts.

REFERENCES

1. Sonia Alleyne, "A Professional Branding Model," *Black Enterprise*, July 2011, p. 67.
2. Scott E. Seibert, J. Michael Crant, and Maria L. Kraimer, "Proactive Personality and Career Success," *Journal of Applied Psychology*, June 1999, pp. 416–427.
3. Scott E. Seibert, Maria L. Kraimer, and J. Michael Crant, "What Do Proactive People Do? A Longitudinal Model Linking Proactive Personality and Career Success," *Personnel Psychology*, Winter 2001, pp. 845–874.
4. Seibert, Kraimer, and Crant, "What Do Proactive People Do?" p. 866.

5. Quoted in Laura Raines, "Mentoring Is Critical for Women to Advance in Careers," *www.acj.com*, May 17, 2011, pp. 1–3. Retrieved November 1, 2012.

6. Gary Kranz, "Employee Engagement: Losing Lifeblood," *Workforce Management*, July 2011, pp. 24–28.

7. Douglas J. Brown, Richard T. Cober, Kevin Kane, Paul E. Levy, and Jarrett Shalhoop, "Proactive Personality and the Successful Job Search: A Field Investigation with College Graduates," *Journal of Applied Psychology*, May 2006, pp. 717–726.

8. Rita Class and Hans De Witte, "Determinants of Graduates' Preparatory Job Behaviour: A Competitive Test of Proactive Personality and Expectancy-Value Theory," *Psychologica Belgica*, Number 4, 2002, pp. 251–266.

9. Coleman cited and quoted in Kaitlin Madden, "Appear Ageless On Your Résumé: Shift Focus to Career Accomplishments," *Career Builder*, January 29, 2012, p. 1.

10. Joanne McCool, "Don't Call Us; We'll Call You or How to Get a Recruiter to Find You on LinkedIn," *www.examiner.com*, March 15, 2010, pp. 1–4. Retrieved October 21, 2011.

11. Les Berglas, "How Do I Get a Headhunter Interested in Me?" *Fortune*, April 12, 2010, p. 40.

12. John H. Zenger, Joseph R. Folkman, and Scott K. Edinger, "Making Yourself Indispensable," *Harvard Business Review*, October 2011, pp. 84–92.

13. Cited in Joann S. Lublin, "Layoff Rumors? Get Ready to Get Busy," *The Wall Street Journal*, August 5, 2008, p. D1.

14. Lublin, "Layoff Rumors?" p. D5.

15. Dana Mattioli, "Layoff Sign: Boss's Cold Shoulder," *The Wall Street Journal*, October 3, 2008, p. D6.

16. Cited in Dennis McCafferty, "Save Your Job," *USA Weekend*, April 16–18, 2010, p. 17.

17. Douglas T. Hall, *Careers In and Out of Organizations* (Thousand Oaks, CA: Sage Publications, 2002).

18. Ans De Vos and Nele Soens, "Protean Attitude and Career Success: The Mediating Role of Self-Management," *Journal of Vocational Behavior*, Volume 73, 2008, pp. 449–456.

19. Patricia Arnstett, "Companies Push Employees to Be Proactive About Health," *Detroit Free Press*, August 19, 2012, pp. 2–3.

20. Jeffrey Pfeffer, "Power Play," *Harvard Business Review*, July–August 2010, p. 90.

21. Von Flagman, "Creating a Niche, and Earning a Promotion," *The New York Times* (www.nytimes.com), March 3, 2012, pp. 1–3. Retrieved September 26, 2012.

22. Denise Campbell, "What's Your Social Media Strategy?" *Black Enterprise*, November 2010, p. 75.

23. "Toot Your Own Horn – the Right Way," *Communication Briefings*, February 2011, p. 1.

24. Quoted in "It's Getting Tougher to Bully Brands," *Bloomberg Business Week*, August 6–12, 2012, pp. 20–24.

25. Peter Montoya and Tim Vandehey, *The Brand Called You* (Tustin, CA: Peter Montoya Publishing, 2005), pp. 11–12, 14.

26. Cited in Debra Auerbach, "Boost Career with a Personal Brand," *Career Builder*, July 15, 2012, p. 1.

27.   William Atkinson, "Turning Stress Into Strength," *HR Magazine*, January 2011, p. 49.
28.   Sabine Sonnentag, "Recovery, Work Engagement, and Proactive Behavior: A New Look at the Interface Between Nonwork and Work," *Journal of Applied Psychology*, June 2003, pp. 518–528.
29.   Berrin Erdogan and Talya N. Bauer, "Enhancing Career Benefits of Employee Proactive Personality: The Role of Fit with Jobs and Organizations," *Personnel Psychology*, Winter 2005, pp. 859–891.
30.   Douglas J. Brown (interview with), "6 Steps to Successful Self-Branding," *Tribune Media Services* (www.chicagotribune.com), August 17, 2012, p. 1. Retrieved August 18, 2012.
31.   Auerbach, "Boost Career with a Personal Brand," p. 1.
32.   Josh Hyatt, "Building Your Brand (and Keeping Your Job)," *Fortune*, August 10, 2010, pp. 72–73.
33.   Erdogan and Bauer, "Enhancing Career Benefits," p. 883.

6. Opportunity recognition, innovation, and proactivity

A key component of proactive behavior is recognizing opportunities that others may have overlooked. If a worker is to be proactive, he or she must identify an opportunity to express proactivity, such as the manager of a tech support center seeing the possibilities of selling cloud backup services to clients who need help in repairing digital devices.

Over 75 years ago when Chester Carlson was studying to become a patent attorney, he was faced with the tedious task of hand copying information from law books at the library. Recognizing that there must be a better way to copy written documents, he decided to build a machine to accomplish the task instead. His xerographic machine led to the founding of what became Xerox Corporation. Although Carlson's Eureka moment is significant, he had been looking for opportunities to find new ways of printing since he was ten years old.[1]

A modern example of opportunity recognition lies behind the Chipotle Mexican Grill. Steve Ellis opened a taqueria in Denver, Colorado, to earn enough money to fund his dream of a full-scale restaurant. As sales soared for his Mexican food, he saw a great opportunity. He pivoted and expanded the burrito restaurant into a chain instead of following through on his plan to open a full-scale restaurant.[2]

The purpose of this chapter is to describe in detail how the proactive personality and proactive behavior contribute to opportunity recognition, and its logical consequence – innovation including creativity. In addition to opinion, some research and theory is available to contribute to understanding the link between proactivity and both opportunity and innovation.

PROACTIVITY AND OPPORTUNITY RECOGNITION

Our analysis of proactivity and opportunity recognition examines three closely related aspects of the same phenomenon: searching for opportunities, seeing and seizing the opportunities sought, and representative examples of opportunity recognition in different domains or fields.

Searching for Opportunities

As mentioned several times, a major characteristic of the proactive person is to actively search for opportunities to engage in constructive behaviors. The checklist presented in Figure 6.1 provides you an opportunity to reflect on your own behaviors and attitudes that suggest a propensity to search for opportunities in your immediate and remote environment. Searching for opportunities requires that the individual proactively scan the environment to find a fit between his or her capabilities and an environmental need. Here is a representative example of the process:

> Company owner Jeffrey Taylor generates revenue by creating 2-D and 3-D animations to illustrate engineering processes and criminal court testimonies. A few years ago, he was thinking about potential new applications for his technology. Discussions with a client soon convinced Taylor of the need to help people visualize the benefits of environmental sustainability. His research then revealed a growing sector that could benefit from the type of cutting-edge visuals his company provides. Taylor's company, CrossPlatform Design L.L.C., is now actively involved in creating green (environmentally friendly) visuals.[3]

Why a person might engage in opportunity searching has been the subject of scholarly investigation.[4] A starting point is that an individual's intrinsic interest in the task at hand might prompt the person to seek creative solutions to problems. The visual presentation specialist mentioned above was most likely strongly interested in making two-dimensional and three-dimensional designs, prompting him to both search for and be receptive to new potential applications of his imaging methods.

A segment of a study conducted by Fierong Yuan and Richard W. Woodman with 238 full-time employees and their direct supervisors in several different industries provides another insight into what might trigger opportunity searching. The industries included generally emphasize innovation: information technology service, computer system development, furniture design and manufacturing, and chemical instruments development and manufacturing. The sample included employees from a broad cross-section of jobs, including technicians, sales and marketing specialists, production supervisors, quality control inspectors, middle managers, and research and development scientists and engineers. Creativity was measured by supervisory ratings.

The variable under study most related to why a person searches for opportunities was "dissatisfaction with the status quo," as measured by responses to the following three statements:

No.	Attitude or behavior reflecting opportunity seeking and recognition	Yes	No
1.	I often question how a process I encounter could be improved.	❑	❑
2.	When I am shopping in a store or online I sometimes wonder why the store does not carry a particular product or provide a particular service.	❑	❑
3.	I enjoy reading about inventions and inventors.	❑	❑
4.	Ideas for improvement related to the job sometimes come to me when I am engaging in leisure activities.	❑	❑
5.	I imagine there are many opportunities in industrialized countries to sell products and services in under-developed countries.	❑	❑
6.	I doubt anything can be done about the problem of so many infants and old people falling down frequently.	❑	❑
7.	My life doesn't need any improvements or changes.	❑	❑
8.	I sometimes wonder how long people are going to put up with having so many e-mail messages to receive and send almost every day.	❑	❑
9.	Why should anybody really care about what might lie at the bottom or under the world's largest oceans?	❑	❑
10.	I have given some serious thought as to what could be done with all the vacant stores in shopping malls.	❑	❑
11.	Finding the Next Big Thing is mostly a matter of luck.	❑	❑
12.	It would be extremely difficult for me to find ways to reduce my living expenses by 2 percent.	❑	❑
13.	At least a few times in my life I have heard "opportunity knocking" and made good use of the situation.	❑	❑
14.	However silly it sounds, the early bird really does get the worm.	❑	❑
15.	Opportunities exist for most people if they just knew where to look and how to seize them.	❑	❑
16.	Now that energy-boosting drinks have been on the market a long time, there are most likely no ideas for another beverage category left.	❑	❑
17.	Looking for ways to recycle garbage is close to being a waste of time.	❑	❑
18.	A productive use of time is to set aside a small period of time each week just to think.	❑	❑
19.	Interacting with coworkers can be an effective way of finding new ideas.	❑	❑
20.	I believe in the old saying, "Necessity is the mother of invention."	❑	❑

Notes: scoring and interpretation: give yourself 1 point for responding "Yes" to the following statements: 1, 2, 3, 4, 5, 8, 10, 13, 14, 15, 18, 19, and 20. Give yourself 1 point for responding "No" to the following statements: 6, 7, 9, 11, 12, 16, and 17. The more of these attitudes and behaviors you scored in accordance with the scoring key, the higher the probability that you are a person who seeks and recognizes opportunities. Scores of 17–20 suggest strong tendencies toward opportunity seeking and recognition, whereas scores of 1–4 suggest weak tendencies toward opportunity seeking and recognition.

Figure 6.1   A checklist of behaviors and attitudes reflecting opportunity seeking and recognition

1. Many things in my department need improvement.
2. The performance of my organization needs to be improved.
3. The performance of my work needs to be improved.

The hypothesis was supported that dissatisfaction with the status quo was positively related to performance outcomes of innovative behavior.[5] The implication is that being dissatisfied with the status quo prompts a worker to search for innovative ways to improve a work process. For example, a quality control inspector might suggest a new way of inspecting components before any defects lead to quality problems in a final product.

Seeing and Seizing Opportunities

Although the difference most likely reflects different points on the same continuum, seeing and seizing opportunities follow searching for them. The marketing manager of a senior living complex might be searching for opportunities to expand the rental base of the complex. One day she reads about the shrinking labor force in the United States, and carefully studies a major reason for the decrease in the labor force – more baby boomers are retiring early. She sees this fact as a possible growth factor for her senior residence complex. She seizes the opportunity to develop a database of young retirees in her geographic region. Next she devises a direct-mail campaign, an e-mail marketing campaign, and a telemarketing program aimed at interesting this pool of early retirees. The marketing manager's proactive thinking eventually pays off as she rents a considerable number of apartments and patio homes.

Opportunity seeking and seizing often stem from a felt need to be more productive, as in "Necessity is the mother of invention." Coastal Contacts, a major player in the North American online contact-lens retail market, held a planning session for revving up growth, but no good idea or plan emerged. As a result, over the next six months, CEO Roger Hardy and his top-management team telephoned customers each week to solicit any of their potential suggestions. This straightforward proactive behavior paid off. To the team's surprise, one recurring theme emerged – customers wanted next-day delivery. Coastal Contacts then started delivering lenses overnight. Sales increased 41 percent in one year in the United States where the new delivery policy was implemented.[6]

The proactive policing style used for many years in New York City provides insight into seeing and seizing opportunity. Crime has decreased 80 percent in New York City since the 1990s. As a result of the decrease in crime, legitimate commerce has flourished in some of the city's poorest neighborhoods, tourism has boomed throughout New York City, and property values have escalated. Major retailers such as Home Depot have moved into neighborhoods once controlled by drug gangs, providing employment for local workers. It has been estimated that the control of crime helped 10,000 black and Hispanic males avoid premature death.

Seeing and seizing opportunities were done with a focus on preventing crimes. "Seizing" in this context referred to taking the opportunity to prevent crime. (Chapter 9 of this book focuses on proactivity and prevention.) In 1994, William Bratton, the New York Police Commissioner at the time, hoped that his proactive methods would prevent future crimes, not simply react to crimes already committed. The drive began by analyzing victim reports daily to target police resources in neighborhoods in which crime patterns were emerging. Leadership at the police department held commanders accountable for the safety of their precincts. The key method of the police was to intervene when they observed an individual acting suspiciously. The person might be asked a few questions, or frisked if legally justified. These proactive methods (often referred to as "Stop-and-frisk") averted a large number of crimes.

Despite the merits of the proactive program in preventing crime, it has been strongly criticized on the basis of civil rights. The specific charge is that the NYPD policy is racist because the majority of people stopped are black, Latino, or a combination of the two. A federal judge overseeing a class-action suit against the NYPD has announced her conviction that the stop-and-frisk policy is unconstitutional. Another dysfunction of the policy is that it may have triggered attacks against police by city residents.[7] For example, during the first seven months of 2012, 10 police officers were shot, more than in the previous four years combined.[8]

Brief Case Examples of Opportunity Recognition and Seizure in a Variety of Domains

In addition to the examples already presented about the close association between proactive thinking and opportunity recognition, additional examples from a variety of domains will help explain further this association. Furthermore, the examples presented in this section are designed to provide insight into various ways in which opportunity recognition takes place, followed by seizing the opportunity.

Seeing the possibilities for selling shoes online
A classic example of seeing an opportunity followed by seizing the opportunity is the behavior of Nick Swinmurn, the founder of the online shoe store, Zappos. (Although CEO Tony Hsieh is usually associated with Zappos, Swinmurn brought him in as the major investor.) In Swinmurn's

words, "I was at the mall and couldn't find the pair of desert boots I wanted. So, I thought, why not do an online shoe store?" Swinmurn seized the opportunity through the business model of going into shoe stores, photographing their stock, and selling the shoes online. Part of Swinmurn's opportunity recognizing was to explain to skeptical investors that at the time 5 percent of all the shoes sold in the U.S. were through mail-order catalogs. The implication was that some customers were already purchasing shoes without trying them on. Zappos became a highly successful enterprise that soon sold a variety of clothing and other merchandise. The company was acquired by Amazon.com in 2009 for $1.2 billion.[9]

Spotting investment opportunities during a recession

According to the research of Ranjay Gulati, Nitin Hohria, and Franz Wohlgezogen, 9 percent of companies emerge from a recession stronger than ever. Leaders at these companies proactively spot opportunities that offer reliable returns in a reasonable period of time. CEOs must exercise cost discipline and financial prudence while detecting these profitable opportunities. The researchers offer the case example of Target, which during the 2000 recession increased its marketing and sales expenditures by 20 percent and its capital expenditures by 50 percent in comparison to pre-recession levels. The company also increased the number of Target stores from 947 to 1107, and added 88 new SuperTarget stores. Additional opportunity seizing included expanding into several new merchandise segments, bolstered by investments in credit-card programs, and developing its online business. To help fund these new opportunities, Target management relentlessly reduced costs, improved productivity, and enhanced the efficiency of its supply-chain operations.[10]

Recognizing a cognitively distant opportunity in retail banking

Cognitive scientist Giovanni Gavetti says that the challenging quest for distant opportunities requires strategic leaders who are both competent economists and psychologists. Gavetti observes that the best opportunities for growth lie on "unoccupied mountain tops," meaning that so far business people have not spotted their potential. Because the unoccupied mountain tops are *cognitively distant* (or far from the status quo) they are difficult to recognize and seize, and therefore competition is weak.

Gavetti offers the historical example of Charlie Merrill, who was able to spot a cognitively distant opportunity – banks as financial supermarkets. Such retail banks would offer a variety of products to a variety of customers. Even though bankers had been scrambling for profits this opportunity had not been spotted before because nobody else had conceived of such a firm. The opportunity seeking and seizing of Merrill did not focus exclusively on the economics of the business. In contrast, he reconceived the banking business through an analogy that contained deep insight that other bankers lacked. An essential part of seizing the opportunity was for Merrill to persuade both internal and external stakeholders, such as customers and capital lenders, that his idea had strong potential.[11]

Seeing the opportunity in disruption

As is well publicized, new technologies can disrupt the well-being of companies as well as entire industries. The shift to digital forms of advertising away from print media is one such telling example. Brian Martin, a consultant to the advertising industry, believes that there is opportunity to be recognized and seized in the moment of disruption. The shift to digital advertising has created a revolution in the field. Advertising's first creative revolution took place soon after television became entrenched into society. Digital has reached a similar degree of saturation. With so much advertising shifting to the Internet, including mobile devices, clients are reaching out for the type of help that advertising agencies can offer. Agencies that spotted this opportunity have survived and prospered.

To capitalize on opportunity within the shift to digital in advertising, the agencies had to quickly recruit professionals who were skilled in the new information technology, but who also understood, and were sympathetic toward, advertising. A case in point is a Boston advertising agency that relocated from a palatial mansion outside the city to an open office in a downtown location. With this shift, social media specialists, creative-advertising specialists, media planners, technologists, and user-experience specialists work in close proximity at modular desks.[12]

Asking the right question to recognize an opportunity in the eyewear business

A frequent antecedent to being proactive is to question why a present condition exists, as was done by the founders of Warby Parker, a firm that sells eyewear online. In 2008, four MBA students at the Wharton School of the University of Pennsylvania were kicking around ideas with two other classmates. They questioned why eye glasses, which are uncomplicated and mass produced, often cost as much as an iPhone. One of the four students, Neil Blumenthal, who had worked at a nonprofit agency that donates glasses to people in developing countries, thought he had an answer. The optical industry is an oligopoly, with a few companies making wide profit margins. Within a year the four students had begun to implement the idea of selling eyewear with a vintage look online. The often boxy style had already gained popularity in hipster neighborhoods. Next, they tested their frames and styles with other students at the Wharton School.

The students also saw the possibilities of a business model that would allow a free home try-on program plus a way of uploading photos on to the company website that would provide a virtual try-on of the eyewear. (After glasses have been tried on and returned, an optical prescription must accompany the order.) The company now also has physical show-rooms in some 10 cities across the United States.

Another factor contributing to the success of Warby Parker also reflects proactivity – the company's social mission. For each pair of glasses sold, the company helps someone in need purchase eyeglasses, though not a Warby Parker creation.[13]

Spotting an opportunity to save money on a major cost driver

Proactivity can translate directly into increased profits, and therefore boost productivity, when an opportunity is sought, found, and capitalized upon to save money on a key expense. Dawn Stokes is now the Chief Accelerator of Total Driving Experience, and was CEO and founder of the predecessor company, Texas Driving Experience. Her present company, as well as the previous company, offers corporate team-building experiences at Texas Motor Speedway in Fort Worth, Texas. The 38 vehicles in the previous company, including 18-wheelers and Corvette Z06 race cars, consumed enormous amounts of fuel. Stokes was refueling her vehicles at local gas stations, usually paying for 1000 gallons at a time. She soon saw an opportunity to reduce the amount of money she was paying for fuel, a major cost driver for Texas Driving. Stokes decided to purchase gas in massive quantities from a fuel distributor and store it onsite. She calculates that she saves between 45 cents and 55 cents a gallon through bulk purchasing, which has added considerably to profits.[14]

Seeing the opportunities based on a personal talent

For some proactive personalities, a business opportunity can stem from a talent that works well in personal life. Janis Spindel, a manufacturer's representative and a small-business owner, observed that she had enormous success in matchmaking for her friends. She finally saw an opportunity for a business when 14 friends she fixed up on blind dates all married the dates in the same year. She founded an upscale dating service for male clients who pay her from $50,000 to $250,000, plus expenses and a marriage bonus, to find them a wife. However, the company also offers more limited services for fees of $5000, and $15,000 to $25,000. Spindel has a database of approximately 12,000 women, and meets as many as possible, including group meetings. One of the growth drivers in her business is that the divorce rate of the marriages she facilitates is close to zero among 1000 marriages. Her unique and expensive matchmaking service has made

Spindel a national celebrity.[15] As with most firms providing personal services, her matchmaking firm receives some negative posts on the Internet.

Coaching businesspeople about the effective use of social media

In the current era businesspeople have scrambled to make effective use of social media to advance their firms. A problem, however, is that the deluge of information leaves many people baffled as to what is valid and relevant. Michael F. Lewis, the chairman and CEO of two business advisory firms, said he took a very proactive approach, and learned a lot about how to listen and monitor all this activity. He assembled his team and made sure that they wanted to be as proactive as possible in reaching clients and potential clients. The basic opportunity Lewis and his team saw was to engage with corporations by helping them develop social media strategy based on their current level of involvement, and their plans for growth.[16] (Lewis's situation is useful to our discussion of opportunity seeking and seizing because he understood explicitly that he was being proactive.)

Recognizing and seizing the opportunity for easier customer payments

Customers of everyday purchases, such as in restaurants, for a long time have been able to pay for these purchases in forms other than cash, including credit cards and debit cards. Twitter founder Jack Dorsey saw an opportunity to make the process even simpler, considering that the vast majority of consumers have mobile electronic devices. The essence of Dorsey's device and company by the same name, Square, is that customers making small purchases such as coffee and meals can pay for their items simply by giving the cashier their name. The app activates the charge to their stored credit card. Dorsey believes, or hopes, that his device will transform the burden of exchanging money for goods and services.[17] Although not publicly stated, it appears that Dorsey also saw and seized an opportunity based on the fact that many people today either lack cash to make minor purchases, or believe that using cash is inconvenient or old-fashioned.

Spotting a gap between the real and the ideal

Seeing an opportunity will often take the form of observing a discrepancy between what exists and what could exist. As a junior at the Wharton School, Jack Abraham became transfixed with the giant gap between online and offline commerce in terms of product knowledge. When people shop online, they can research products in many ways, yet it is sometimes difficult to know which store has which product in a particular size or color in stock. (We say *often* because online retailers such as Amazon.com and Walmart.com provide ample details about which items are in stock.) With the assistance of others, Abraham developed Milo, a website that lists in-store product inventories for over 50,000 retail stores, featuring over three million products from a variety of retailers. The vision for the new firm was to "bring every product on every shelf in every store in the physical world onto the Internet." Whether or not such an ambitious vision could ever be attained, Milo was sold to eBay for $75 million in 2010.[18]

Seeing an opportunity in a megatrend

Proactive thinking in the workplace sometimes takes the form of seeing an opportunity within a megatrend, and then preparing to capitalize on that opportunity. An exemplary case is Peter Löscher, chief executive of Siemens, who observed a few years ago the explosive growth of megacities. At that time close to 51 percent of the world's 6.9 billion people lived in cities, yet the trend is that, by 2050, approximately 70 percent of the population will inhabit urban areas. Much of the growth is predicted to be in emerging markets such as Asia, Africa, and Latin America. Siemens manufactures heavy equipment and machinery, including electrical transformers, and computer-operated trains necessary for building cities.

Löscher believed that the explosive growth of these cities will power Siemens's sales and earnings for the rest of the century. To seize this larger-scale opportunity, Löscher created a new division named Infrastructure & Cities. Already an enormous unit, with 81,000 employees, it sells electrical equipment, building technology, smart grid applications, and other industrial products targeted at urban areas.[19] The sales of the Infrastructure & Cities sector continue to grow as the world becomes more urbanized, validating Löscher's seeing and seizing an opportunity.

Seeing and seizing an opportunity in the LGBT market

Yet another telling example of seeing and seizing an opportunity was the initiative taken by American Airlines to reach out to the LGBT (lesbian, gay, bisexual, and transgender) market. For many years the airline had taken the initiative to welcome gay and lesbian travelers, but the LGBT marketing program was more explicit. The opportunity recognized was the growing acceptance of all sexual preferences in society, and therefore less concern about offending many heterosexual customers by appealing to the LGBT market. The specific initiative occurred when George Carrancho was appointed as the National Sales and Marketing Manager, LGBT Community for American Airlines.

In 2009 he said: "Even as the rest of American Airlines is shrinking, the Rainbow Team is growing. Our revenue from aa.com/rainbow and our newsletter subscribers have doubled this year." The company participates in as many gay-themed national events as possible, from Human Rights Campaign dinners to rodeos, thereby attracting many visitors. Five years later the Gay and Lesbian Travel, American Airlines website was still operating and drawing many fliers, suggesting that the airline did spot a good business opportunity.[20]

Seeing and seizing an opportunity for enhancing personal wealth
Many people saw opportunities to increase their wealth through real estate ownership during the five-year decline in real estate values that began in 2008. Most homeowners and would-be homeowners were frightened by the decline, instead of seeing and seizing the opportunity. Yet the downturn in the real estate market also spawned opportunities for people with good credit ratings to buy homes at low prices and on favorable terms from homeowners eager to sell. For example, a San Francisco Bay Area married couple purchased a new townhome in 2011 for $430,000. The same model had listed for $730,000 at the top of the market a few years earlier. Furthermore, they were able to negotiate a $15,000 closing cost credit from the builder, who needed to move excess inventory.[21] The link to productivity is that by seeing and seizing an opportunity, some home investors made more productive use of their money.

CREATIVITY, INNOVATION, AND PROACTIVITY

Creativity and innovation are entire fields of study within themselves, with the two processes being closely related depending on how they are defined. As used here, *creativity* refers to the production of novel and useful ideas. *Innovation* takes creativity one step further by referring to the process of creating new ideas and implementing them, usually for a commercial purpose. Both innovation and creativity therefore suggest developing useful ideas. The purpose of the present discussion of creativity and innovation is to focus on their proactive components. The previous discussion in this chapter is closely related because both creativity and innovation imply that people who are creative and/or innovative have sought an opportunity.

Creativity and Proactivity

Creativity involves a heavy component of proactivity, as the individual with a proactive personality consciously or automatically scans the environment to seek alternative solutions to a problem. Here we examine the relationship between creativity and proactivity as demonstrated by three research studies, and a sampling of creative ideas suggesting the relationship.

Three studies about the relationship between creativity and proactivity

Study with retail workers in Taiwan   A team of four researchers attempted to understand how the proactive process contributes to employee creativity. To achieve this understanding, they took into account how employees exchange information with each other, as well as a psychological safety perspective. The latter suggests that employees are motivated to create and innovate when the interpersonal atmosphere is safe for employees taking intellectual risks. Data were collected from a chain of 174 stores in Taiwan that specializes in women's and baby products. An interview with a company executive indicated that employee creativity was welcomed, such as contributing ideas for product promotions. Questionnaires were used to measure proactivity, trust, and demographic factors. Store managers rated employees on their creativity. A total of 190 matched employee–manager pairs were used in data analysis.

Proactive personality was measured through a standard research measure, similar to the questionnaire presented in Chapter 1 of this book (Figure 1.1). A four-item scale was used to measure information exchange. A sample item was, "I interact and exchange ideas with people from different units of the company" (rated on a seven-point continuum from *strongly disagree* to *strongly agree*). A 13-item scale was used to measure employee creativity, with a sample item being, "Comes up with new and practical ideas to improve performance" (rated on a seven-point continuum for *strongly disagree* to *strongly agree*). Trust relationships were measured separately for interactions with the store manager and colleagues, on a seven-point continuum also. A sample item is "My manager and I can freely share our ideas, feelings, and hopes." (The number of items in the scale was not reported by the researchers.)

The results of the study were statistically significant but small in terms of magnitude, as follows:

1. Proactive employees engage in more information exchange with co-workers. (A proactive employee is one with a relatively high score on the proactive personality test.)
2. Proactive employees build relationships of trust with managers and colleagues, and do so partially through information exchange.
3. Trust relationships are conducive to creativity.
4. Exchanging information with colleagues enhances creativity through fostering relationships of trust.

A key conclusion to the study points to the key contribution of proactive personality to employee creativity: proactive personality → information exchange → trust → creativity.[22]

Study in South Korea   A field study with a sample of 157 employee–supervisor pairs in South Korea also found a strong link between employee creativity and proactive personality. Two moderating factors were also examined: the creativity requirements of the position and the extent of supervisory support for employee creativity. The results of the study revealed that proactive personality was positively associated with employee creativity, as measured by supervisory ratings of creativity and also company records of creative suggestions. In addition, the job creativity requirement and supervisor support for creativity jointly influenced, or moderated, the relationship between proactive personality and employee creativity. The specific findings were that proactive employees exhibited the highest creativity when the creativity requirements of the job and supervisor support for creativity were both high.[23]

Study in U.S. management consultancies   A study with 456 supervisor–employee pairs in four consulting firms examined how employees use the proactive behavior of feedback seeking as a strategy to enhance their creative performance. The study focused on knowledge workers because creating new knowledge and approaching work creatively is important for success in management consulting. Five independent variables were studied. One variable was a measure of the extent to which the workers exhibited an innovative cognitive style. Originality is a key part of the innovative cognitive style. A second variable was the perceived organization support for creativity, such as "Creativity is encouraged at my company." The three other variables dealt with feedback seeking in terms of (a) frequency of feedback inquiry, (b) frequency of feedback monitoring, and (c) breadth of feedback inquiry. The dependent variable creative performance was measured by supervisory ratings on 13 items, such as "Comes up with creative solutions to problems."

A conclusion derived from a multitude of analyses is that individuals can enhance their own creative performance by actively seeking feedback on their work from various sources. The proactive behavior of actively seeking feedback is important because the external sources may not always provide their feedback spontaneously or at the right time. It is also likely that the external sources may not be aware of the employee's need for advice and guidance. Key findings of the study leading to the conclusions were that employees' cognitive style and perceived organization support affected two patterns of feedback seeking. The patterns were propensity to inquire for feedback and the propensity to monitor the environment for indirect feedback. An innovative cognitive style and perceived organization support for creativity enhance creative performance in part because they lead to more feedback seeking.[24]

Two examples of creative ideas suggesting proactivity

A recurring theme of this chapter is that creativity involves proactive thinking and behavior. A few notable examples will help reinforce this point. The first example is the development of the Red Bull energy drink that spawned an industry of similar caffeine-laced soda beverages. The creator of Red Bull was the late Chaleo Yoovidhya, who in Thailand in the 1960s began tinkering with a formula for an energy-boosting drink, somehow predicting that the world was ready for such a beverage. About ten years later, he developed his recipe for Krathing Daeng, or Red Bull in English. The drink was welcomed by truck drivers and construction workers who had helped propel Thailand's economic boom of about 40 years ago. Part of Chaleo's proactive approach was in marketing the beverage. Instead of focusing on the capital of Bangkok, he pushed into the provincial market first, gaining a footing by distributing free samples to truck drivers. Later, Chaleo teamed up with an entrepreneur from Austria who launched marketing campaigns based on extreme sports such as motocross and snowboarding.[25]

Today many car-rental companies offer consumers an opportunity to share a vehicle that essentially equates to renting a vehicle in a city for as little as one hour. Not long ago the idea that you could entice upwardly mobile professionals to share cars would have seemed unrealistic. Scott Griffith, founder of Zipcar, proactively recognized that many drivers already shared movies via Netflix and streamed music rather than purchasing a CD. His creative idea was that sharing a car is the natural extension of a hip, financially wise, and environmentally conscious urban lifestyle. Many urban dwellers have infrequent need for a car and do not want to own one. Also included in the creative idea of a Zipcar is that people have access to the vehicles parked on a street or in a parking lot rather than having to go through a car-rental kiosk. Griffith also engaged in the creative process of combining ideas. To share a Zipcar, the customer has to make use of a mobile app, so Griffith combined the idea of a potential consumer desire to use but not own a car with the fascination for smart phones of so many consumers. Zipcar is now owned by the large car-rental agency Avis, and is part of a growing car-sharing industry.[26]

Innovation and Proactivity

Given that creativity leads to innovation, it follows that innovation has a strong component of proactive thinking and behavior. Ronald M. Shaich, chairman and co-chief executive of Panera Bread, believes that innovation is part of an organization's *discovery muscle*. To exert this discovery muscle, people within the company have to believe that they have to be proactive in the sense of figuring out where the world is going and how the company can get there, and then deciding on which direction to take.[27] Innovation is important at the level of the individual, the team, and the organization, but also at the level of society. Economists and business leaders across the economic spectrum have believed for many years that innovation can lead a country out of an economic downturn. New products, services, and ways of doing business will create enough growth to facilitate prosperity.[28] And, to be innovative, somebody has to reach out into the environment to figure out what products and services people need or want.

Our discussion of the link between proactivity and innovation focuses on the proactive components of the process of innovation, and two examples of innovation based on simplicity.

Proactive elements within the innovation process
In this section we illustrate several examples of how proactivity is included in the process of innovation.

1. Reaching out to network members for innovative ideas. Marc Dienoff, the founder of Salesforce.com is highly regarded for his innovative thinking, particularly because he was a pioneer in selling software that is downloaded from the Internet (part of cloud computing). Dienoff states that he aggressively hangs out with young entrepreneurs in order to stay abreast of innovations which might lead to more innovations of his own. When asked why he hung out with a specific entrepreneur, Dienoff replied, "He grew up on the Internet. I didn't. He is the next generation of innovation." At the time Salesforce.com was figuring out how to borrow the entrepreneur in question's ideas to make software more fun to share.[29] The point here is that Dienoff's proactive behavior of reaching out to network members feeds him ideas for innovation.

2. Proactively ask questions. Many years ago, Peter Drucker identified the power of provocative questions. "The important and difficult job is never to find the right answers, it is to find the right question," he wrote. Innovators regularly ask questions that challenge common wisdom. Often they question what would happen if they took a particular course of action. To give an historically important example, Michael Dell said that the idea for founding Dell Computer emerged from his asking why a computer costs five times as much as the sum of its parts. In pondering the answer to the question he hit upon his revolutionary business model of selling custom-configured computers over the phone.[30]

3. Small group of people with a difficult-to-understand idea.   Eric Schmidt, now executive chairman of Google, Inc., believes that the story of innovation has always been a small team of people who have a new idea. Frequently that idea is not understood by colleagues and their executives. Not only does the group proactively happen upon an idea, but they have to take the initiative to persuade managers that their idea has potential commercial value.[31] An example might be a team of Google workers pushing forth the idea of medical professionals using a Google product to help make diagnoses of difficult conditions while a patient is undergoing surgery.

4. Taking the initiative to cast aside traditional ideas and thinking.   A tired saying about creativity is that it requires thinking outside the box, yet this statement has merit. The editors of *Fast Company*, a magazine that features innovation and information technology, predict that the dominant organizations of the future will be those who are willing to scrap conventional ideas.[32] One well-publicized example is that when Tom Szaky was a college freshman he founded Teracycle, one of the pioneering companies in making products out of garbage. For example, Skittles wrappers are fused to become a kite, and Honest Tea containers have been converted into a laptop computer case. Rather than only salvaging what was useful in waste, such as extracting useful steel from scrapped vehicles, Szaky sought to convert garbage into useful products. His idea for bringing about innovation at Teracycle is to let anyone who has a product idea to make something out of that idea. The focus is on doing something useful with a creative idea (which could be considered a definition of innovation).[33]

5. A willingness to take risks.   As mentioned in Chapter 1, a willingness to take risks is an attribute of the proactive personality. Similarly, to innovate, organizations must be risk takers. A twist on this idea is that amid worries that many workers are becoming less innovative, some companies are rewarding employees for their mistakes or high risk taking. Research support for this practice stems from evidence that innovations are frequently accompanied by a high failure rate. Innovation researcher Judy Estrin notes that failure, and how companies deal with it, are a big part of innovation. Failures caused by negligence are bad, but learning from failure can help the individual and the organization. It is also well documented that successful inventors and innovators tend to be those with the most failures.[34] We have heard frequently about how Thomas Edison had dozens of failures leading to a useful version of a light bulb. Also, the much-heralded Steve Jobs had a few key product failures associated with his innovations including the Apple Lisa and the Newton Message Pad.[35]

Innovation based on simplicity

Innovation triggered by proactive thinking sometimes is based on a simple idea, and despite the simplicity contributes substantial value. The first example of how innovation can stem from recognizing a simple idea comes from the production of shrimp. For many years, the United States was dependent on other nations for shrimp production. Searching for ways to increase shrimp yields, scientists embraced a technology in which shrimp are farmed indoors, in large, rectangular tubs of water, laid out side by side. Known as *raceway technology*, this method does not produce enough seafood to be cost-effective. (The term "raceway" refers to the fact that the water in the tubs circulates in a direction that resembles horses on a racetrack.)

Addison L. Lawrence, a scientist at the Texas Agrilife Research Mariculture Laboratory, developed a simple idea that proved to be revolutionary – stacking the tubs on top of one another like shoe boxes. In this manner, the concept of *super-intensive stacked raceways* came into being, making it possible to produce up to one million pounds of shrimp annually per acre of water. This compared to the 50,000 pounds produced by the original raceway system, and the 20,000 pounds produced by natural ponds. Lawrence claims that anything that is really good and patentable is quite simple.

Lawrence's simple ideas still required some advanced technology because stacking the tubs would only work if the tubs were lighter. The solution Lawrence found with the help of others was to use less water in the tubs, after discovering that the shrimp could survive in eight to ten inches of water. Using less water made the tubs lighter.[36]

An approach to innovation based on simplicity is *jugaad*, a frugal form of innovation. *Jugaad* is a Hindu word that refers to an improvised or makeshift solution to a problem using scarce resources. A more formal definition of *jugaad* is that it is a "frugal, flexible, and inclusive approach to problem solving and innovation." For example, washing machines are used to mix up yogurt drinks. The innovative thinking inherent in such a contraption is that an individual or group somewhere along the way scanned the environment to derive a new commercial use for an existing machine.

The major application of *jugaad* is to meet customer needs inexpensively and rapidly. This application occurs because it is innovation driven by scarce resources and attention to a customer's immediate needs, not particularly a desire to lead an improved lifestyle. A hypothetical example might be refurbishing older hearses into delivery trucks for small-business owners who cannot afford to purchase a standard delivery truck.

According to a Cisco systems executive, Wim Elfrink, innovation in India focuses on affordability and scale. A particularly successful application of *jugaad* is the electrocardiogram in a backpack developed by GE Healthcare's Indian engineers.[37] The compact EEG points to the theme of this chapter: somebody sees an opportunity to meet a need, and then develops a creative idea into a successful commercial product.

SUGGESTIONS FOR APPLICATION

1. When identifying an opportunity, it is helpful to define the opportunity clearly so other people perceive the same opportunity, and will work with you to capitalize on your opportunity finding.[38] For example, a facilities technician might tell her boss, "I see an opportunity for the owners of this building to save thousands of dollars in utility costs simply by installing a large garden on the roof. At the same time, many tenants might become more loyal because their building is environmentally friendly."

2. Opportunity recognition is a valuable behavior, but it is not sufficient for converting the idea into a positive change for a person's employer or making an entrepreneur successful. Also needed is the willingness to persistently pursue turning the idea into reality. Samer Kurdi, chairman of the global board, Entrepreneurs' Organization, writes that "Great ideas are abundant, but it's what we decide to do with them that counts."[39]

3. Fashion designer Liz Lange advises us of a fundamental way of finding opportunities that lead to innovation: as you go about daily life, routinely ask yourself, "Isn't there a better way?" Frequently, the answer is "Yes."[40] This type of thinking led to ATMs when the assumption was questioned that to withdraw and deposit funds, a teller was needed for every transaction. At the same time the ATM developers were looking for an opportunity to reduce the costs of operating a bank.

4. Another fundamental way of finding opportunities is to listen carefully to customers, or workers who come into frequent contact with customers. Collin Wheeler, at age 23, founded 123JUNK, an enterprise that provides the means to get rid of unwanted household items that trash companies will not pick up. Wheeler and his team sort their junk into what can be donated to charities and what can be recycled. As with most entrepreneurs, Wheeler spotted an opportunity. While working for a moving company, his customers often asked him what they should do with those items the company didn't want to move. He became convinced there was a market for these services, so he became a junk man.[41]

Manufacturing workers who interact with customers may know what takes too long to accomplish, what parts or products are too expensive, and what causes problems. This information can lead to finding opportunities, such as replacing plastic packaging with paper because customers dislike dealing with plastic wrappings.

5. To strengthen the relationship between a worker's proactive tendencies and creativity, it is helpful for the position to explicitly require creativity solutions to problems, and for the supervisor to encourage creative problem solving.

SUMMARY

A key component of proactive behavior is recognizing opportunities that others may have overlooked. Searching for opportunities requires that the individual proactively scan the environment to find a fit between his or her capabilities and an environmental need. A study suggested that being dissatisfied with the status quo prompts a worker to search for innovative ways to improve a work process.

Seeing and seizing opportunities follows searching for them. Opportunity seeking and seizing often stem from a felt need to be more productive. Opportunity recognition and seizure have been practiced in a variety of domains in business, including seeing the opportunity within a disruption. Seeing an opportunity will often take the form of observing a discrepancy between the real and the ideal.

Both innovation and creativity suggest developing useful ideas. Creativity involves a heavy component of proactivity, as the proactive personality consciously or automatically scans the environment to seek alternative solutions to a problem. A study showed that proactive employers engage in more information exchange with coworkers, and that this exchange enhances creativity through fostering relationships of trust. Another study showed that proactive employees were the most creative when the creativity requirement of the job and supervisory support for creativity were high. A study of management consultants found that individuals can enhance their own creative performance by actively seeking feedback on their work from various sources.

Innovation also has a strong component of proactive thinking and behavior. To be innovative somebody has to reach out into the environment to figure out what products or services people need or want. Proactivity is included in the process of innovation in several ways: reaching out to network members for innovative ideas; proactively asking questions; small groups of people with a difficult-to-understand idea; taking the initiative to cast aside traditional ideas and thinking; and a willingness to take risks.

Innovation can also be based on recognizing a simple idea. An important example is the Indian process of *jugaad*, a form of frugal innovation involving an improvised or makeshift solution to a problem.

When identifying an opportunity it is helpful to define the opportunity clearly so other people will perceive the same opportunity and want to contribute. Asking "Isn't there a better way?" can lead to opportunity finding, as can listening to customers and employees who are in contact with customers. Employee creativity is likely to be enhanced when the job requires creativity and the supervisor supports creativity.

REFERENCES

1.   "How to Come Up with a Great Idea," *The Wall Street Journal*, April 29, 2013, p. R1.
2.   "How to Come Up with a Great Idea."
3.   Maya Payne Smart, "The Business of Green," *Black Enterprise*, June 2010, pp. 104–111; www.crossplatformdesign.com. Retrieved May 1, 2013.
4.   Literature reviewed in Feirong Yuan and Richard W. Woodman, "Innovative Behavior in the Workplace: The Role of Performance and Image Outcome Expectations," *Academy of Management Journal*, April 2010, p. 323.
5.   Literature reviewed in Yuan and Woodman, "Innovative Behavior in the Workplace," p. 333.
6.   Verne Harnish, "Five Ways to Get Your Strategy Right," *Fortune*, April 11, 2011, p. 42.
7.   Heather MacDonald, "How to Return New York City to the Street Gangs," *The Wall Street Journal*, August 11–12, 2012, p. A.15.
8.   Joe Kemp, "A Year of Danger for NYPD Officers as 12 Unlucky Cops Were Shot in 2012," *Daily News* (www.nydailynews.com), December 9, 2012, p. 1. Retrieved June 7, 2013.
9.   Dinah Eng, "Zappos's Silent Founder," *Fortune*, September 3, 2012, pp. 19–22. The quote is from p. 21.
10. Ranjay Gulati, Nitin Nohria, and Franz Wohlgezogen, "Roaring Out of Recession," *Harvard Business Review*, March 2010, p. 68.
11. Giovanni Gavetti, "The New Psychology of Strategic Leadership," *Harvard Business Review*, July–August 2011, pp. 118–121.
12. Cited in Danielle Sacks, "Mayhem on Madison Avenue," *Fast Company*, December 2010/January 2011, p. 142.
13. Susan Berfield, "A Startup's New Prescription for Eyewear," *Bloomberg Businesswseek*, July 4–July 10, 2011, pp. 49–50; www.warbyparker.com. Retrieved May 2, 2013; "What Eyewear Startup Warby Parker Sees That Others Don't," *Knowledge@Wharton* (http://knowledge.wharton.upenn.edu). Retrieved May 8, 2013, pp. 1–4.
14. Andrea Cooper, "Think Fast," *Entrepreneur*, September 2008, pp. 19–20.
15. Anne Fisher, "The Executive Matchmaker: Janis Spindel," *Fortune*, June 23,

2008, p. 69; www.janisspindelmatchmaker.blogspot.com, February 21, 2013. Retrieved June 1, 2013.

16. "Social Media in the C-Suite: Listening, Learning and Creating a Strategy from the Top Down," *Knowledge@Wharton* (http://knowledge.wharton. upenn.edu), October 12, 2011, pp. 1–2.

17. Ellen McGirt, "Square: For Making Magic Out of the Mercantile," *Fast Company*, March 2012, pp. 83–84.

18. Danielle Sacks, "EBay's Shop Boy," *Fast Company*, July/August 2011, p. 100; Leena Rao, "Confirmed: Ebay Acquires Milo for $75 Million. Investors Make a Killing," *http://techcrunch.com*, December 2, 2010, p. 1. Retrieved June 18, 2013.

19. Daniel Fisher with Naazheen Karmalli and Gady Epstein, "Urban Outfitter," *Forbes*, May 11, 2011, pp. 90–92.

20. Kate Rockwood (interviewer), "Partnering With Pride," *Fast Company*, November 2009, p. 21; *American Airlines: Gay and Lesbian Travel* (www. aa.com). Retrieved May 3, 2013.

21. Tara-Nicholle Nelson, "When Opportunity Comes Knocking," *Black Enterprise*, July 2012, pp. 72–30.

22. Yaping Gong, Siu-Yin Cheung, Mo Wang, and Jia-Chi Huang, "Unfolding the Proactive Process for Creativity: Integration of the Employee Proactivity, Information Exchange, and Psychological Safety Perspectives," *Journal of Management* (http://www.sagepublications.com), August 10, 2010, pp. 1–19. Retrieved May 16, 2012.

23. Tae-Yeol Kim, Alice H. Y. Hon, and Deog-Roe Lee, "Proactive Personality and Employee Creativity: The Effects of Job Creativity Requirement and Supervisor Support for Creativity," *Creativity Research Journal*, Issue 1, 2010, pp. 37–45.

24. Katleen E. M. De Stobbeleir, Susan J. Ashford, and Dirk Buyens, "Self-Regulation of Creativity at Work: The Role of Feedback-Seeking Behavior in Creative Performance," *Academy of Management Journal*, August 2011, pp. 811–831.

25. James Hookway, "Creator of Red Bull Energy Drink Spawned an Industry," *The Wall Street Journal*, March 10, 2012, p. B9.

26. Paul Keegan, "The Best New Idea in Business," *Fortune*, September 14, 2009, p. 44; Jason Voiovich, "The Hope for Zipcar: Be Less Like Avis, More Like Redbox," *DuetsBlog* (www.duetsblogcom), January 29, 2013, pp. 1–3. Retrieved May 30, 2013.

27. Cited in Adam Bryant, "Your Company Can Deliver, but Can It Discover?" *The New York Times* (www.nytimes.com), July 21, 2012, p. 2. Retrieved May 31, 2013.

28. Michael Mandel, "Can America Invent Its Way Back?" *Businessweek*, September 22, 2008, p. 052.

29. Victoria Barret, "Mister Disrupter," *Forbes*, August 8, 2011, p. 84.

30. Cited in Jeffrey H. Dyer, Hal B. Gregersen, and Clayton M. Christensen, "The Innovator's DNA," *Harvard Business Review*, December 2009, p. 63.

31. "How Google Fuels the Idea Factory," *Businessweek*, May 11, 2008, p. 054.

32. "The Word's Most Innovative Companies," *Fast Company*, March 2011, p. 65.

33. Tom Szaky, "What's In Your Waste Can?" *Executive Leadership*, March 2012, p. 3.

34. Sue Shellenbarger, "Better Ideas through Failure," *The Wall Street Journal*, September 27, 2011, pp. D, D4.
35. Chandra Steele, "7 Steve Jobs Products that Failed," *www.premag.com*, August 28, 2011, p. 1. Retrieved June 17, 2013.
36. Nicole LaPorte, "In the School of Innovation, Less is Often More," *The New York Times* (www.nytimes.com), November 5, 2011, pp. 1–3. Retrieved June 6, 2013.
37. Reena Jana, "From India, the Latest Management Fad," *Bloomberg Businessweek*, December 14, 2009, p. 057; Ian Wylie, "Jugaad Innovation: How to Disrupt-it-Yourself," *Google Think Insights* (www.google.com/think), December 2012, pp. 1–6. Retrieved May 15, 2013.
38. Judy Dobles, "6 Steps to Capitalizing on an Opportunity," *Democrat and Chronicle*, October 30, 2012, p. 5B.
39. Cited and quoted in "How to Come Up with a Great Idea," p. R1.
40. Cited and quoted in "How to Come Up with a Great Idea," p. R1.
41. Heather Huhman, "CEOs under 25: Collin Wheeler," www.sanfranciscoexaminer.com, April 30, 2009. Retrieved May 25, 2013. See also Retrieved July 2, 2013.

7. The entrepreneurial personality, behavior, and proactivity

A major manifestation of the proactive personality and behavior is entrepreneurship, particularly in the sense of developing an innovative business. Entrepreneurship is considered an asset for society because so much new employment is created through the efforts of entrepreneurs. Approximately 60 to 80 percent of new employment in the United States is created by small businesses.[1] An unknown number of these small businesses are novel enough enterprises to be considered true entrepreneurships. For example, when two people open a café, the activity might not be classified as entrepreneurship but rather as merely small-business ownership.

Successful entrepreneurs tend to be proactive, particularly with respect to being creative and adventuresome. The potential contribution of entrepreneurs in society, as well as their personality, behavior, and proactivity are illustrated by how, in recent years, entrepreneurs have helped rebuild the deteriorating city of Detroit, Michigan. At its depth of despair the population of Detroit had plummeted 25 percent, and the city had more than 10,000 vacant lots. Furthermore, Detroit declared bankruptcy in 2013.

Dan Gilbert, the founder of Quicken Loans, was one of the entrepreneurs who applied his imagination and proactivity to help in the slow process of rebuilding the once highly respected metropolis. The lease on Quicken company headquarters in the suburbs was due to expire in 2010. Gilbert, whose family had roots in Detroit, took the initiative to begin the restoration. Quicken loans rented space in a building and invested $30 million in making the space stylish and upbeat, with several thousand people working there by 2013. Gilbert also played an active role in helping recruit other companies and creating a downtown retail experience. Another initiative was to offer internships to students, with 600 interns from across the country. Gilbert reasoned that a big selling point to the young generation would be to help rebuild a city and help thousands of needy people in the process.[2]

In this chapter we explore the link between entrepreneurship and proactivity by focusing on a description of the entrepreneurial personality, entrepreneurial thinking and personal characteristics, and entrepreneurial risk taking.

THE ENTREPRENEURIAL PERSONALITY

As a starting point in understanding the entrepreneurial personality, you are invited to take the quiz presented in Figure 7.1. The proactive personality has long been associated with tendencies toward entrepreneurship, suggesting that the entrepreneurial personality might be a manifestation of proactivity. Entrepreneurial behavior can be characterized as taking the lead to accomplish a venture. J. Michael Crant surveyed 181 undergraduate and MBA students, and found a positive relationship between the proactive personality and intention to become a business owner.[3]

A study conducted a few years later with 215 small-business presidents found that the president's degree of proactive personality was positively and significantly related to entrepreneurial behavior. The proactive personality scores of the presidents were positively associated with increases in company sales, and with an aggressive entrepreneurial posture. Analysis of the data also found that a proactive personality was related to starting rather than buying or inheriting a business, and with the number of businesses started.

Indicate on a scale of 1 to 5 the extent of your agreement with the statements below: agree strongly (AS), agree (A), neutral (N), disagree (D), disagree strongly (DS).

No.		AS	A	N	D	DS
1.	I have actually started a business of my own.	5	4	3	2	1
2.	I have thought several times at least of starting a business of my own.	5	4	3	2	1
3.	So many new products are being introduced practically every week that it seems senseless to bother dreaming up an idea for another new product.	1	2	3	4	5
4.	I enjoy the challenge of meeting new people and explaining what I do.	5	4	3	2	1
5.	I get excited about thinking of a new idea for a product or service.	5	4	3	2	1
6.	Casino gambling is a major waste of time.	1	2	3	4	5
7.	Betting money on sports is exciting and fun.	5	4	3	2	1
8.	Taking care of administrative details is boring for me.	5	4	3	2	1
9.	I am (or would be) comfortable working outside of regular working hours.	5	4	3	2	1
10.	The best job for me would be one that offers a stable salary, regular working hours and vacations, and a guaranteed pension.	1	2	3	4	5
11.	Self-employment fits (or would fit) my personality.	5	4	3	2	1

12.	What a horrible life it would be for me to get paid strictly on commission.	1	2	3	4	5
13.	I enjoy the challenge of selling my ideas and myself to people I have not met before.	5	4	3	2	1
14.	I need at least eight hours of sleep and regular rest breaks during the day to perform well.	1	2	3	4	5
15.	If I personally knew a family that had been victims of a disaster, I would be willing to attempt to raise money for that family.	5	4	3	2	1
16.	I enjoy purchasing lunch from a street vendor when the opportunity arises.	5	4	3	2	1
17.	If you are not a scientist or an engineer it is useless to try to invent something that is intended for the marketplace.	1	2	3	4	5
18.	Most people who become rich and famous got there by luck.	1	2	3	4	5
19.	I would enjoy the experience of working on developing new products in a company department located away from where most employees worked.	5	4	3	2	1
20.	If I were self-employed or worked from home for an employer, I would probably start my workday at about 10 a.m.	1	2	3	4	5

Notes: scoring and interpretation: add the numbers that you have circled.
85–100 The results suggest that you have many of the proactive tendencies of an entrepreneurial personality. You probably enjoy risk taking and change, and would be willing to take the risk of earning your income through self-employment.
50–84 You most likely have average tendencies toward being an entrepreneurial personality. You probably would not enjoy a career filled with risk and uncertainty.
20–49 Your personality makeup most likely does not resemble that of an entrepreneurial personality. You might place a high value on stability and security. A regular paycheck is probably quite important to you.

Figure 7.1   My tendencies toward being an entrepreneurial personality

Because proactivity reflects the individual's orientation toward the environment, a strongly proactive president creates an organization that frequently scans the environment along with a bold and aggressive approach toward the market. The increase in sales associated with proactivity suggests that proactive entrepreneurs are aggressively developing the firm as a strategic approach to the marketplace.[4] Another example of a president engaging in entrepreneurial behavior would be for him or her to start a new venture for the small business, such as a childcare center establishing an adult-care center.

In this section we examine the entrepreneurial personality from four perspectives: entrepreneurial leadership and the proactive personality; the Da Vinci-type personality; the interests of the entrepreneurial personality; and the potential downside to the entrepreneurial personality.

Entrepreneurial Leadership and the Proactive Personality

Another way of framing the link between entrepreneurship and the proactive personality is to focus on entrepreneurial leadership, which refers to the entrepreneur's role in leading his or her organization. Leon C. Prieto argues that proactive personality appears to have potential for providing additional insight into how personality traits are related to entrepreneurship. The natural link, as already stated and implied, is that entrepreneurship is inherently proactive – to be an entrepreneur one has to scan the environment to find an opportunity, and then capitalize on the opportunity. Individuals with a proactive personality may be more inclined to mobilize resources and gain the commitment required for value creation that the entrepreneur requires.[5] Dan Gilbert, the Quicken founder who wanted to help rebuild Detroit, used his influence to help gain commitment from Chrysler, Twitter, and Blue Cross and Blue Shield to move people into the new complex. He also gained the commitment of many restaurants to join the mother tenants.[6]

Proactive personality types may have a strong desire to become entrepreneurial leaders in order to create value for the firm. An assistant manager at a large restaurant, for example, might explore the possibilities of establishing a team-building component based on the preparation of gourmet meals. The program would be sold to organizations, as has been done successfully by a handful of elite restaurants. Such behavior reinforces the notion that proactive people are often successful in leadership roles partially because of their desire to take action and create a positive change in their work environment.[7]

An analysis of the entrepreneurial personality prepared by R. Elizabeth C. Kitchen includes three traits linked to entrepreneurial leadership and proactivity.[8] First, being a successful entrepreneur requires creativity and innovative ability, both necessary for introducing a new product or service, or taking an existing product or service and making it better. (This topic has already been explored in Chapter 6.) Secondly, flexibility is an important trait for entrepreneurs because it helps them adapt to circumstances, or "go with the flow." An entrepreneurial venture will not always go as planned, and the entrepreneur will have to react to the problem, and proactively seek a new path. A classic example is minoxidil, originally used to treat high blood pressure. However, patients and health care professionals observed that hair growth was a side effect of the treatment. This unanticipated side effect led to the development of a topical solution applied to the head for the treatment of male-pattern baldness, with Rogaine being the most recognized brand of minoxidil.[9] The message is that the product development specialists were entrepreneurially minded and flexible. Flexibility and creativity, as in this instance, can be closely related because a creative solution is often needed to be flexible.

Thirdly, entrepreneurs are adventuresome, which is a variation of risk taking. The individual with a strong entrepreneurial personality is typically adventuresome and welcomes challenges. Being adventuresome is particularly important because the entrepreneur will often confront a situation outside his or her comfort zone, such as having to pitch an idea to a group of unfriendly venture capitalists.

The Da Vinci-Type Personality

The entrepreneurial personality has also been reframed as the Da Vinci-type personality in reference to the great artisan Leonardo Da Vinci. A person with this personality type has been observed as (a) liking thrill, excitement, and risk; (b) being a highly creative problem solver; (c) being impulsive; (d) being ambitious and industrious; (e) having considerable energy to pursue personal interests; and (f) having a strong desire to be the hero or heroine in an emergency. Richard Branson, the founder of the Virgin Group that includes an investment in commercial space launches, and extreme thrill seeking in personal life, is cited as an example of the Da Vinci personality type. According to Garret Lo Porto, Branson's temperament has facilitated his having a propensity for risk taking, thrill seeking, and being a brilliant entrepreneur.[10]

Although the Da Vinci-type personality has not been the subject of formal research, it fits well the thrust of the entrepreneurial personality with its emphasis on creativity and thrill seeking.

Interests and the Entrepreneurial Personality

Although interests are different from personality traits they often reflect personality traits. For example, a person who is strongly introverted may gravitate toward occupational interests for which introversion is well suited, such as highly analytical work. As a result many chemists and computer coders are introverted. With respect to having entrepreneurial interests as an adult, many entrepreneurs were interested in business as a child, including managing a paper route or selling cookies door to door. In school, many future entrepreneurs seek entrepreneurial roles such as founding a club or leading fund drives. In general, a natural inclination of past interest in entrepreneurship is a positive predictor of later success as an entrepreneur.[11]

The Potential Downside of the Entrepreneurial Personality

Although the entrepreneurial personality traits fueling proactive behavior are generally perceived as positive, according to Donald F. Kuratko a darker side of entrepreneurial behavior also exists. The problem stems from the energetic drive of successful entrepreneurs, meaning that they can be proactive to a dysfunctional extent.[12] Forty years ago, Manfred Ket de Vries cited specific negative factors within the entrepreneurial personality that could dominate behavior. Although all of these factors can be positive in an optimum amount, potential dysfunctions are also present. Here we describe the potentially negative personality factor most closely related to the proactive personality, *high confrontation with risk*.

Entrepreneurs have a strong tendency toward risk taking, and usually enjoy taking risks. Higher risk often results in higher reward, propelling the risk-prone personality to be bolder in taking risks. Entrepreneurs face several risks that can be grouped into four areas. First is *financial risk*, where the entrepreneur places considerable personal money, borrowed money, or corporate money at stake. Many families have gone through bankruptcy because the entrepreneur within the family borrowed heavily to fund a project that failed. Second is *career risk* in which the entrepreneur fails on a new venture, and therefore loses out on promotion and suffers a loss of credibility. For example, a corporate entrepreneur might champion a new venture that fails totally, and he or she is no longer considered for any further promotions or other advancements, and might be fired.

Third is *family and social risk*, centering on the tremendous amount of energy and time devoted to an entrepreneurial pursuit that results in alienation from the family. For instance, the entrepreneur might work 80 hours per week to found and launch a new business. *Psychic risk* refers to the entrepreneurial leader being able to handle any of the other risks mentioned. A failed risk can be a devastating blow to some entrepreneurs, such as borrowing heavily to fund a new venture, working 90 hours a week, and winding up bankrupt and divorced because of the venture.[13]

ENTREPRENEURIAL THINKING AND PERSONAL CHARACTERISTICS

A logical extension of understanding the entrepreneurial personality is a study of entrepreneurial thinking and personal characteristics that especially reflect proactive behavior. Topics selected here to illustrate entrepreneurial thinking and characteristics include the entrepreneurial spirit, social entrepreneurship, and seeing derivative opportunities.

The Entrepreneurial Spirit

The term *entrepreneurial spirit* appears to be a global term that refers to a variety of traits, behaviors, and attitudes that propel a person into entrepreneurial actions. The 10-year-old child who walks around the neighborhood picking up discarded bottles and cans on the lawns and streets to later get refunds is said to have an entrepreneurial spirit. And the 50-year-old CEO of a manufacturing company who decides to create a separate division to provide machine maintenance services to other companies is also said to have an entrepreneurial spirit. All of the previous traits and behaviors mentioned so far in this chapter would therefore be part of the entrepreneurial spirit. Here we look at a few aspects of entrepreneurial thinking and personal characteristics that could be considered part of the entrepreneurial spirit.

A key component of the entrepreneurial spirit is a passion for founding an enterprise, along with a passion for the enterprise once founded. The potential link between passion and proactivity is that passion contributes to the perseverance aspect of the proactive personality. According to an analysis by the editors of *Entrepreneur*, no person embodies the word "passion" as much as Richard Branson, founder of the Virgin megabrand. Starting in 1970, the Virgin group has steadily expanded to more than 200 companies, including music publishing, mobile phones, retail stores, and space travel. "Businesses are like buses," Branson once said. "There is always another one coming."[14]

Another major way in which the passion of the entrepreneur expresses itself is the love of the product or service being offered. One example is that John Schnatter, the founder of Papa John's Pizza, appears to believe that his pizza is the tastiest and the best buy among its many competitors. Another example is the unswerving devotion Bill Gates had for Word, PowerPoint, and Windows during his active days at Microsoft Corp.

The phenomenon of many entrepreneurs founding a series of companies suggests that when the passion begins to fade for one enterprise, the entrepreneur becomes restless and founds another enterprise. A possible example is Marc Andreessen, who has founded or co-founded a series of successful enterprises, including Netscape (the pioneering Internet browser), Andreessen Horowitz (a Silicon Valley venture capital firm), Ning (a consumer Internet company), and Opsware (datacenter automation software).[15]

Another manifestation of the entrepreneurial spirit is to rarely take no for an answer with respect to pursuing an enterprise in which the entrepreneur sees value. Often the entrepreneur or prospective entrepreneur will see value in his or her ideas that others overlook. The people saying that the idea won't work include family members, friends, potential partners, and often venture capitalists and other lenders. In contrast, the entrepreneur might detect a niche in the market that is not evident to others. A classic example is that the entrepreneur who originally sold mattresses over the phone (1-800-Mattress) was told by many people that his idea was preposterous. Nobody would purchase a mattress without first at least touching it to determine the degree of firmness, even if talking with a bedding consultant on the phone. The company lasted 33 years, and grew to a substantial size before ultimately landing in bankruptcy.[16]

In many cases the naysayers to the entrepreneur's idea are thinking too broadly. Most critics focus too much on economic conditions and not enough on whether the proposed business can meet an unsatisfied customer demand. An example is that Ann Patchett, a best-selling author, decided to open a bookstore in downtown Nashville, Tennessee. People she talked to rejected her idea, pointing out that two major bookstore chains in Nashville had failed. They also reasoned that book stores had become virtually obsolete in the Internet age. Yet Patchett reasoned that the two stores were more than 30,000 square feet each and profitable, and had closed because of corporate problems. Patchett believed that she could earn a good living by opening a bookstore of 2500 square feet. The store she founded, Parnassus Books, is thriving and expanding, indicating Patchett's entrepreneurial spirit of not listening to naysayers.[17]

Social Entrepreneurship

A complex way in which proactivity and entrepreneurship are linked is that many businesspeople reach out into the environment to find new ways of doing social good. The term *social entrepreneurship* combines the passion of a social mission with an image of discipline, innovation, and determination often associated with high-technology firms.[18] Stated more simply, social entrepreneurship is an entrepreneurial approach to social problems such as homelessness, contaminated drinking water, and extreme poverty. Although social entrepreneurship has several meanings, in the context here it refers primarily to businesspeople who take an entrepreneurial approach to solving social problems. The social entrepreneur is therefore an entrepreneur with a social mission.

Altruistic payoffs
A key aspect of social entrepreneurship in contrast to entrepreneurship in general is that social entrepreneurship addresses important social needs in a way that is not dominated by direct financial payoffs to the

entrepreneur.[19] Successful social entrepreneurship offers non-financial rewards, such as pride and the satisfaction of having helped people in need. In addition, social entrepreneurship offers satisfaction of the need for achievement that has long been said to motivate entrepreneurs. Satisfaction of the power need is also possible when the impact of social entrepreneurship is major, such as developing a foundation for cancer research.

The social entrepreneur seeks an opportunity to help others, but the social improvements that come about because of the entrepreneurial venture may be difficult to measure, unlike the market's reaction to a product or service innovation. J. Gregory Dees writes that it is inherently difficult to measure social value creation. He asks how much value is created by reducing pollution in a given stream, saving the spotted owl, or providing companionship to seniors. At times social entrepreneurs pay for their investments with company funds, but at other times they rely on the contribution of philanthropists.

Social entrepreneurship can be combined with business entrepreneurship, with Toms Shoes being a much-publicized example. Blake Mycoskie, the founder of Toms Shoes, short for "Tomorrow's Shoes," once thought during a vacation in Argentina, "Why not create a for-profit business to help provide shoes for poor Argentinian children?" Mycoskie soon founded Toms Shoes, based on the stipulation that when a customer purchases one pair of the company's shoes, Toms gives a pair of shoes to a poor child somewhere in the world. In one year with the help of charities and other groups, its giveaways surpassed one million pairs of shoes.[20]

Proactive elements of social entrepreneurship
An expanded definition of social entrepreneurship helps us understand its proactive elements. According to Dees, social entrepreneurs are change agents in the social sector by means of the following:

- adopting a mission to create and sustain social value;
- recognizing and relentlessly pursuing new opportunities to support that mission;
- engaging in a process of continuous innovation, adaption, and learning;
- acting boldly without being limited by resources currently at hand;
- exhibiting a heightened sense of accountability to the constituencies served and for the outcomes created.

This multi-faceted definition is really an ideal to strive for, and the closer a person gets to satisfying all these conditions, the more he or she fits the model of an effective social entrepreneur. The individuals who are more innovative in their work and create more meaningful social improvements are perceived as more entrepreneurial.[21]

The idea that social entrepreneurs are change agents in the social sector provides additional insight into their proactive personality and behavior. Social entrepreneurs are reformers and revolutionaries with a social mission, such as Muhar Kent, the chairman and CEO of the Coca Cola Company, who founded the Coca-Cola African Foundation to improve drinking water and sanitation in under-developed countries within Africa. One of the goals of the foundation is to reduce the number of children who die from preventable diseases.[22]

A similar social entrepreneurship initiative took place when the Peace Corps announced a strategic partnership with the Water and Development Alliance (WADA). The latter is a long-standing public–private partnership between the U.S. Agency for International Development (USAID) and Coca Cola. The purpose of this three-party alliance is to improve local capacity to deliver sustainable water supply sanitation and hygiene (WASH) services for the reduction of waterborne disease around the world. WADA works with the Peace Corps WASH initiative to raise awareness and build capacity among Peace Corps and community trainers around sustainable water supply and sanitation services, as well as improved hygiene behaviors.[23]

Although Kent works with a team of executives in this large-scale social entrepreneurship initiative, he receives credit for identifying a critical social need and taking effective action. Critics might say that because Coca-Cola promotes the consumption of some beverages that are non-nutritious, they are merely conducting a public-relations campaign to improve their image through promoting safe water and hygiene. Despite this criticism, Kent and his colleagues have accomplished an important act of social entrepreneurship.

In the role of change agent, social entrepreneurs make fundamental changes in the social sector, and attack the underlying causes, rather than only treating symptoms. Finding ways to provide clean water, for example, is preferable to only treating people for the disastrous effects of contaminated water such as dysentery and cholera.

Another manifestation of proactivity among social entrepreneurs is that they recognize and relentlessly pursue new opportunities. As Dees explains, where others see problems, entrepreneurs see opportunities. Social entrepreneurs typically have a vision of how to achieve improvement and they fiercely want their vision to be implemented. The more effective social entrepreneurs combine persistence with a willingness to make adjustments along the way. Rather than surrendering when they encounter an obstacle, social entrepreneurs ask, "How can we surmount this obstacle? How can we make this work?"[24]

Compassion as a driver of social entrepreneurship

A recent model of social entrepreneurship emphasizes that compassion encourages social entrepreneurship. Compassion contains a strong element of proactivity because to be compassionate is to reach out to another person to satisfy his or her desire to be understood and receive sympathy. The developers of the research-based model in question, Toyah L. Miller, Matthew G. Grimes, Jeffery S. McMullen, and Timothy J. Vogus, posit that three mechanisms transform compassion into social entrepreneurship. Compassion, in their model, is viewed as prosocial (helping others) motivation that connects an individual with a suffering community, and triggers sensitivity to the pain and needs of others. The three mechanisms are integrative thinking, prosocial cost–benefit analysis, and commitment to others' suffering, as described below:[25]

1. Compassion and integrative thinking   Compassion serves as a prosocial motivator that drives the potential social entrepreneur to search for solutions that promise collective gains rather than individual interests. Prosocial motivation also facilitates the individual proactively paying attention to information about others' perspectives such that he or she can better understand the issue from their perspective and identify more ways to offer constructive help. The business executive with prosocial motivation might send e-mails to social workers and ask, "To what extent is it true that in some of the city neighborhoods, the children are so hungry that they cannot concentrate on learning at school?" The enhanced perspective increases cognitive flexibility, willingness to take risks, and openness to the possibility that a problem is complex. As a result, the individual expands his or access to ideas and potential solutions.

Compassion also facilitates integration of various perspectives to deal with a social issue because it moves a person away from the advocacy of a single perspective that would deter the person from looking at other perspectives. Strong prosocial motivation engenders consideration of a wider range of actions to reduce the suffering of other people. In the example at hand, the person might ask, "What are some workable alternatives to relieving hunger among elementary school students?"

In short, the research behind this model suggests that because compassion is a type of prosocial motivation it causes stronger receptivity to diverse information. In turn, new ideas and problem-solving approaches are recombined, leading to a constructive solution.

2. Compassion and prosocial cost–benefit analysis   According to the model being described, a compassionate person does not think exclusively in terms of personal gain. Compassion results in a more prosocial cost–benefit analysis in which the outcomes for other people are valued more highly than "What's in it for me?" As a result, the perceived benefits of acting to alleviate the suffering of others are increased. When the suffering of others is perceived to be unfair and unjust, the compassionate person is led to characterize beneficiaries as more needy and worthy of help, thereby increasing the perceived benefits of acting on their behalf.

Compassion leads the actor to recognize that a wide range of benefits are possible when acting to help others, such as alleviating pain and suffering, bringing joy to others, and giving people resources to begin improving their lot in life. Compassion can also lead to an "emotional tax" in the form of guilt stemming from not aiding community members. The emotional tax can be a cost because not helping others hurts the individual. Compassion also can enhance the proactive behavior of taking risks that are consistent with the value of wanting to help others. One risk might be being perceived as a "do gooder" who should stay at home instead of getting involved in a community where he or she does not belong.

3. Compassion and the commitment to alleviate suffering   Compassion as a prosocial motivator enhances the dedication to a cause or moral principle. At the same time compassion leads to a commitment to the people who benefit from the compassionate person's efforts, and a willingness to persevere in the face of negative feedback. Compassion can lead to emotional ties that become symbols of group membership, and encourage the social entrepreneur to focus on the goal of alleviating suffering within that group. The alleviating of suffering produces emotional energy which in turn reinforces commitment to those with whom the person is connected. A key point here is that emotional connection to others' suffering can reinforce desirable aspects of a prosocial self-identity that is oriented toward the alleviation of the suffering another person, or group, might be experiencing.

Recognizing problems in society

A basic explanation as to why social entrepreneurship takes place is that an enterprising, proactive individual recognizes a problem in society, and decides to alleviate the problem. For example, an executive might receive information from the human resources department and hiring managers that many job applicants are turned away because of limited reading ability. As a result, the executive initiates an adult literacy program in the community. Perhaps the programs sponsored by Coca-Cola Company to increase the supply of drinking water and improve sanitation stemmed from the recognition of problems in society.

A specific example of a successful business executive becoming a social entrepreneur is Susan L. Taylor, who for 40 years was a major force at *Essence* magazine. By age 35, Taylor had become editor in chief of the fashion, lifestyle, and beauty magazine. In 2006, Taylor founded a nonprofit, the National CARES Mentoring Movement, and four years later she began investing all her work time into the organization. CARES recruits and connects black mentors with local organizations that serve young people, and mentoring organizations in an effort to facilitate the academic and social success of black children. The societal problem Taylor recognized was that an estimated 58 percent of black fourth graders were functionally illiterate at the time. Mentors are asked to invest one hour per week to help guide a vulnerable young person. Part of the goal of CARES was to recruit 1 million black mentors, and the organization has made considerable progress toward that goal.[26]

Seeing Derivative Opportunities

Entrepreneurs by nature seek opportunities, as has been mentioned many times in this book. Further insight into the proactivity of entrepreneurs can be found in a refinement of opportunity seeking we refer to as "finding derivative opportunities." (We are not referring to the investment category of financial derivatives.) A derivative opportunity is much like finding an opportunity within an opportunity, or innovatively seeing the opportunity to expand services already being provided. A slightly humorous example regards hair salons that in recent years have offered esthetic services, including the removal of facial hair and skin care. The opportunity within an opportunity has been to offer women, as well as some men, hair-removal services suited for wearing a bikini in public. Although this service peaks during summer vacation time, the fact that people take vacations at different times during the year has made these so-called "Brazilian" hair-removal treatments a year-round business. Dermatologists have noted that this entrepreneurial venture brings risks to the clients, in the form of sexually transmitted infections facilitated by the removal of hair around the genital area.[27]

The executive recruiting business (often referred to as "headhunting") offers another example of the entrepreneurially minded person finding a derivative opportunity. The income from executive recruiters traditionally stems from employers who pay them to find qualified candidates. These firms in the past did not represent job seekers, and did not accept payment from them. An executive recruiter in Kansas City saw an opportunity to change the traditional model and generate income from job hunters. The change took place in two steps. First, they began offering a free-to-individuals career portal at www.mylandajob.com. The site aggregates position posting from 1100 job boards and provides free articles, audios, and webinars, and a one-time résumé review. Secondly, the firm offers one-on-one career counseling for individual clients for a fee. A senior recruiter of the firm thereby shifts from recruiter to career coach for selected clients.[28] Even if a handful of other firms are seeing and acting upon the same derivate opportunity it still represents entrepreneurial, proactive thinking and behavior.

ENTREPRENEURIAL RISK-TAKING BEHAVIOR

Earlier in the chapter we described risk taking as a key entrepreneurial trait. Here we focus more on the risk-taking behavior that typically stems from the trait of risk taking that is often combined with thrill seeking. Risk taking is characteristic of both the traditional version of an entrepreneur and the corporate entrepreneur. In a discussion of how professional women can better succeed in the workplace, Angela Brady, CEO of WellPoint, said, "Be open to opportunity and take risks. In fact, take the worst, the messiest, the most challenging assignment you can find, and then take control."[29]

Mark Zuckerberg, the founder of Facebook, could be considered the world's best-known entrepreneur. At the same time he is a corporate executive, and therefore takes risks as an entrepreneurial business founder and a corporate executive. In addition to being inventive, Zuckerberg displays the entrepreneurial behavior of taking the risk of changing the direction of the enterprise. Changing direction, with its attendant risk taking, is crucial because a company that fails to catch the next wave can falter badly. At one time the powerful IBM suffered because it dismissed the relevance of personal computers. Soon, however, IBM became a dominant player in the field of small computers. During a period beginning in 2011, Zuckerberg was determined not to be a company losing out on implementing a new technology development.

The shift in direction under consideration was that Facebook had now to embrace apps (the computer applications used on mobile devices). Instead of attempting to reach the broadest possible audience with a dynamic product, Facebook needed to select one operating system to demonstrate what it could accomplish in mobile phones. "I can't overstate how much we had to retool the whole company's redevelopment process," said Zuckerberg. He soon introduced Facebook Home, a new way to provide its customers with a strong Facebook experience on mobile phones.

The risks in this change of direction by Zuckerberg and Facebook were considered huge. Facebook Home made Zuckerberg and the company dependent on Android, the operating system owned by its intense rival, Google Inc. Zuckerberg also risked alienating key partner Apple, by focusing resources on the iPhone manufacturer's major competitor, Google.[30] Yet, as a world-class entrepreneur, Zuckerberg was willing to accept the risks.

Entrepreneurial risk taking can sometimes ward off potential future problems. By taking a risk in the present, a bigger future risk can be avoided. A relevant case is that of Bill Perkins of the Bill Perkins Automotive Group in Michigan. In April 2009, General Motors announced that it would terminate the Pontiac line of automobiles. The problem Perkins faced was that 60 percent of his revenue came from the sale of Pontiacs. With three locations in Michigan, Perkins had to figure out how his business could survive without the Pontiac brand. A risk Perkins had taken earlier with his dealership prevented a calamity. He had the foresight to reinvest profits in his business by purchasing the buildings in which his dealerships were located. Had GM owned the properties, eviction would have been a possibility after the Pontiac line was discontinued.[31] Also, owning was less expensive than renting, making it easier for Perkins to survive with his remaining lines, Buick, Chevrolet, and GMC. A few years later he owned two Chevrolet dealerships. Of note, having foresight is a proactive behavior because one anticipates problems in advance.

SUGGESTIONS FOR APPLICATION

Thinking and behaving entrepreneurially can often enhance the productivity of individuals and organizations. The following are suggestions for behaving more entrepreneurially in the context of working for an organization. Several of these suggestions might be applicable also to the self-employed entrepreneur.

1. *Be willing to take risks.* Risk taking is characteristic of self-employed entrepreneurs and entrepreneurial thinkers within the organization. The innovation championed by the entrepreneurial thinker may fail, losing money for the firm and credibility for the innovator. Risks exist even when the entrepreneurial venture succeeds. Once implemented, innovation eventually becomes standard company practice. Then the entrepreneurial thinker may feel compelled to develop another idea

that could be rejected, or eventually fail if accepted. A plausible suggestion for becoming more of a risk taker is to begin taking small risks and observe the positive and negative consequences. If you savor the rewards of success and can absorb pain from losses, your risk-taking propensity may increase.

2. *Learn to function with a minimum of structure.* A successful entrepreneurial thinker within an organization has to learn to operate with less structure than another professional in a more traditional role. As a result, the person engaged in entrepreneurial activity within the organization may have fewer rules, regulations, and policies for guidance.

3. *Learn to use informal influence processes.* Professionals engaged in an entrepreneurial activity, such as developing a new product or service, face the same key challenges as other types of project leader. Instead of using formal authority to get the resources and cooperation they need, they often have to rely on informal influence processes. For example, it may be necessary to deliberately compliment others to gain their cooperation when they are not part of your team. Learning to use informal influence well is important for another reason. Employees who are attracted to work on an entrepreneurial project within a firm may not respond well to formal authority because they dislike hierarchy.

4. *In a large organization, maintain a professional management style.* Entrepreneurial thinkers are known for their resistance to professional management techniques such as maintaining careful controls and delegating responsibility. Many small-business entrepreneurs hire professional managers to run their operation once it achieves substantial growth. Such practice in recent years has been referred to as hiring "adult supervision." Because large, complex organizations prefer all units to be professionally managed, it is the entrepreneurial project leader's advantage to practice professional management. In general this refers to following the fundamentals of planning, organizing, leading, controlling and rational decision making.

SUMMARY

A major manifestation of the proactive personality and behavior is entrepreneurship, particularly in the sense of developing an innovative business. Successful entrepreneurs tend to be proactive, particularly with respect to being creative and adventuresome. The proactive personality has been long associated with tendencies toward entrepreneurship, suggesting that the entrepreneurial personality might be a manifestation of proactivity. A study showed that the extent to which a company president had a proactive personality was positively related to entrepreneurial behavior, including starting rather than buying or inheriting a business.

Entrepreneurial leadership is linked to the proactive personality, with such personality types having a strong desire to become entrepreneurial leaders in order to create value for the firm. Proactive people are often successful in leadership roles, partially because of their desire to take action and create a positive change in their work environment. Proactive traits of entrepreneurial leaders include creativity and innovative ability, flexibility, and being adventuresome.

The Da Vinci-type personality (a) likes thrills, excitement, and risk, (b) is a highly creative problem solver, (c) is impulsive, (d) is ambitious and industrious, (e) has considerable energy to pursue personal interests, and (f) has a strong desire to be heroic in an emergency. Interests may also gravitate a person toward entrepreneurship, particularly as reflected in early interests in entrepreneurship.

A darker side of entrepreneurship also exists, especially with respect to an energetic drive that can be dysfunctional, particularly with respect to taking too many risks. Higher risk often results in higher rewards, propelling the risk-prone personality.

"Entrepreneurial spirit" is a global term that refers to a variety of traits, behaviors, and attitudes that propel a person into entrepreneurial actions. A key component of the entrepreneurial spirit is a passion for founding and enterprise, along with a passion for the enterprise after it is founded. Passion is also reflected in a love of the product or service offered by the entrepreneur. Perhaps the reason for serial entrepreneurs is that they lose passion for their present company.

A complex way in which proactivity and entrepreneurship are linked is that some businesspeople reach out into the environment to find new ways of doing social good. Social entrepreneurship is an entrepreneurial approach to a variety of social problems. The social entrepreneur addresses important social needs in a way that is not dominated by direct financial payoffs. The social improvements that come about because of the entrepreneurial venture may be difficult to measure.

Social entrepreneurship can sometimes be combined with business entrepreneurship, such as giving to charity with each unit sold. Social entrepreneurs are change agents, adopting and pursuing a mission to create and sustain social value. The more effective social entrepreneurs combine persistence with a willingness to make adjustments along the way.

A recent model of social entrepreneurship emphasizes that compassion encourages social entrepreneurship. According to the model, three mechanisms transform compassion into social entrepreneurship: integrative thinking, a prosocial cost–benefit analysis, and a commitment to alleviate suffering. A basic explanation as to why social entrepreneurship takes place is that an enterprising, proactive individual recognizes a problem in society, and decides to alleviate the problem.

Derivative opportunity seeking is another part of the entrepreneurial personality. A derivative opportunity is much like finding an opportunity within an opportunity, or innovatively seeing the opportunity to expand services already being provided. Risk taking is both an entrepreneurial trait and a behavior. Both traditional entrepreneurs and corporate entrepreneurs take risks. Entrepreneurial risk taking can sometimes ward off future risks.

Thinking and behaving entrepreneurially can often enhance the productivity of individuals and organizations. Suggestions for behaving entrepreneurially in the context of an organization include (a) be willing to take risks, (b) learn to function with a minimum of structure, (c) learn to use informal influence processes, and (d) in large organizations, maintain a professional management style.

REFERENCES

1. Brad Sugars, "How Many Jobs Can Your Startup Create this Year?" *Entrepreneur.com*, January 11, 2012, p. 1.
2. Chuck Salter, "A Love Story," *Fast Company*, May 2013, pp. 110–111.
3. J. M. Crant, "The Proactive Personality Scale as a Predictor of Entrepreneurial Intentions," *Journal of Small Business Management*, July 1996, pp. 42–49.
4. Richard C. Becherer and John G. Mauer, "The Proactive Personality Disposition and Entrepreneurial Behavior among Small Company Presidents," *Journal of Small Business Management*, Issue 1, 1999, pp. 28–36. Part of this analysis is as synthesized from Kilian Werenfried Wawoe, "Proactive Personality: The Advantages and Disadvantages of an Entrepreneurial Disposition in the Financial Industry," Doctoral Dissertation, Amsterdam, Holland: Vrije Universiteit, 2010, p. 17.
5. Leon C. Prieto, "Proactive Personality and Entrepreneurial Leadership: Exploring the Moderating Role of Organization Identification and Political Skill," *Academy of Entrepreneurship Journal*, July 1, 2010, pp. 1–16.
6. Salter, "A Love Story," p. 111.
7. Prieto, "Proactive Personality and Entrepreneurial Leadership," p. 9.
8. R. Elizabeth C. Kitchen, "The Entrepreneurial Personality," *www.brighthub.com*, December 26, 2009, pp. 1–2. Retrieved April 5, 2013.
9. Omudhome Ogbru, "Minooxidil, Rogaine," *MedicineNet.com* (www.medicinenet.com), p. 1. Accessed May 10, 2013.
10. Garret Lo Porto, *The Da Vinci Method* (Concord, MA: Media for Your Mind, Inc., 2005).

11. Carol Roth, "Do You Have what it Takes to be an Entrepreneur?" *www. entrepreneur.com*, November 8, 2011, pp. 1–3. Retrieved March 14, 2012.
12. Donald F. Kuratko, "Entrepreneurial Leadership in the 21st Century," *Journal of Leadership and Organizational Studies*, No. 4, 2007, pp. 1–11.
13. Manfred F. R. Ket de Vries, "The Dark Side of Entrepreneurship," *Harvard Business Review*, November/December 1985, pp. 160–167.
14. Cited in "Spirit of the Entrepreneur: These 5 Characteristics Will Take You Far as You Start Your Business," *www.entrepreneur.com*, February 26, 2008, pp. 1–2. Retrieved February 13, 2013.
15. "Marc Andreessen Background/Biography," *ChubbyBrain* (www.chubby-brain.com), pp. 1–2. Retrieved May 10, 2013.
16. Tiffany Kary, "Dial-a-Mattress, 1-800 Mattress File for Bankruptcy (Update 2)," *Bloomberg News* (www.bloomberg.com) May 24, 2009, pp. 1–2. Retrieved March 12, 2012.
17. Chuck Green, "When Entrepreneurs Don't Take No for an Answer," *The Wall Street Journal*, April 29, 2013, p. R5.
18. J. Gregory Dees, "The Meaning of 'Social Entrepreneurship'," published by the Kaufman Center for Entrepreneurial Leadership, October 31, 1998, p. 1.
19. Johann Mair and Ignasi Marti, "Social Entrepreneurship Research: A Source of Explanation, Prediction, and Delight," *Journal of World Business*, Issue 1, February 2006, pp. 36–44.
20. Philip Delves Broughton, "Doing Good By Shoeing Well," *The Wall Street Journal*, September 9, 2011, p. A17. Book review of Blake Mycoskie, *Start Something that Matters* (New York: Spiegel & Grau/Random House, 2011).
21. Dees, "The Meaning of 'Social Entrepreneurship'," p. 4.
22. "WaterAid Joins Forces with the Coca-Cola Africa Foundation to Bring Safe Drinking Water," *Financial News Making Money* (www.finchannel. com), May 11, 2013, pp. 1–3. Retrieved May 21, 2013.
23. "Peace Corps, USAID and Coca-Cola Announce Partnership to Strengthen Training on Water Supply, Sanitation and Hygiene in Developing Nations," *Peace Corps* (www.peacecorps.gov). Retrieved May 11, 2013.
24. Dees, "The Meaning of 'Social Entrepreneurship'," p. 5.
25. Toyah L. Miller, Matthew G. Grimes, Jeffery S. McMullen, and Timothy J. Vogus, "Venturing for Others with Heart and Head: How Compassion Encourages Social Entrepreneurship," *Academy of Management Review*, October 2012, pp. 616–640.
26. LaToya M. Smith, "Backtalk with Susan L. Taylor," *Black Enterprise*, November 2010, p. 96; *www.caresmentoring.org*. Retrieved May 12, 2013.
27. Melissa Healy, "'Brazilians' and Other Forms of Pubic Hair Removal May Carry Risk," *Los Angeles Times* (www.latimes.com), March 18, 2013, p. 1. Retrieved April 17, 2013.
28. Diane Stafford, "Headhunters Take Talents to Career Coaching," *McClatchy Newspapers* (www.miamihearld.com), September 11, 2011, p. 1. Retrieved November 14, 2012.
29. Quoted in John Bussey, "How Women Can Get Ahead: Advice from Female CEOs," *The Wall Street Journal*, May 18, 2012, p. B2.
30. Facts and quotes from Jesse Hempel, "The Second Coming of Facebook," *Fortune*, April 29, 2013, p. 74.
31. Alan Hughes, "Defensive Driving: Bill Perkins Positions his Dealerships to Survive the Auto Industry Wreckage," *Black Enterprise*, February 2010, p. 67.

8. Business strategy and proactivity

Business strategy has a variety of meanings, with most of them referring to an integrated, overall concept of how the firm will achieve its objectives. To develop this overall concept or plan, the strategist must be proactive about the future and point the firm in the right direction. To develop strategy is an inherently proactive process. In a sense, the strategic leader helps the organization invent the future instead of reacting only to problems facing the firm in the present. For example, strategists at the major soft-drink companies in anticipation of a growing demand for healthier soft drinks have increased their production of non-carbonated, low-calorie, fruit-flavored beverages.

The school reformist, Michelle Rhee provides an example of strategic, proactive thinking at the highest level (or "very big thinking"). Rhee's first two major initiatives toward educational reform were as CEO of the New Teacher Project and as Washington D.C. city's school chancellor. In 2011, Rhee crystalized her plan to set up a new organization, not as a charity but as a political-advocacy and membership group. The organization, labeled Students First, would rely on funding and Rhee's star power. Rhee planned to raise $1 billion in contributions and recruit 1 million supporters in one year. The main points of Students First were to change the tenure and seniority rules in public schools, giving parents more choice in what schools their children would attend. She also wanted mayors rather than school boards to control schools, and advocated more fiscal responsibility by school administrators. Part of Rhee's strategic vision was to rely on grassroots support, with thousands of small donors and campaign workers.[1]

The grand-scale strategic thinking built into Students First, fell short of its fundraising goals and grassroots support during its first several years of existence, and Michelle Rhee has evoked some negative reaction. For example, a group called New Yorkers for Great Public Schools, a union-backed parents' coalition, contends that Students First has not been effective.[2] Nevertheless, what Rhee is doing with her organization illustrates a proactive strategy to tackle a major problem. And in the long run, her proactive stance may prove beneficial to school systems and their students.

In this chapter we describe various aspects of business strategy that

Following is a list of statements related to strategic thinking. Respond "Agree" or "Disagree" to each statement.

No.	Statement in relation to strategic thinking	Agree	Disagree
1.	Every action I take should add value for our customers, clients or the public.	❏	❏
2.	Everyday frustrations usually make it difficult for me to think about the purpose of what I am doing.	❏	❏
3.	It is the job of top management only to worry about strategy. I have my own job to worry about.	❏	❏
4.	The future takes care of itself if you do your job well.	❏	❏
5.	A vision plays an important role in guiding the actions of workers.	❏	❏
6.	Whatever will be, will be. You can't control the future.	❏	❏
7.	It makes good sense for management to ask itself, "What business are we really in?"	❏	❏
8.	I see a lot of value in a team of people going offsite for a couple of days to contemplate the future of the company.	❏	❏
9.	Giant, successful companies such as Microsoft, IBM, GM, and Procter & Gamble should have no concern about their future.	❏	❏
10.	I like the idea of a company asking dozens of employees what other products and services the company should offer in the future.	❏	❏

Note: scoring and interpretation: strategic thinking is reflected in a response of "Agree" to statements 1, 5, 7, 8, and 10, as well as "Disagree" to statements 2, 3, 4, 6, and 9. If you scored in the strategic direction for 8 or more of these statements you probably have strong tendencies toward strategic thinking.

Figure 8.1   The strategic thinking checklist

illustrate its proactive nature, and how this proactivity often enhances organizational performance and productivity. As a starting point in the study of proactivity and strategic thinking, you are invited to take the self-assessment quiz presented in Figure 8.1.

PROACTIVE ELEMENTS OF BUSINESS STRATEGY

Business strategy is a broad field of study in itself. Here we look at the proactive elements of business strategy from seven different perspectives, all centering on the theme that strategy is a proactive process.

The Contribution of Strategic and Proactive Thinking

Strategic and proactive thinking are related because strategy involves proactivity, but sometimes proactive thinking is more straightforward than being part of an elaborate business strategy. Here we look at the two categories separately.

The contribution of strategic thinking

Strategic thinking, including the ability to proactively search for new directions for an organization, is a highly valued and relatively rare ability. Indra Nooyi, the CEO of PepsiCo, once said that the most overrated skill is running a business. To her, the most important skill for any CEO is strategic acuity. She recalls that when she was going to run the European business in 1996, Roger Enrico (the PepsiCo CEO at the time) said, "I'm pulling that. You're going to stay back." His explanation was, "I can get operating executives to run a P&L [profit and loss]. But I cannot find people to help me re-conceptualize PepsiCo. That's the skill in shortest supply."[3]

The most elegant contribution of strategic thinking for a business enterprise is for the strategic leader to point the organization to prosper in a space or niche that others have not yet discovered. "Blue Ocean Strategy" is the term suggested by W. Chan Kim and Rene Mauborgne to define a strategy that makes the competition irrelevant because others have not yet discovered the market space. The challenge is that in an established industry, companies compete with each other for portions of available market share, such as pharmaceutical companies competing to sell over-the-counter pain relievers. The competition is so intense that some firms obtain such a small market share they lose money and/or go out of business. This type of industry is described as a "red ocean," representing the bloody competition among the sharks. A blue ocean exists where no firm currently operates, enabling the company to expand without competition – assuming a true demand exists for the company's product or service.[4]

Blue Ocean Strategy is not simply an opinion expressed by two consultants. The strategy resulted from a decade-long study of 150 strategic moves spanning 30 industries over the period of 1880 to 2000. A foundation example of the Blue Ocean Strategy in action is Cirque du Soleil, a Quebec, Canada, company that substantially changed the nature of a declining circus industry in the 1980s. Based on conventional strategy analysis the circus industry was in rapid decline. Star performers had too much power over a circus. Alternative forms of entertainment from sporting events, video games, and the home entertainment industry were relatively inexpensive and gaining share of the entertainment market. Another pressure on the industry was that animal rights groups were objecting strongly to the way in which circuses treated animals. Cirque du Soleil placed itself in a blue ocean by eliminating the animals and reducing the importance of individual stars.

The company created a new genre of entertainment that combined dance, music, and acrobatic and athletic skill to appeal to an upscale adult audience that had lost interest in the traditional circus. Even the name *cirque* is innovative because it is the French word for both circus and circle, so the troupe offered a new concept still tied to the past, at least for people who know French. (Also, many children are thrilled by the amazing feats performed by Cirque du Soleil performers.)

Blue Ocean Strategy is complex, with consulting firms offering programs for its implementation. However, the four actions that can help a firm create a Blue Ocean Strategy point to the proactive thinking required. The actions are dictated by answering the following questions:

1. *Which of the factors that the industry takes for granted should be eliminated?* Management at Cirque du Soleil eliminated animals, star performers, and the three separate rings.
2. *Which factors should be reduced well below the industry standard?* Cirque du Soleil downplayed much of the thrill and danger associated with conventional circuses, yet still retained a dose of danger in some of the acrobatics.
3. *Which factors should be raised well above the industry's standard?* Cirque du Soleil enhanced its uniqueness by developing its own tents rather than by performing within the confines of existing physical structures, such as a downtown arena.
4. *Which factors should be created that the industry has never offered?* Cirque du Soleil transformed the meaning of a circus by introducing dramatic themes, artistic music and dance, and a more upscale, refined environment that lacked the traditional smell of a circus.[5]

Kim and Mauborgne believe that the leading companies of the future will succeed not by battling competitors but by proactively identifying and creating these blue oceans. The authors also recommend that business leaders should focus less on their present customers and more on non-customers and potential new customers. Intentionally or unintentionally, leadership at Research in Motion and Apple Corp. hit upon a Blue Ocean Strategy – the development of the Blackberry and iPod, respectively. Two examples of companies intentionally using the Blue Ocean Strategy are Pitney Bowes and Nintendo.

Michael Citrelli, the former CEO of Pitney Bowes, said that his company created the Advanced Concept & Technology Group, a unit responsible for identifying and developing new products outside the existing product line. An example of the Blue Ocean Strategy stemming from this group was the development of a machine that enables customers to design and print their own postage from desktop computers.

The Nintendo Wii and DS that company leadership designed to target audiences that are not traditionally known to play video games are examples of the Blue Ocean Strategy. By simplifying its interface, and by marketing software to complement daily life (such as improving a tennis stroke), rather than create escapist experiences (such as violent video games), Nintendo has sparked greater mainstream appeal than any previous console. Nintendo has often struggled to keep up with the demand for Wii and DS.[6]

The contribution of proactive thinking

Proactive thinking, whether or not it can be considered true business strategy, can make a key contribution to a company's survival and reputation. An important example is that a company leadership taking a proactive stance would recall a faulty line of products rather than wait for customers to complain and deal with the issue when facing pressures of a lawsuit. This type of proactive behavior took place in 2002 when the Toro Company, Exmark Manufacturing, and Dixon Industries Inc. collectively recalled 62,000 faulty commercial riding mowers that had an exhaust system problem. The three companies worked proactively and directly with their dealers, distributers, and customers during the recall campaign to fix or replace the faulty units already on the market.[7] In 2012 and 2013, Toro proactively recalled riding mowers again; this time approximately 3700 mowers were recalled. The problem was that the idler pulley could rub against the mower's fuel tank, posing a fire threat, but no incidents were reported.[8] As a formal business strategy, a proactive recall might be classified as part of a high-quality or brand leadership strategy.

Identifying a Major Need for Change

Another important link between business strategy and proactivity is that the proactive thinker must identify what situation or condition needs changing before developing a strategy to bring about the change. Waiting until an emergency presents itself, such as a supplier going out of business, to bring about change could be considered reactive. Yet scanning the environment for needed change can be considered both strategic and reactive. In this section we examine identifying a major need for change (or a need for a major change) from three related perspectives: recognizing the need for change at the core of the enterprise; a proactive search for growth; and taking the offense to improve business.

Recognition for change at the core of the enterprise

Part of being a strategic thinker is knowing when it is time to change a core business, such as General Electric wondering if the manufacture of light bulbs is still a good idea. An in-depth study of 25 companies by strategy consultant Chris Zook discovered that it is possible to measure the vitality of a business core.[9] If the measurement suggests that the core needs reinvention, it may be best to mine hidden assets. Some of the 25 companies were in a crisis mode when they began the process of redefining themselves. According to Zook's research, five diagnostic questions can be asked to recognize early signs of erosion, as follows:

1. *What is the state of our core business?* Take a careful look at profitability, market share, customer retention rate, measures of customer loyalty and advocacy, and share of disposable income.
2. *What is the state of our core differentiation?* Take a careful look at metrics of differentiation, relative cost position, business models of emerging competitors, and whether differentiation is increasing or decreasing.
3. *What is the state of our industry's profit pools?* Take a careful look at size, growth, and stability, share of profit pools captured, shifts and projections, and high costs and prices.
4. *What is the state of our core capabilities?* Take a careful look at an inventory of key capabilities, relative importance, and gaps in comparison to competitors and future core needs.
5. *What is the state of our culture and organization?* Take a careful look at loyalty and involuntary turnover, capability and stress points, agreement in the pursuit of objectives, motivation to perform well, and bottlenecks to growth.

If the comprehensive and complex task of finding answers to these questions suggests that the core business is weakening, it would be time to locate a hidden asset to be the centerpiece of a new strategy. Developing such a new strategy would take courage and proactivity, much like a large retail chain discovering that its core asset was its hundreds of store locations, not the stores themselves. The chain would then obtain much of its profits from selling and/or leasing the many locations after closing the stores.

In 20 of the 25 companies Zook studied, a hidden asset proved to be the centerpiece of a new strategy. The hidden assets tended to fall into three categories. The first was *undervalued business platforms*, which refers essentially to a business unit, or parts of several units, that is undervalued and underutilized. An example is the GE Capital unit of General Electric that was not considered important for many years, but then recognized for its potential. GE Capital became a major source of the parent company's revenue for many years until weakened temporarily by the financial crisis that began in 2008.

The second category was *untapped insights into consumers.* It is possible that one neglected customer segment could be a source of unprecedented growth. DeBeers had been long known as a supplier of diamonds, to both merchants and end consumers. Leaders at DeBeers soon recognized that this high brand recognition could be a source of new revenues. The company stepped up its brand further through advertising. DeBeers also developed new product ideas for its distributors and jewelers, and sponsored ad campaigns to reach consumers. The company diamond business has increased tenfold. DeBeers still sells rough diamonds, but its core has shifted to serving consumers and customers.

The third category of hidden assets was *underexploited capabilities.* Sometimes individual companies combine a few business processes to create difficult-to-replicate competitive advantage. Although Amazon. com may not have been hurting at the time of the Zook study, it proves to be an excellent example of combining capabilities to generate new sources of revenue. Amazon began as an online distributer of books and music. Along the way it developed outstanding capabilities in displaying products, storing and shipping them, and receiving payments. Amazon soon evolved into a distributer of thousands of products, including those of other merchants and competitors.

The key point for our purposes about finding hidden assets to launch a new strategy is that the person (or people) in charge has to think proactively about these assets. Even searching for the opportunities within hidden assets is proactive.

The proactive search for growth into adjacent space

The search for growth possibilities within the organization is an effective proactive strategy, but the search into adjacent markets can also be effective. To learn more about how to sustain profitable growth Chris Zook and James Allen conducted a five-year study of corporate growth with a sample of 1850 companies. The researchers tracked specific growth initiatives and linked them back to company performance. The research led to two major conclusions. First was that the most sustained, profitable growth occurs when a company extends beyond the boundaries of its core business into adjacent space. For example, an established manufacturer of the alternative energy source of turbines might expand into the manufacture of solar panels.

Secondly, certain successful companies profitably outgrow their competitors by developing a formula for expanding these boundaries, in predictable ways that can be repeated many times. The average company has a success rate of approximately 25 percent in launching new initiatives. Companies that have discovered a repeatable formula have a success rate of approximately 50 percent, and some drove their success rate to 80 percent of new initiatives. The repeated acts include moving into new geographic areas, as well as applying a successful business model to new segments. A basic business model for many appliance stores has been to charge for the installation of complicated consumer electrical equipment such as television sets that are linked to satellite systems and computers. Installation services are so profitable that they led to a few major electronic stores developing services, such as the Geek Squad. The squad is composed of technicians who visit homes to help with the installation and servicing of a variety of consumer electronic devices. For example, many consumers need help dealing with the complexities of a newly purchased smart phone.

Zook and Allen have developed six suggestions a company can use to successfully take the initiative to be successful in an adjacent business. The suggestions stem from an evaluation of 181 moves into adjacent space.

1. *Expand along the value chain, despite this being one of the most challenging adjacency moves.* Apple Corp. originally sold its consumer products through intermediaries such as computer and electronic stores but was highly successful in launching its own retail outlets which co-existed with other distribution channels.
2. *Develop new products and services.* Several major manufacturers of telecommunication equipment, including Xerox Corporation, enhanced their revenues by moving into the space of consulting and information technology services. Xerox purchased Affiliated Computer Services, a company that performed mostly back-office work for other companies, and ACS soon became a major revenue source for Xerox.
3. *Use new distribution channels.* With so many distribution channels available, it requires serious proactive thinking to find a new channel for a product or service, especially with so many products and services being sold online as well as in physical stores. An unusual example is that a group of face-lift specialists, Lifestyle Lift, have opened stores in upscale shopping plazas across the United States to increase market penetration.
4. *Enter new geographies.* The globalization of business is so widespread that selling in other countries barely qualifies as proactive thinking any longer. What is proactive, however, is to identify potential markets in under-developed countries where competitors have not yet

ventured. Procter & Gamble, for example, has been diligently pursuing the sale of their products in poor, emerging-market countries for years with some success.

5. *Address new customer segments, often by modifying a proven product or technology.* To develop its business, leadership at Charles Schwab expanded its advisory service for discount brokerage services to target high net-worth individuals. This initiative is notable because serving high net-worth individuals overcame the traditional thinking that Charles Schwab was geared to investors with moderate incomes.

6. *Move into "white space" with a new business built around a strong capability. (This is the most rare and difficult adjacency move to identify and implement.)* "White space" in this context refers to a new business possibility that competitors have not yet identified. A classic example is that American Airlines created the Sabre reservation system, a spinoff that is considered to be more valuable than the airline itself. Sabre, in turn, moved into adjacent areas such as the online travel agent, Travelocity.[10]

All these strategies and tactics for moving into adjacent space required a careful exploratory search of the environment to see what might be feasible. Sometimes the proactive adjacent move can prove to be a failure, such as the one-time move of McDonald's into the children's clothing market, and Xerox attempting to become a computer manufacturer.

Taking the offense to improve business

During poor business conditions, a natural response for top-level managers is to search for ways to reduce expenses to meet current sales volume. A more proactive response to the same negative conditions is to accept the challenge of finding a way to improve business conditions. The downturn signals that change is needed, and the proactive solution is to find an initiative that strengthens rather than weakens the firm. For example, during a recession a moderately priced restaurant might suffer from decreased revenue. A proactive solution would be to begin a program of selling meals from a truck, a type of business that often prospers during a recession.

An example of the strategy of taking the offense took place when Randy Cohen, the founder of Ticket City, a ticket broker in Austin, Texas, laid off workers and reduced the pay of managers during a recession. Cohen then came across an article about his once growth-oriented company, entitled "Don't Be Afraid." The contents of the article triggered him into realizing that he had slipped into a defensive mode. Cohen's proactive response was to hire 10 new people and invest in marketing, which resulted in a one-third increase in revenues and a substantial increase in profits. A further initiative was to sponsor a new nationally televised college Bowl Game, the Ticket City Bowl.[11]

Disruption as a Strategy

A recurring theme in strategic thinking is to discover ways to disrupt the business activities of other companies or to ward off being disrupted by new competitors. As the terms were originally developed by Clayton Christensen and Michael E. Raynor, the strategic thinker has to distinguish between *sustaining* innovations and *disruptive* innovations. Sustaining innovations are those that improve a product to appeal to the most demanding customers. Both incremental improvements and breakthroughs qualify as sustaining innovations. Among these would be improving the gas mileage and dashboard command system on a luxury sedan or sports car. A disruptive innovation, in contrast, is aimed at serving a market of new or less demanding customers with a product that may be inferior, or easier to use.[12] Among the many disruptive innovations in modern times have been personal computers disrupting mainframe computers, smart phones disrupting expensive cameras, cell phones disrupting watches, and manufactured patio homes replacing larger, standard homes.

Asking if disruption is feasible

To understand whether disruption is feasible, Christensen and Raynor ask a set of questions:

- Is there a large population of people who historically have not had the money, equipment, or skill to do this thing for themselves?
- Are there customers at the low end of the market who would be happy to purchase a product with less, but adequate, performance if they could purchase it at a lower price?
- Is the innovation disruptive to *all* of the significant competitors in the industry?[13] *All* may be difficult to attain, as illustrated by how cell phones and smart phones have heavily disrupted the market for low-priced and medium-priced watches. Many people whose primary goal in using watches is to tell the time no longer purchase watches – they simply access their phone to tell the time. Nevertheless, the fashion watch industry is booming with customers who wear watches as jewelry or as a status symbol of affluence. Many affluent people wear watches that cost as much as or more than the average price of a new automobile, even though less expensive devices are available for telling the time.

Identifying disruptive changes

A key strategic and proactive skill for the executive or marketing specialist is to identify company- or industry-disrupting changes that are approaching that could help or damage the company. Consultants Michael Birshan and Jayanti Kar explain that these insights do not emerge automatically.[14] Consider the challenge of technological disruption. For many executives, being promoted requires a deep understanding of industry-specific technologies, such as those embedded in the company's products or in manufacturing techniques. To be promoted, less knowledge is required of cross-cutting technology trends such as the impact of social media and nanotechnologies. Another problem is that many senior executives are content to delegate thinking about cutting-edge technology developments to the company chief information officer or chief technology officer. Of concern is that it is precisely such cross-cutting technology trends that have the highest probability of upending value chains, transforming industries, and radically improving sources of profit and competitive advantage.

To become more proactive in identifying disruptions some executives choose to spend one or two weeks visiting a technology hub, such as Silicon Valley or Cambridge, Massachusetts, to meet companies, investors, and academics. Other executives ask a more technophile member of the team to stay current with the issues and brief them periodically. Another approach is to develop reverse mentoring relationships with younger colleagues who are specialists in technology and innovation. It is also helpful to observe directly what customers are doing with technology, such as using their smart phones at a retail store to make price comparisons.

Finding a useful disruptive technology is more likely to develop from looking at new sources of competition than the traditional source of competition often found through competitive intelligence. Birshan and Kar offer the example of the mining industry in which developed-world major players (such as Anglo American, BHP Billiton, and Rio Tinto) that have long competed with each other globally, now must also take into account competitors from Brazil, China, India, and elsewhere.

Picking up weak competitive signals is often the result of careful practice – a systematic updating of insights into competition as an ongoing part of developing strategy. Questions such as the following might be asked to gather insights into being disrupted or creating disruptions:

- Who is well positioned to play in emerging business areas?
- If new technologies are involved, what are they, and who else might master them?
- Who seems poorly positioned, and what are the implications for competitive balance in the industry or for acquisition opportunities?

Executives who focus competitive reviews on questions like these will often achieve insights of substantially more value than would be possible through the common practice of periodically examining the financial and operating results of competitors. The team is more likely to develop a disruptive strategy if it meets regularly to communicate about current and potential future strategies. The communication sessions can include a dramatic touch, such as holding and feeling a competitive consumer product.

Two examples of successful disruptions
Two examples from substantially different industries will help illustrate the proactive thinking involved in disruptive changes. The first example is James Dyson, the founder and CEO of Dyson, a manufacturer and seller of a bagless vacuum cleaner. Dyson has been regarded as a disrupter because of his creativity in product design. Although a bagless vacuum cleaner was not a new concept, Dyson found a niche in the bagless vacuum cleaner field by making his cleaner easier to use, particularly in emptying the chamber containing the vacuumed dirt. Part of Dyson's proactivity is his persistence. He believes that no one has the right idea at the beginning. He explains that he made 5127 prototypes of the bagless vacuum before he got it right.[15]

An information technology example of disruption is the open source software company, MySQL. The company is now owned by Oracle Inc., and offers for sale many commercial versions of its product. Founder Simon Phipps notes that rather than competing head on with companies that were one thousand times their size, he focused on the underserved market of Web developers. He decided early in developing the new software that he could not compete successfully on features. The space he identified was to compete on ease of use, performance, and cost, using a strategy of co-existence rather than replacement. A key component of his disruptive strategy was to serve the underserved. For many website developers, MySQL was their first database. Today, many of the world's largest and fastest-growing organizations, including Facebook and Zappos, rely on MySQL to save time and money by powering their high-volume websites, business-critical systems, and packaged software.[16]

Reinvention of the Organization as a Strategy

A courageous business strategy is to reinvent the organization in response to perceived negative trends or forces in the outside world. The reinvention strategy is proactive to the extent that the leader or leadership team perceives the need for reinvention before the organization is in crisis. A strong example of reinvention has taken place five or six times at Cisco Systems under the leadership of its chairman and CEO John Chambers. He emphasizes that a company has to change before the need for change becomes obvious, and that the toughest thing is when you see the warning signals that others don't. One of the examples he presents took place during 2011, when everybody else became quite optimistic about the economy. He saw business from state governments starting to slow, meaning that Cisco would lose on potential sales to the states.

In a 2012 reinvention, Chambers was moving Cisco away from being a router and switch company for the Internet, and using the company technology to changes areas like health care and education. In a two-year period Cisco gained market share in areas others said the company did not fit. Chambers emphasizes that he does not like change, but must accept the inevitable when market conditions warrant changing. A major part of the challenge is that it takes three to five years to drive a new strategy through the company.[17]

Burberry, the British company famous for trench coats, is also heralded for its successful reinvention. According to one analysis, the following are five ways the iconic British brand reinvented itself over a six-year period, after losing some of its competitiveness and market share. The problems included copies of its trademark tartan, mass-market designs produced by franchises, and too little presence at discount outlets.[18]

- Rule 1: *Reignite the passion.* Leadership at Burberry understood that the company needed bigger aspirations and goals powered by passion. They achieved this by making the Burberry brand the core focus and informing executives that art, not business, would drive the major decisions. Workers at all levels were inspired to design beauty into every facet of the business.
- Rule 2: *Refresh the brand core.* The company focused on constant brand refreshing, charting a sustainable growth path through one collection after another. Every new handbag, jacket, trench coat or dress surprised and delighted large numbers of customers.
- Rule 3: *Reinvent the brand experience.* Burberry gave customers total access to the brand using any electronic device, on multiple platforms, anywhere, anytime. As a result of these efforts, Burberry became the dominant luxury brand on Facebook. Runway shows were streamed in real time, with allowance for home delivery before collections arrived at stores.
- Rule 4: *Reinforce a balanced culture.* A balanced culture in the thinking of Burberry leadership refers to not having a single way of thinking, working, and doing. People were hired who had both high cognitive intelligence and emotional intelligence. Cross-disciplinary

collaboration between right-brain and left-brain specialists was encouraged, as was cross-department mentoring. The balanced culture is said to have contributed to innovative decisions and designs.

- Rule 5: *Reimagine the future.* In addition to clear, creative vision for top-level managers, a Strategic Innovation Council pools the inter-disciplinary and intergenerational wisdom and experience of many of Burberry's most competent workers to sense what the future will bring.

The reinvention or revitalization of Burberry is instructive in understanding how proactive strategy can revitalize a business enterprise. Denise Cooper, chief reinvention officer for an HR consulting firm, explains that company executives know it is time for reinvention when they have doubts about the strategic plan of their business. Another warning signal is when the executives wonder if they have the right talent on board to deliver excellent financial results into the future. Cooper offers four suggestions for reinventing the enterprise, as follows:[19]

1. *Get clear.* The executive leading the reinvention should be explicit on what he or she wants to accomplish, and what his or her role will be in the transformation. The executive might also think through how much he or she is attached to the status quo.
2. *Align your leadership team.* Successfully reinventing a business requires the collective effort, ownership, and personal accountability of the top management team. If they are unable to separate themselves emotionally from the status quo, the initiative will stall. In-person discussions about the need for reinventing the company will be helpful in dealing with resistance to change.
3. *Start small with multiple projects through the company.* After the leader initiating the reinvention and the top-management team have a clear understanding of the desired end result, the leader should initiate small projects, and connect and build upon each initiative. For example, an ailing product might be revitalized. The gradual approach will provide the opportunity to evaluate responses to change, risk, and failure.
4. *Tackle the excuses.* The leader sparking the reinvention may be ready for grand changes before others in the organization. As a result, the leader might encounter a variety of excuses, including: "We're too busy." "We've done this before and it didn't work." "With all our priorities, how can we afford this?" It is important for the leader of the reinvention to realize that excuses are often a plea for him or her

to present answers that inspire people to rise above their self-interest and achieve something of value for the common good.

Dealing Proactively with Complementors

Strategic thinking can be directed at dealing with other enterprises the company neither buys from nor sells to. *Complementors* are companies that, acting alone, provide complementary products and services to mutual customers. The value of a company's products or services can be enhanced by these complementary products or services.[20] At the most elementary level, submarine sandwich and pizza shops that sell many subs for take-out have additional sales if situated adjacent to a beers-of-the-world store. People who purchase beer will often want to purchase sub sandwiches and pizza, particularly if convenient. The relationship will be symbiotic if purchasers of sub sandwiches and pizza purchase beer frequently. On a more sophisticated level, Intel and Microsoft neither buy nor sell from each other directly, but they are in business together. Intel chips are used inside the Windows operating system.

Although the label *complementor* is relatively new, complementary products and services have been recognized for a long time. Night clubs profit greatly from conventions, and people are more willing to attend business and professional conventions if they know the night life at the convention city is exciting. Hotels and theme parks share the same customers. Home improvement stores profit greatly from real estate sales, and people are more likely to purchase older homes if home improvement stores are available.

The strategic and proactive aspects of complementor relationships take place when the strategist searches for complementary products and services, and attempts to enhance relationships with the complementors. As explained by David B. Yoffie and Mary Kwak, a major reason why relationships with complementors have to be managed is that discord can develop. The issue of pricing best illustrates the potential problem. Ideally a company manager would like to price his or her goods and services high while the complementors price them low. Airline executives, for example, would be happy to see vacation lodgings prices quite low, while destination resorts would like to see quite low airfares. And SUV dealers would like gasoline prices to stay low, while gasoline dealers would like the price of SUVs to stay low.

When the relationships between complementors are natural and unforced, such as purchasers of holiday trees purchasing tree decorations, and customers purchasing trees so they can buy tree decorations, not much strategic thinking is required. Several suggestions for taking the initiative to enhance relationships with complementors when there might be potential discord are described next.[21]

The first step in taking the initiative to manage relationships with complementors is to understand in-depth their strategies and goals, their existing capabilities, their incentives for cooperation, and any potential areas of conflict. For example, about 60 percent of new automobiles come equipped with radios capable of receiving non-fee broadcast stations as well as satellite stations. If after the free-trial period, not enough new-vehicle purchasers subscribe to the satellite stations, the satellite radio providers may not want to continue their investment of installing these radios in the new vehicles. However, even if many purchasers of new vehicles do not intend to continue with the satellite service, they still demand a new vehicle with satellite capability. Both the manufacturer and dealer, and the satellite radio provider benefit, assuming that the manufacturer and dealer get a small commission on the stream of revenues from the satellite subscriptions.

The second step is to understand the business model of competitors, and then try to gain the upper hand. One approach to gaining the upper hand is to use *hard power* – resorting to inducements or coercion to get what you want. Sony at one time was successful in attracting developers to its video games by reducing by 50 percent industry-standard licensing fees.

If the strategist wants to build more constructive long-term relationships with complementors than by using hard power, a shift to *soft power* tactics is advised. Soft power relies on indirect means of persuasion. Skillful implementers of soft power get others to want what they want instead of forcing or bribing them to do so. A general approach might be to give another company an incentive to build a complementary product by giving them access to your customer base. A specific approach might be an automobile manufacturer reaching out to the satellite radio providers to ask how the two of them could cooperate to increase the percentage of long-time subscribers to satellite radios. At the same time, the automobile manufacturer might suggest a plan whereby dealers, in their routine follow-up e-mail surveys to car buyers, could ask about satisfaction with the satellite radio service.

Our purpose here is not to elaborate on the intricacies of complementor relationships, but to observe that it takes proactive thinking and behavior to build relationships with strategic business partners over whom you have no direct control.

The Proactive Development of a Quality Strategy

A basic business strategy is to offer goods or services of higher quality than does the competition. Many business leaders continue to emphasize quality even if there is a less explicit emphasis today on formal quality programs. A strategy of quality is particularly proactive when a company strategist recognizes that by providing higher quality, the company might gain advantage. Although company leadership would hardly receive much recognition today for taking the initiative to develop a quality strategy, it has worked well in the past.

As the world was emerging from the Great Recession in 2010, Ford Motor Co. was experiencing a sales surge that dealers attributed to the company's emphasis on advanced technology and factory-built quality. Dennis Snyder, a Ford dealer in Albuquerque, N.M., and past chairman of Ford's National Dealer Council, noted, "We started another quality initiative in the late '90s, but we were doing it one line at a time." Manufacturing plants were operating at top speed and were pushing dealers to take everything they produced. Dealers would be loaded with a 150-day supply of vehicles that would sit on the lots and not receive the needed maintenance attention. Ford was just jamming products onto dealers' showrooms and lots, he explained.

Following this strategy, rattles, squeaks, malfunctioning handles and mechanical glitches were repaired after customers found them. From the customer's perspective, quality was an afterthought. The company dropped to a low point in the automotive industry's quality ratings, and Ford was losing money on warranty repairs.

As chairman, William Clay Ford enhanced the company quality initiative, getting everyone involved, from production technicians to top-level executives. The projects saved Ford more than $675 million worldwide within two years. With Alan Mulally, the former Boeing Co. executive joining Ford in 2006, the quality initiative was pushed even further. Mulally also proactively responded to customer concerns and demands, environmental sustainability, and gave the vehicles the feel of a smart-phone app. Under the One Ford quality plan, Mulally combined the best of Ford's North American and European styling and engineering. The quality initiative was further implemented by using high-tech testing to assure vehicles were delivered to dealers with many fewer warranty-repair problems.[22]

Using Design to Seek Competitive Advantage

Good design can be strategic when it is used to gain competitive advantage, and it requires proactive thinking and behavior to visualize how improved design, or a radically new design, might give a company an edge. Thomas Watson, Jr., the legendary IBM executive, told a business school audience in 1973 that good design is good business. Watson had long recognized the possible competitive advantage of good design, going back to 1954 when he recruited a designer to reinvent the street-level showroom of IBM's Manhattan headquarters. Good design today is seen as highly profitable, as in the premium price paid for Apple Corp. products.

Good design is strategic to the extent that the design is focused on grabbing customer attention and loyalty. Another reason for the importance of design is what happens in manufacturing a basic product when it becomes a commodity that is now made in a lower-wage country. At the same time distribution channels might now be placed on the Internet. These forces combine to bring competitive advantage to design which can help build customer relationships. (Of course, in this age of brand piracy a design can be copied.)

Another reason for being proactive about design is that an alluring design can deliver a sustainable edge. Other features such as functionality are of obvious importance, but good design builds loyalty.[23] Many observers have remarked that the simplicity of design of the Google home page has contributed substantially to its dominance as a search engine. Leadership at Google intuitively knew that the front-page design could give the company a competitive edge, and therefore invested substantial resources, including top in-house talent, in developing the home page.

Strategic design, or design specifically developed to increase revenue, applies to basic as well as high-tech industries. A few years ago, strategists at McDonald's decided to reshape the concept of selected McDonald's restaurants through redesign. The proactive change was to expand the fast food restaurant concept to create a place to relax and enjoy time in the restaurant. The new design was created to expand the experience after customers have eaten their meal. Customers had the opportunity to watch television, and use the Wi-Fi connections. Many of the new restaurants resemble community centers or cafés. Again, we emphasize *selected* because the vast majority of McDonald's restaurants cater to people who eat quickly and leave, use the drive-through service, or take the food off the premises.

The basic strategic thought behind the McDonald's redesign was expressed by chief operating officer Don Thompson (who later became CEO). "People eat with their eyes first. If you have a restaurant that is appealing, contemporary, and relevant, both from the street and the interior, the food tastes better."[24] It most likely would have been a strategic error for McDonald's executives to have redesigned all its restaurants because untold millions of people throughout the world like the basic McDonald's restaurant.

Being strategic about design is a continuing process, because the strategist has to take the initiative to call for a redesign, or an adaptation of the design over time. For example, the luxury vehicles carrying the Lincoln brand were redesigned in appearance in 2012, because the long-standing design had lost much of its appeal. Spearheaded by a chief designer hired from rival Cadillac, the redesign boosted sales, including attracting more customers who are not seniors.[25]

SUGGESTIONS FOR APPLICATION

A major career skill to develop is to become a strategic, proactive thinker. Strategic thinkers are valued in the executive suite, as well as at other organizational levels. The following are a few suggestions for developing strategic thinking skills:

1. *Train yourself to look at the overall perspective and the consequences of your actions.* A strategic thinker takes into account the implications of his or her actions throughout the organization, also referred to as "systems thinking." For example, a non-strategic thinker might say, "Why spend money planting trees on our property? We must cut expenses." The strategic, long-term point of view would be, "If we can find the money to plant trees now, our facility will be more attractive to customers, employees, and potential employees in the future."

2. *Constantly question your own opinions.* Develop the habit of searching for opinions contrary to yours to sharpen your insights. You might think, for example, that the product or service you are championing has a glorious future and no major changes are needed. Seek different opinions to verify your thinking. Interacting with people from different disciplines and different political perspectives can help you question your own opinions.

3. *Recharge your brain and body regularly.* Strategic thoughts are the most likely to emerge when you feel relaxed enough to carefully reflect on the present and the future.

4. *Anticipate the future with a broad perspective.* Engage in such activities as looking for game-changing information at the periphery of your industry and building external networks. In this way you might be able to identify disrupters early.

5. *Think critically by challenging common wisdom about your organization or organizational unit.* A company might have a stable group of suppliers, but it would still be helpful to ask what the company would do if a few of these suppliers went out of business at once. Be proactive about developing contingency plans to deal with such a difficult-to-manage turn of events.

SUMMARY

The business strategist must be proactive about the future and point the firm in the right direction. Strategic thinking, including the ability to proactively search for new directions for an organization, is a highly valued and relatively rare ability. The most elegant contribution of strategic thinking is for the leader to point the organization to prosper in a space that others have not yet explored. The Blue Ocean Strategy makes the competition irrelevant because others have not yet discovered the market space. The actions to take to implement the Blue Ocean Strategy stem from answering four questions, including: Which factors should be raised well above the industry standard? Which factors should be created that the industry has never offered?

Proactive thinking can make a key contribution to a company's survival and reputation, such as company leadership taking a proactive stance to recall a faulty line of products rather than waiting for complaints. The proactive thinker must identify what situation or condition needs changing before developing a strategy to bring about the change. Part of being a strategic thinker is to know when it is time to change a core business. One of the questions to ask is, "What is the state of our core differentiation?"

A hidden asset within a core business can be the centerpiece of a new strategy. Hidden assets tend to fall into the categories of (a) an undervalued business platform, (b) untapped insights into consumers, and (c) unexploited capabilities. These hidden assets have to be thought about proactively. This most sustained profitable growth occurs when a company extends beyond the boundaries of its core business into adjacent space. Certain successful companies profitably outgrow their competitors by developing a formula for expanding these boundaries, in predictable ways that can be repeated many times. Two suggestions for growth into adjacent space are (a) expand along the value chain, and (b) address new customer segments, often by modifying a proven product or technology. Taking the offense during poor business conditions can sometimes be profitable.

A disruptive innovation is aimed at serving a market of new or less demanding customers with a product that may be inferior, or easier to use. To understand whether disruption is feasible, it helps to ask if there are customers at the low end of the market who would be happy to purchase a product with less, but adequate, performance at a lower price. A key strategic and proactive skill for the executive or market specialist is to identify company- or industry-disrupting changes that are approaching that could help or damage the company. To become more proactive in identifying disruptions, some executives visit technology hubs or consult with specialists in technology and innovation. Looking at new sources of competition can be helpful.

A courageous business strategy is to reinvent the organization in response to perceived negative trends or forces in the outside world. The reinvention strategy is proactive to the extent that the leader or leadership team perceives the need for reinvention before the organization is in crisis.

Strategic thinking can be directed at dealing with complementors – companies acting alone that provide complementary products or services. Complementary products and services have been recognized for a long time, such as printers and ink cartridges. The strategic and proactive aspects of complementor relationships take place when the strategist searches for complementary products and services, and attempts to enhance relationships with complementors. Both hard-power and soft-power tactics can be used to build these relationships.

A strategy of quality is particularly proactive when a company strategist recognizes that by providing higher quality, the company might gain advantage. Good design can be strategic when it is used to gain competitive advantage, and it requires proactive thinking and behavior to visualize how improved design, or a radically new design, might give a company an edge.

A major career skill to develop is to become a strategic, proactive thinker. Suggestions for developing strategic thinking skills include (a) train yourself to look at the overall perspective and the consequences of your actions, (b) anticipate the future with a broad perspective, and (c) think critically about challenging common wisdom about your organization or organizational unit.

REFERENCES

1. Jeff Chu, "Forget $100 Million: Michelle Rhee Wants to Spend a Billion!" *Fast Company*, February 2011, p. 96.
2. "Michelle Rhee's StudentsFirst Influence Targeted In Report By New York Group," *Huff Post Politics* (www.huffingtonpost.com), May 10, 2013, pp. 1–3. Retrieved May 22, 2013.
3. Cited in Patricia Sellers, "The Queen of Pop," *Fortune*, September 28, 2009, p. 108.
4. W. Chan Kim and Rene Mauborgne, "Blue Ocean Strategy," *Harvard Business Review*, October 2004, pp. 76–85.
5. Alan Murray, "What is Blue Ocean Strategy?" *The Wall Street Journal* (http://guides.wasj.com), April 7, 2009, pp. 1–2. Retrieved May 25, 2013.
6. "Blue Ocean Strategy," http://vectorstudy.com/management, pp. 1–12. Retrieved May 16, 2013.
7. Brian Bass, "Examples of Organizations That Use Proactive Stances,"

Demand Media (http://smallbusienss.chron.com). Retrieved May 16, 2013.

8. "Toro Recalls Zero Turn Riding Mowers Due to Fire Hazard," *United States Consumer Safety Commission* (www.epsc.gov), May 9, 2013, pp. 1–2. Retrieved May 16, 2013.

9. Chris Zook, "Finding Your Next Core Business," *Harvard Business Review*, April 2007, pp. 66–75.

10. Chris Zook and James Allen, "Growth Outside the Core," *Harvard Business Review*, December 2003, pp. 57–64. Most of the examples presented in the description of the research are new.

11. Verne Harnish, "Five Ways to Get Your Strategy Right," *Fortune*, April 11, 2011, p. 42.

12. Clayton Christensen and Michael E. Raynor, *The Innovator's Solution: Creating and Sustaining Successful Growth* (Boston: Harvard Business School Press, 2003); Simon Phipps, "Disruption as a Business Strategy," *InfoWorld* (http://.infoworldl.com), July 7, 2009, pp. 1–2. Retrieved February 15, 2013.

13. Christensen and Raynor, *The Innovator's Solution.*

14. Michael Birshan and Jayanti Kar, "Becoming More Strategic: Three Tips for Any Executive," *McKinsey Quarterly* (www.mckinseyquarterly.com), July 2012, pp. 1–5. Retrieved January 13, 2013.

15. Christina Chaey et al. (interviewers), "The Disrupters," *Fast Company*, December 2001/January 2012, p. 109.

16. Simon Phipps, "Disruption as a Business Strategy, " http://www.mysql.com. Retrieved May 18, 2013.

17. Diane Brady (as told to), "John Chambers," *Businessweek Bloomberg*, August 27–September 2, 2012, p. 76.

18. Idris Mootee, "The Five Rules of Business Reinvention: What Can You Learn from Burberry?" *Innovation Playground* (http://mootee.typepad.com), June 4, 2012, pp. 1–7. Retrieved December 15, 2012.

19. Denise Cooper, "How Can You Reinvent Your Business?" *Task* (www.task.fm), 2012. Retrieved January 15, 2013.

20. David B. Yoffie and Mary Kwak, "With Friends Like These: The Art of Managing Complementors," *Harvard Business Review*, September 2006, pp. 88–98.

21. Yoffie and Kwak, "With Friends Like These," pp. 91–96.

22. Holly Ocasio Rizzo, "On Track to Tale Back Auto Market," *Hispanic Business*, November 2009, pp. 36–41. The quote is from p. 38.

23. Cliff Kuang, "Good Design is Good Business," *Fast Company*, October 2012, pp. 78–89.

24. Quoted in Ben Paynter, "McDonald's $2.4 Billion Makeover," *Fast Company*, October 2010, pp. 104–112; "New McDonald's Restaurant Design," http://retaildesigns.blogspot.com, April 27, 2012, pp. 1–3. Retrieved April 14, 2013.

25. "Redesigning the Lincoln," *CBS News* (www.cbsnews.com), December 2, 2012, pp. 1–2. Retrieved April 15, 2013.

26. Suggestions 2 through 5 are based on Paul J. H. Schoemaker, "6 Habits of True Strategic Thinkers," Inc. (www.inc.com), May 20, 2012, pp. 1–5 and Shaun Rein, "Three Keys to Improving Your Strategic Thinking," *Forbes.com* (www.forbes.com), November 9, 2010, pp. 1–2. Retrieved June 1, 2013.

9. Problem prevention and proactivity

A major component of the proactive personality is to take action to influence the environment. One of many ways to influence the environment is to prevent problems from taking place. Problem prevention contributes to productivity because many problems, such as having a serious accident, reduce productivity. In recent years, Somali pirates have been stepping up their attacks against cargo ships, including hostage taking. To deal with modern pirates, ship owners, often encouraged by their insurers, have resorted to a variety of old and new tactics, including razor wire, fire hoses, safe rooms, long-range acoustic devices, and laser dazzlers.

All of these methods have some utility in reacting to pirate attacks. Yet, Lars Gustafson, senior vice-president of marine practice at Marsh insurance brokerage, found that proactivity about piracy pays bigger dividends. He explains that, "Not one ship has been taken that has an armed security team on board." For a tanker moving across a high-risk sea, an armed, four-person security team costs about $30,000. Although this is expensive, insurers are willing to discount premiums by as much as $20,000 for employing a security team. A tally showed that the armaments both counter-attacked and prevented piracy. In 1000 passages in treacherous waters, there were 90 encounters with pirates. Seventy-two were blocked simply by showing arms. Three other attacks were deterred by warning shots fired into the air, and 15 by single shots fired near the pirate vessel.[1] Other methods to help prevent attacks from sea pirates include avoid discussing a ship's route or cargo while in port, avoiding bottle necks in shipping lanes, and searching the ship before leaving port for the presence of unauthorized passengers.[2]

The aspects of problem prevention covered in this chapter are divided into the following sections: proactivity and early-warning signals; planning and problem prevention; the prevention of moderate-intensity problems; and crisis prevention and proactive thinking.

PROACTIVITY AND EARLY-WARNING SIGNALS

A key perspective about problem prevention is to be on the lookout for early signals of pending problems, including a crisis. To personalize the meaning of early-warning signals, you are invited to take the quiz presented in Figure 9.1. The Institute for Crisis Management has demonstrated that the majority of crises are in fact *smoldering crises* that, with proper vigilance, could have been detected in advance. According to ICM

Rate your reactions to each of the following statements using the five-point scale: Disagree strongly (DS), Disagree (D), Neutral (N), Agree (A), Agree Strongly (AS).

No.	Statement	DS	D	N	A	AS
1.	If I saw even an ounce of fluid under my car, I would check under the hood (or have somebody else check) for a problem.	1	2	3	4	5
2.	If I smelled even a trace of smoke in my living quarters, I would search all around to see if there was a fire somewhere in my home.	1	2	3	4	5
3.	It's human nature to complain, so why take every minor customer complaint seriously?	5	4	3	2	1
4.	If I were an office manager and I noticed that our use of pens, pads, and ink cartridges had increased substantially, I would regard it as an ordinary fluctuation in demand.	5	4	3	2	1
5.	If three talented people left the organization, it would most likely mean that the company is creating voluntary turnover problems.	1	2	3	4	5
6.	If I were a hotel manager, I would study carefully the answers the guests left on the survey cards in the room or online after they returned home.	1	2	3	4	5
7.	If I saw the "check engine service" light flash on my vehicle dashboard more than once, I wouldn't worry about it for now.	5	4	3	2	1
8.	If I saw graffiti about my approach to work on a restroom wall, I would regard it simply as a joke.	5	4	3	2	1
9.	People who present scientific evidence about global warming should be dismissed as radicals or alarmists.	5	4	3	2	1
10.	Negative write-in comments on employee attitude surveys should be taken seriously.	1	2	3	4	5

Notes: scoring and interpretation: add the numbers you have circled to obtain your total score.

45–50 You have strong positive attitudes toward seriously considering early-warning signals, and therefore are likely to resolve many problems at their earliest stage.

36–44 You have an average tendency toward taking early-warning signals seriously.

10–35 You are probably not paying careful enough attention to early-warning signals of problems. Take minor negative tendencies more seriously to see if they are true indicators of upcoming problems.

Figure 9.1   The early-warning index

data, about two-thirds of crises fit into this predictable category.[3] For example, an early-warning signal that a company could face bankruptcy in the near future might be the first time the company borrows money to meet operating expenses.

Erika James and Lynn Perry Wooten believe that early-warning signals are often overlooked by management because the latter believes that serious problems only happen to other people. At the same time, members of the management team may use the defense mechanism of denial to preserve a pristine image of themselves and their organizations even in the face of contrary evidence.[4] Crisis consultant Tony Jaques reminds us that even though looking for early-warning signals is necessary to avoid major problems, it is not an easy task.[5] When the French bank Société Générale lost $7 billion (4.9 million euros) from the activities of a rogue trader in 2008, an independent panel later found that the company failed to act on 75 early-warning signals over a period of 18 months.[6]

An attempt has been made to help decision makers identify danger signals and respond to them based on *complexity science*. Among the key propositions of complexity science are that systems have many interacting elements, and that the whole is greater than the sum of the parts. David J. Snowden and Mary E. Boone have built what they label the "Cynefine Framework" that includes suggestions about dealing with early signals of problems.[7] Here we describe the basis of the framework as it relates to signal detection and taking the appropriate action. From our perspective, detecting the signals might be described as *proactive* whereas responding to them might be described as *reactive*.

1. *Simple contexts.* Such contexts assume that an ordered universe exists, where cause-and-effect relationships can be perceived and right answers can be determined based on facts. The danger signals in a simple context include (a) complacency and comfort, (b) a desire to simplify complex problems, (c) entrained thinking, (d) no challenge of received wisdom, and (d) overreliance on best practice if the context shifts. (Entrained thinking is a conditioned response that occurs when people are blocked from new ways of thinking because of perspectives they acquired in the past. In effect, the thinking drags itself along.) To respond to these danger signals, the decision maker is advised to (a) create communication channels to challenge orthodoxy, (b) stay connected without being a micromanager, (c) not assume that events are simple, and (d) recognize both the value and limitations of best practice.

2. *Complicated contexts.* As with simple contexts, complicated contexts assume that an ordered universe exists where cause-and-effect relation-

ships are perceptible, and facts lead to the right answers. The danger signals of a complicated context include (a) experts who are overconfident in their own solutions or in the efficacy of past solutions, (b) analysis paralysis, (c) expert panels, and (d) exclusion of viewpoints of non-experts. To respond to these danger signals, the decision maker is advised to (a) encourage all stakeholders to challenge expert opinions to combat entrained thinking, and (b) use experiments and games to force people to think in non-traditional ways.

3. *Complex contexts.* Such contexts are unordered because there is no apparent relationship between cause and effect. The way out of problems is based on emerging patterns. The danger signals in a complex context include (a) temptation to retreat to habitual, command-and-control leadership style, (b) temptation to look for facts rather than letting patterns emerge, and (c) desire for accelerated resolution of problems or exploitation of opportunities. To respond to these danger signals, the decision maker is advised to (a) be patient and take the time to reflect on the problem, and (b) use approaches that encourage interaction to facilitate the emergence of patterns.

4. *Chaotic contexts.* As with complex contexts, chaotic contexts are unordered because there is no apparent relationship between cause and effect. The danger signals in a chaotic context include (a) applying a command-and-control leadership style longer than needed, (b) emphasizing the "cult of the leader," (c) missed opportunity for innovation, and (d) chaos that keeps going. To respond to these danger signals, the decision maker is advised to (a) establish mechanisms, such as parallel teams, to take advantage of opportunities afforded by a chaotic environment, (b) encourage advisers to challenge your point of view after the crisis has abated, and (c) work to shift the context from chaotic to complex.

A decision maker who wanted to use the Cynefine Framework to help detect early-warning signals of problems could get some clues as to where these signals might lie. For example, the decision maker might conclude that problems were brewing if management team members were becoming too complacent about the competition and viewpoints of non-experts were being excluded from problem solving.

A classic example of detecting an early-warning signal, followed by taking constructive action, took place at Ford Motor Co. in 2006. CEO Alan Mulally sensed that a recession might be on the way because automobile sales were taking a slight dip, and dealer inventories were moving up slightly. Using Ford's assets as collateral, Mulally decided to borrow $23.6 billion from banks. Accumulating so much debt was a difficult decision, but it helped the company weather the recession, and to survive without requiring financial assistance from the federal government.[8]

Another example of the importance of looking for early-warning signals took place at a small enterprise named The FruitGuys. As a small-business owner and a pilot, the father of Chris Mittelstaedt taught him the importance of being alert to early indications of trouble. The dotcom bust of 2008 severely damaged Mittelstaedt's regional fruit delivery business, leaving his company with $50,000 of bad debt after many customers went bankrupt, and Mittelstaedt with $100,000 of personal debt. As a result, the importance of staying alert to early-warning signals took on extra meaning. Mittelstaedt says that his company was growing so fast at the time that he wasn't paying enough attention to his dashboard or thinking macro-economically. He eventually recovered by restricting The FruitGuys to include a tighter credit policy, more variable costs, and expansion into national markets.[9]

PLANNING AND PROBLEM PREVENTION

The most systematic way to prevent problems is to plan so carefully that problems do not occur. Three questions are important for the preventive planner:

- How can we position ourselves to minimize problems?
- What could possibly go wrong with what we want to accomplish?
- How can we prevent things from going wrong?

The preventive planner must keep problem prevention in proper perspective because all problems cannot be prevented, so it is better to focus on problems of higher potential damage. For example, a human resources director might not be able to prevent all problems of political incorrectness (such as a sales representative describing an Asian as an *Oriental*). Yet the director might attempt to prevent as much discrimination in hiring as possible, such as not discriminating against job applicants who are seniors.

In this section we describe a few useful planning techniques to help prevent problems: scenario planning, assuming that Murphy's Law is true, and visualization.

Scenario Planning to Help Prevent Problems

Forecasting is a way of predicting what will happen in the future. To make effective use of such knowledge it is helpful to plan how to respond to the forecasted events. *Scenario planning* is the process of preparing responses to predicted changes in conditions.[10] With scenario planning, you prepare for what the future might look like, and then do something proactive about what negative events could take place. The practice of scenario planning was pioneered in the U.S. military in the 1950s, and gained popularity in a few major business corporations in the 1970s. With the turbulence in recent times, including the airplane attacks on the World Trade Center on September 11, 2001, scenario planning has made a comeback.

A good use of scenario planning would be to figure out in advance how to deal with a serious disruption in business such as that caused by a hurricane. At the same time it would be helpful to plan for a substantial increase in business such as that caused by a hurricane. A building-supply company might face the latter problem.

One of many companies making serious use of scenario planning is JDS Uniphase Corp, a manufacturer of fiber-optic telecommunications equipment. A few years ago, as input from sales representatives showed early signs of a decrease in demand, company management started planning for the worst-case scenario. Sales orders also began to decrease. The company then decided to kill some products, combine two of its divisions, outsource more manufacturing to contractors, and close three factories with seven research and development sites, eliminating 400 jobs.[11] It is possible also for scenario planning to lead to optimistic outcomes, such as a baby-products company preparing for a forecasted surge in births.

Assuming that Murphy's Law is True

The primary version of Murphy's Law states, "If something can go wrong, it will." Although probably intended as a whimsical statement, the law serves as a useful reminder that potential problems cannot be avoided. Believing in Murphy's Law would lead a person to make contingency plans, such as purchasing a cloud-computing back-up service. Another proactive example of using Murphy's Law would be to cross-train employees and identify successors for key positions, to help cope with voluntary turnover, which is almost inevitable.

Believing in Murphy's Law is an effective mental set for problem prevention because you are likely to plan a solution to deal with the inevitable problem of something going wrong. Along these lines, many company-sponsored outdoor events such as picnics and receptions are backed up with tents. In this way the event can still proceed in case of heavy rain, hail, or a broiling sun. A dose of pessimism makes a person more predisposed to believing in Murphy's Law.

Murphy's Law can also be regarded as another statement of the *law of unintended consequences.* The key point of the law is that, quite often, when you try to do something to benefit others, you create unintended and unanticipated problems. Proactivity contributes to dealing with unintended dysfunctional consequences by anticipating what might go wrong and building controls to help reduce the possibility of the negative taking place.

A frequently observed unintended negative consequence is that men who take erectile-dysfunction drugs experience a doubled or tripled risk of acquiring a sexually transmitted disease. The finding is based on a study of 1.4 million men aged 41 or older at 344 different major employers conducted by researchers from the Massachusetts General Hospital in Boston. A contributing factor is that primary care physicians do not typically talk to older men about safe sexual practice, partly because older men run a lower risk than younger men of acquiring a sexually transmitted disease. Yet just by virtue of asking for an erectile-dysfunction drug, these men are in a high-risk category. The reason is that men who engage in behavior such as unprotected, promiscuous sex are more likely to seek out erectile-dysfunction drugs. A potential control would be to provide sex counseling to recipients of the erectile-dysfunction drugs.[12]

A business example of unintended consequences is that some companies try to reduce overheads by offering a generous program of severance pay to employees who leave voluntarily. The generous severance pay might be considered an initiative to help the individuals who leave as well as the company. However, an unanticipated problem can be that many of the more capable employees join other firms or use their severance pay to help fund becoming a business owner. There can be a brain drain that weakens rather than strengthens the firm. A proactive antidote to the problem would be to offer retention bonuses to some of the best performers.

Despite the advantages of positive thinking, a modicum of negative thinking enhances the ability to prevent problems. A potential downside of optimism is that it can lead a person to not fear risks, such as the possibility of being fired for poor performance. Also, being a little pessimistic about the future can sometimes help us reduce anxiety about potential worse-case scenarios.[13] For example, a job seeker might land a position with a start-up company that has earned hardly any revenue. Thinking about the problems of working for a company that never gets off the ground, such as not getting paid, may help that person be less anxious about the prospects of failure.

Pessimists think frequently about what could go wrong. They worry about negative outcomes others would not think of, such as five members of the executive team crashing in the same airplane. As a consequence, they are proactively arriving at solutions to problems just in case the worst-case scenario does happen.

Martin Seligman, director of the Positive Psychology Center at the University of Pennsylvania, places the need for balance between optimism and pessimism in these words: "The idea that optimism is always good is a caricature. It misses realism, it misses appropriateness, it misses the importance of negative emotion."[14]

Visualization to Prevent Future Problems

Visualization has become a multipurpose behavioral technique for achieving better results. The technique has also been referred to as "imagery rehearsal" and "mental practice," and has been used to enhance performance in a variety of settings, including sports.[15] To visualize, you create an image in your mind of what you would like to accomplish. The more senses that are incorporated into the visual image, the stronger its power. The visualizer might see, taste, hear, smell, and touch a goal. Visualization is used to prevent problems by visualizing all the problems that could occur with a new process, procedure, or product the person is developing. Corrective action in the form of a change in procedure could be made in advance. For example, the customer service manager might visualize how customers will react when they have to make 10 entries on the automated touch-tone system to answer an account inquiry. The service manager might also visualize being seated at the telephone, punching buttons and listening to complicated directions for six minutes to find out if a particular check had been cashed.

Another application of visualization would be to imagine what type of negative scenarios a person being interviewed might create for the team. The interviewer might think, "She seems so self-centered and narcissistic. I can just see her at meetings demanding so much attention for her ideas. And she would be frequently searching for compliments from the other team members. I think we should speak to a few people who know her before the team extends her an invitation to join us."

Visualization can also be used as a method of preventing problems by empathizing with the people implementing your process, procedure, product, or service. If you imagine how they would react, you might be able to prevent a problem. For example, the developer of a website for an investment company might anticipate that it would be too difficult for most people to figure out how to transfer money from one account to another. As a result, she would search for a way to simplify the process.

THE PREVENTION OF MODERATE-INTENSITY PROBLEMS

Problem prevention and opportunity seeking are both proactive actions that occasionally blur in distinction. Consider a business executive who is looking for ways to prevent poor business conditions or a flattening in sales. The executive might proceed to look for an opportunity to buffer against a downturn or a leveling off of sales. A case in point is the actions taken several years ago by Jack Ma, the founder of Chinese e-commerce company Alibaba.com, to enhance sales. As the economic crisis of 2009 lingered, he expanded aggressively overseas. He predicted that as people lost their jobs, many would enter self-employment and would want to connect with manufacturing distributors worldwide. His goal at the time was to reduce Alibaba's reliance on The People's Republic of China and turn the site into a global marketplace for importers and exporters. Ma correctly predicted that his model would work in India, in Japan, in Mexico, as well as almost anywhere. Ma's planning to succeed and prevent problems worked well, as within a few years Alibaba.com had become the world's biggest e-commerce (with some retailing included) site in terms of financial volume.[16]

In this section we describe a variety of proactive measures designed to prevent problems of less-than-crisis proportions. Crisis prevention is covered later in the chapter, although a given problem might lie in the middle of the continuum between a severe problem and a crisis.

Policies and Procedures for Problem Prevention

Policies and procedures can be helpful in preventing problems, and a few illustrative examples are presented here.

Accident prevention
Workplace accidents create human, financial, and public relations problems, and therefore are worthy of substantial preventive measures. Ambulance workers, medics, physicians, physician assistants, and nurses, among others, react to the suffering and sadness involved in an accident. Managers and human resource specialists, as well as healthcare professionals, can get involved in proactive accident strategies. Proactive monitoring provides feedback on safety performance before an accident or health problem occurs. The monitoring involves measuring compliance with the performance standards that have been established. The primary purpose of proactive monitoring is to measure success and to reinforce positive achievements. Two basic examples of proactive accident-prevention

techniques would be to (a) install flooring that is skid resistant when wet, and (b) use safety devices to assure that desktop printers cannot provide electric shocks.

One of the recommended procedures for preventing accidents is to implement checklists consisting of a series of simple questions developed by someone familiar with the risks in an area or activity. The checklist serves to focus attention on possible risks and how each risk could be identified and controlled.[17] An example for an athletic facility would be: "Are there any bolts used for holding down temporary structures that protrude from the ground still present after the structure has been removed? Search the facilities and remove any such bolts immediately."

An instructive example of the need for proactivity in managing accidents takes place among teenage workers. Teenagers are far more likely to be injured at work, although they work fewer hours and are forbidden by law to work at high-risk jobs. According to the National Institute for Occupational Safety and Health, approximately 200,000 workers less than 18 years old are injured on the job each year in the U.S. Close to 70,000 of these workers were injured seriously enough to require a visit to a hospital emergency room.

One approach to accident prevention is to screen applicants for drug use and criminal records because they might be risk takers. The harsh logic here is that a person not hired cannot have an accident at the enterprise of the employer. Basic safety training can be an effective measure for teenage workers, including instruction in the use of protective equipment, how to extinguish fires, and CPR. As the St. Louis Zoo, no person under age 18 is permitted to drive a vehicle or operate power equipment. These last two measures fall into the category of initiatives to prevent accidents, as does basic safety training.[18]

Preventive maintenance

Preventive maintenance is central to avoiding many problems. The term refers to the systematic inspection, cleaning, lubricating, and servicing of equipment. A classic management handbook defines preventive maintenance as "the art and science of discovering and diagnosing incipient failures – a breakdown about to happen."[19] Preventive maintenance is inherently proactive because you resolve potential problems proactively rather than react to them after they have taken place.

Through preventive maintenance inspections, many minor malfunctions can be discovered and corrected before they develop into breakdowns and emergencies. Without preventive maintenance, breakdowns might account for 85 percent or more of the time of maintenance technicians. When preventive maintenance is working well, the amount of time technicians spend on breakdowns can often be reduced to 15 percent. Preventive maintenance might be less important with electronic equipment than with machinery with many moving parts, but it is still important. For example, desktop computers are more likely to stay in working order if unnecessary programs that accumulate and obsolete files are occasionally purged from the hard drive.

A more complicated example of the importance of preventive maintenance related to information technology is the concept of *technical debt.* The problem refers to the "long-term consequences of poor design decisions in architecture and of customization, shortcuts and work-arounds in the code base that accumulate over time." As time passes by, software systems that are not properly maintained become more complex and their structures deteriorate. To prevent problems of technical debt it is recommended that the software development staff communicate openly with business executives about potential problems. Implementing best practices and training software developers are also effective preventive measures.[20]

Although preventive maintenance is a concept linked closely to machines, it also applies to people and services. For example, giving people encouragement, emotional support, and recognition will keep them performing well longer than if they are neglected. Preventive maintenance can be applied to services before deterioration into full-blown problems. An example would be looking for potential queuing problems when there is a peak demand for a service, such as people lining up to purchase refreshments at a concert or sporting event. A few extra temporary workers during times of peak demand can lead to greater sales volume and less customer frustration.

Appointment of chief health policy officer

A concern of many manufacturers of snack food and carbonated beverages is that they will receive considerable negative publicity because the food they offer the public is not nutritious. To be proactive about the potential problem in 2007, PepsiCo Inc. appointed Derek Yach, a former executive director of the World Health Organization and a nutrition expert. His position was soon upgraded to senior vice-president for global health. The goal of Yach and his colleagues is to create healthy options while making the less-healthy beverage and food offerings healthier. The idea of healthier foods is not to replace standard products from PepsiCo, but to meet all kinds of consumer demands. At the same time, company leadership will fend off in advance complaints that the company does not care about good nutrition.[21]

Prevention of Ethical Problems

Working toward becoming a more ethical organization has been a major concern of many types of organization in recent years. A strategic approach to ethical problems is to prevent them from happening rather than taking action to deal with them when they have arisen. Two important preventive approaches are establishing written codes of ethical conduct, and providing training in ethics and social responsibility.

Establishing written codes of ethical conduct
Many organizations use written codes of conduct as guidelines for ethical and socially responsible behavior. Such guidelines continue to grow in importance because workers in teams have less supervision than previously. Regardless of the industry, most codes deal with quite similar issues. Patricia Breeding, integrity compliance officer for Covenant Health, in Knoxville, Tennessee, says, "They all address conflicts of interest, gifts and things like vendor relationships. They use the word 'customer' in one and 'patient' in another but they're all about doing the right thing."[22]

Prohibition of bribery of government or corporate officials is being incorporated more frequently into ethical codes to combat potential major problems. For example, in 2011 U.S. regulators accused IBM of 10 years of bribery in Asia, contending that employers handed over shopping bags filled with cash in South Korea. IBM allegedly also arranged junkets for government officials in China in exchange for millions of dollars in contracts. IBM agreed to pay $10 million to settle the civil charges, which alleged that more than 100 employees of IBM subsidiaries were involved in the bribes.[23] (This case is remarkable because IBM has a positive reputation for ethics and social responsibility.)

Providing training in ethics and social responsibility
Forms of ethics training include messages about ethics and social responsibility from company leadership, classes on ethics at colleges, and programs with exercises in ethics. These training programs reinforce the idea that ethically and socially responsible behavior is both morally right and good for business. Training programs in ethics and social responsibility are most likely to be effective when the organizational culture encourages ethical behavior.

Caterpillar Inc., the manufacturer of construction and mining equipment, exemplifies a modern approach to training in ethics. During the annual training, all 95,000 employees ponder a series of questions presented to them either via the Internet or on paper. The scenarios, written in-house, encourage workers to consider the best way to behave in a particular situation. Employees are able to consult the code of ethics as they reflect on the scenarios. One scenario involves a plant-floor employee adding a cleansing agent used by other employees to the agent the employee is presently using. One of the alternatives is "Check with an environmental health and safety group to ensure the combination is safe."[24]

The Caterpillar example is instructive with respect to the challenges of preventing ethical problems. Although the training program may prevent many problems, the success rate is less than perfect. In 2011, Caterpillar was accused of demoting an executive who discovered a $2 billion tax-avoidance maneuver. The company was charged by an executive of using offshore subsidiaries in Switzerland and Bermuda to avoid $2 billion in U.S. income tax through a tax and financial statement fraud. A Caterpillar spokesperson said the company did nothing illegal with respect to tax payment.[25]

Prevention of Online Reputation Problems

A widespread problem that requires prevention is receiving unjustified negative publicity from customers, consumers, present employees, and past employees. Many websites designed for the purpose of publishing reviews of products and services are easy targets for intensely negative postings about a business firm. According to an eMarketer.com survey, 83 percent of consumers reported that online reviews influence their perceptions about business enterprises.[26] Many suggestions are available to help deal with a negative review, such as interacting in a constructive way with the poster of the negative comment. Our focus, however, is on the prevention of online reputation problems, as follows:

- *Company management must work extra hard to create fans and to deal openly with issues that make people dislike the company.* A clothing manufacturer that outsources manufacturing to low-wage countries such as Bangladesh can address the issue by setting higher health, safety, and wage standards to minimize negative publicity over the Internet.
- *Create a website that facilitates having a good reputation.* The title on the pages of the website should contain key words that will help you rank high in search results. This will help push negative reviews off the first page of search engine results. For example, a basement waterproofing company might include the two following terms in its webpage titles, "Dry basement," "Getting rid of harmful mold."
- *Purchase a set of potential negative domain names, such as http://*

companynameexploitscustomers.com. In this way, the critics will not be able to launch such a site. For example, Wal-Mart Stores, Coca-Cola Company, and Whole Foods Markets own the domain name for their brand ending in "sucks.com."[27]

Cost Cutting as Problem Prevention

In Chapter 6 we mentioned spotting an opportunity to save money as a factor that contributed to the productivity of a race-driving, team-building enterprise. A variation on this theme is to prevent a financial problem within an organization by proactively cutting costs before the company has to do so as a reactive measure. The case example chosen here to illustrate cost cutting as problem prevention is that of Greg Babe, the CEO of Bayer MaterialScience North America. He was surprised and shocked by a global executive committee proposal that his headquarters be closed. Babe turned the negative news into an opportunity to completely reshape his company, with an emphasis on cost cutting.

Babe's initiative was to assemble a war-room team of four competent and experienced managers. He assigned the team the full-time mission of assembling a picture of the company's costs that was clear enough to build a transformative cost-cutting plan. The team assembled what was referred to as a "cost cube": expense data capable of being organized and segmented along a number of different dimensions. A moment of insight took place when the team recognized that the cost structure should be determined by how the management team wanted to expand the business, not by a predetermined cost-reduction target.

The cost-cutting exercise became a growth initiative. Instead of simply eliminating a chunk of overhead, everything about the business would be redesigned to build in flexibility. The dual purpose was to profitably survive a business downturn (reactive) but more importantly to prepare for future growth (proactive). An analogy Babe used in communicating with all employees was that "We should really fix our roof while the sun is shining and not wait until the rain pours down."

Babe convinced North American headquarters management to give his division $70 million to help him cut $100 million from the $400 million in overhead costs, as well as completely transform the business. The cost-cutting plan did create the hardship of laying off hundreds of employees. The more positive side of the restructuring included retraining 1000 employees, outsourcing many operations, and modifying the company's product offerings. Specific examples of cost cutting included a more automated way of receiving money from customers, and canceling several much-loved projects because they probably had limited commercial potential.[28] So in this example, costs had to be cut to survive in the short term, as well as preventing future problems and enhancing opportunities.

CRISIS PREVENTION AND PROACTIVE THINKING

An organizational crisis has been defined in many ways, but a representative definition developed by Ericka James and Lynn Perry Wooten is as follows: "An emotionally charged situation that, once it becomes public, invites a negative stakeholder reaction, and thereby has the potential to threaten the financial well-being, reputation, or survival of the firm or some portion thereof."[29] Earlier in the chapter we described looking for early-warning signals as a key strategy for preventing problems, including crises. As Jaques notes, crisis preparedness is not the same as crisis prevention. The former refers to such methods as system planning, manuals, war-rooms, and check-lists that inform people on what to do when a crisis strikes. Crisis prevention refers to such strategies and tactics as risk assessment, environmental scan-ning, and anticipatory management.[30] Here we describe two other strategies and tactics for decreasing the probability that a crisis will take place.

Disaster Planning

Planning for a disaster does not prevent a crisis, but it helps lessen the intensity of a future crisis. In a sense, some of the worst consequences of a crisis can be prevented, including reducing the number of deaths and injuries that might otherwise take place. A case in point is the dis-aster planning of George Boué, the vice-president of human resources at Stiles Corp., a real estate management company. Stiles is located in Fort Lauderdale, Florida, a geographic area prone to hurricanes. Boué says that skillful crisis management involves establishing an effective team in advance and thinking through what might be needed. For Stiles that takes the form of having counselors on call, cleanup crews, and roofers under contract. Assuring that building structures are as hurricane resistant as possible is another preventive measure. Boué says that every contingency cannot be anticipated, but having a team in place and a careful disaster plan is an important initiative.[31]

Closely related to disaster planning is for an organization to build up cash reserves. An organization can easily enter a crisis mode if it faces a financial crisis based on such negative events as a massive product recall or a class-action suit encompassing thousands of employees and/or custom-ers. Another example of a cash-draining crisis would be for a judge to rule that a technology or pharmaceutical company was guilty of patent violation. The company would therefore have to both stop selling a product and make a huge cash settlement to the company suing over the patent violation. In the opinion of John O. Whitney, nothing is more important for a successful turnaround than cash. Financial managers therefore have to devise a system for gathering accurate information about the company's true cash picture.[32]

Preventing Workplace Violence

A recurring crisis is workplace violence, when the violence involves serious injury or death. Violence has become so widespread that homicide is the fourth leading cause of workplace deaths, with about 500 workers murdered each year in the United States. According to the Bureau of Labor Statistics Census of Fatal Occupations, homicides account for about 10 percent of all fatal workplace injuries [33] Homicide is the leading cause of death for women in the workplace. Most workplace deaths result from a robbery or commercial crime. Many of these killings, however, are perpetrated by a disgruntled worker or fired employee harboring an unresolved conflict. As companies have continued to reduce their workforce despite being profitable, these incidents have increased in frequency.

Programs to prevent violence

Many organizations have installed programs to help prevent violence in the workplace. According to the Federal Bureau of Investigation, supervisors and their employees can take certain actions to reduce these incidents of violence. First, it is critical to understand that workplace violence does not happen randomly. Rather, perpetrators usually display some behaviors of concern. Thus, awareness of these indicators and the subsequent implementation of an action plan to de-escalate potentially violent situations are essential components of workplace violence prevention.

Behaviors of concern can help workers recognize potential problems with fellow employees. If a coworker begins acting differently, determining the frequency, duration, and intensity of the new, and possibly troubling, behavior can prove helpful. Specific behaviors of concern that should increase vigilance for coworkers and supervisors include sadness, depression, threats, menacing or erratic behavior, aggressive outbursts, references to weaponry, verbal abuse, inability to handle criticism, hypersensitivity to perceived slights, and offensive commentary or jokes referring to violence. These behaviors – when observed in clusters and coupled with diminished work performance (as manifested by increased tardiness or absences, poor coworker relations, and decreased productivity) – may suggest a heightened potential for violence.

Relationship problems (e.g., emotional/psychological or physical abuse, separation, or divorce) can carry over from home to the work setting. Certain signs that may help determine if a coworker is experiencing such difficulties include disruptive phone calls and e-mails, anxiety, poor concentration, unexplained bruises or injuries, frequent absences and tardiness, use of unplanned personal time, and disruptive visits from current or former partners. Other predictors of workplace violence include the following employee behaviors and verbal expressions: talk about weaponry, paranoid (highly suspicious) or antisocial behavior, reference to not being heard by management, expression of extreme desperation, history of violence, and being a loner who does not fit into the group. Multiple behaviors such as those just described might be reported to the manager or human resource professional. No single behavior is more suggestive of violence than another. All actions have to be judged in the proper context and in totality to determine the potential for violence.

Intervention

Intervention strategies must take into account two aspects of the workplace violence spectrum: action and flash points. An action point is the moment when an individual recognizes that an employee may be on the path toward committing some type of violent act in the workplace and subsequently takes action to prevent it. Action points offer an opportunity for coworkers to intervene before a situation becomes dangerous. When an action point has been identified, fellow employees can intervene in a number of ways. First, they can talk with the person and "check in" to see if everything is all right. Allowing people to vent about stressful life situations can help them release tension. This type of intervention should be used cautiously. If the individuals display potentially threatening behaviors of concern, vigilant coworkers should report these directly to a supervisor.

Workers also can relay information regarding questionable behaviors to their human resources or security department, ombudsman, or employee assistance program. Moreover, if employees feel unable to directly approach someone about a coworker, they can communicate their concerns via an e-mail or text message. Companies have used drop boxes, 24-7 tip lines, and ethics hotlines to allow employees to report suspicious behavior while maintaining their anonymity.[34]

SUGGESTIONS FOR APPLICATION

1. An effective way of preventing problems not already mentioned in this chapter is to accurately forecast potential problems, using whatever

forecasting techniques are available. Contingency planning begins with forecasting. Based on past experience, managers and corporate professionals should estimate the types of normal-scale problems and crisis that could occur. For example, a pharmaceutical company might predict future recalls based on the percentage of previous recalls. A practical example of proactive problem prevention is that many consumer products have tamper-resistant packaging to prevent poisoning of the contents of packages on store shelves.

2. Although it might be possible to find a mathematical model or statistical forecasting technique to uncover which types of problem might require prevention, quite often a judgmental technique will suffice. A judgmental forecast is a prediction based on a collection of subjective opinions, including crowdcasting (obtaining hundreds of opinions online). For example, employees throughout the organization might be asked their opinion about potential problems facing the company.

3. In terms of forecasting major problems, it is important not to cry wolf too often. Forecasts of impending crises will ultimately be ignored if too many past predictions were made of crises that did not materialize.

SUMMARY

Problem prevention contributes to productivity because many problems, such as having a serious accident, reduce productivity. A key perspective about problem prevention is to look out for early signals of pending problems. Early-warning signals are often overlooked by management because they believe that serious problems only happen to other people. Looking for these signals can be difficult.

An attempt has been made to help decision makers identify danger signals and respond to them based on complexity science. A framework related to signal detection includes simple, complicated, complex, and chaotic contexts. Each context has its own danger signals and responses to those danger signals. An example of a danger signal is complacency and comfort, and an example of responding to a danger signal would be to challenge orthodoxy.

The most systematic way to prevent problems is to plan so carefully that problems do not occur. A good question to ask would be, "What could possibly go wrong with what we want to accomplish?" Scenario planning is the process of preparing responses to forecasted changes in conditions. A good use of scenario planning would be to figure out in advance how to deal with a serious disruption in business such as that caused by a hurricane.

Believing in Murphy's Law would lead a person to make contingency plans, such as purchasing a cloud-computing back-up service. The law is also an effective mental set for problem prevention because you are likely to plan a solution to deal with the inevitable problem of something going wrong. The key point of the law of unintended consequences is that quite often when you try to do something to benefit others, you create unintended and unanticipated consequences. A modicum of negative thinking enhances the ability to prevent problems.

Visualization is used to prevent problems by visualizing all the problems that could occur with a new process, procedure, product, or service the person is developing. Corrective action in the form of a change in procedure could be made in advance. Visualization can also be used as a method of preventing problems by empathizing with the people implementing your process, procedure, product, or service.

Problem prevention and opportunity seeking are both proactive actions that occasionally blur in distinction. Policies and procedures for problem prevention include (a) accident prevention, (b) preventive maintenance, and (c) appointment of a chief health policy officer. Prevention of ethical problems includes (a) establishing written codes of ethical conduct, and (b) providing training in ethics and social responsibility.

A widespread problem that requires prevention is receiving unjustified negative publicity from customers, consumers, present employees, and past employees. One preventive measure is for company management to work extra hard to create fans and to deal openly with issues that make people dislike the company. Cost cutting can sometimes be used for problem prevention by proactively cutting costs before the company has to do so as a reactive measure.

Crisis prevention includes looking for early-warning signals. Disaster planning can prevent some of the worst consequences of the disaster, and building up cash reserves is included as part of the planning. Preventing workplace violence includes programs to predict violence, and intervention techniques.

An effective way of preventing a variety of problems is to accurately forecast potential problems. Contingency planning begins with forecasting. Quite often a judgmental forecast, including crowdsourcing, will be effective in predicting problems.

REFERENCES

1. Bryan Keogh, Oliver Suess, and Jesse Westbrook, "The Arms Race Against the Pirates," *Bloomberg Businessweek*, April 28–May 1, 2011, p. 55.

2. Tracy V. Wilson, "How Pirates Work," *HowStuffWorks* (http://people. howstuffwork.com), Retrieved May 22, 2013.
3. *www.crisisexperts.org*, cited in Tony Jaques, "The Leadership Role in Crisis Prevention," in Andrew J. DuBrin, editor, *The Handbook of Research on Crisis Leadership in Organizations* (Cheltenham, UK/Northampton, MA, USA: Edward Elgar, 2013), p. 274.
4. Erika James and Lynn Perry Wooten, "Leadership as (un)Usual: How to Display Competence in Times of Crisis," *Organizational Dynamics*, Number 2, pp. 141–152.
5. Jaques, "The Leadership Role in Crisis Prevention," p. 281.
6. N. Clark, "Société Générale Posts Record Loss on Trading Scandal, Subprime Exposure," *International Herald Tribune* (www.iht.com), February 21, 2008. Retrieved January 9, 2013.
7. David J. Snowden and Mary E. Boone, "A Leader's Framework for Decision Making," *Harvard Business Review*, November 2007, pp. 68–76.
8. Alex Taylor III, "Fixing Up Ford," *Fortune*, May 25, 2009, p. 46.
9. Amanda C. Kooser, Lindsay Holloway, Nichole L. Torres, and Sara Wilson, "Young Millionaires," *Entrepreneur*, September 2009, p. 69.
10. Cari Tuna, "Pendulum Is Swinging Back on 'Scenario Planning,'" *The Wall Street Journal*, July 6, 2009, p. B6.
11. Tuna, "Pendulum Is Swinging Back on 'Scenario Planning.'"
12. Study cited in David Gutierrez, "Men Who Take Viagra Have 200 Percent Increased Risk of Sexually-Transmitted Disease," *Natural News.com* (www. naturalnews.com), October 30, 2012, pp. 1–4. Retrieved March 13, 2013.
13. Oliver Burkeman, "The Power of Negative Thinking," *The Wall Street Journal*, December 8–9, 2012, p. C3.
14. Quoted in Annie Murphy Paul, "The Uses and Abuses of Optimism (and Pessimism)," *Psychology Today*, November/December 2011, p. 63.
15. Stephen Kraus, "Visualization for Success," *DotFit* (weww.dotfit.com), Copyright 2008–2013, pp. 1–2. Retrieved April 21, 2013.
16. Esmé E. Depres, Mehul Srivastava, and Manuel Baigorri, "At Alibaba, Investors Come Last," *Businessweek*, August 17, 2009, p. 049.
17. www.Accident course homefreeUK.net/mike.everly/download/oc.pdf, pp. 1–8. Retrieved May 20, 2013.
18. Alice Andors, "Keeping Teen Workers Safe," *HR Magazine*, June 2010, pp. 76–80.
19. Sylvan L. Kapner, "Maintenance Management," in H. B. Maynard, editor-in-chief, *Handbook of Business Administration* (New York: McGraw-Hill, 1967), Section 7, p. 57.
20. Bill Roberts, "Debt Crisis," *HR Magazine*, March 2012, pp. 87–90. The quote is from p. 87 of the same article.
21. Nanette Byrnes, "Pepsi Brings in the Health Police," *Bloomberg Businessweek*, January 25, 2010, pp. 50–51.
22. Quoted in Joanne Lozar Glenn, "Making Sense of Ethics," *Business Education Forum*, October 2004, p. 10.
23. Jessica Holzer and Shayndi Raice, "IBM Settles Bribery Charges," *The Wall Street Journal*, March 19–20, 2011, p. B1.
24. Jean Thilmany, "Supporting Ethical Employees," *HR Magazine*, September 2007, p. 108.
25. Peter S. Green, "Caterpillar Accused of Demoting Executive Discovering

$2 Billion Tax Dodge," *Bloomberg* (www.bloomberg.com), July 8, 2011, pp. 1–6. Retrieved May 3, 2013.

26. Tasha Cunningham, "Protect Your Online Business Reputation," *Miami Herald* (www.miamiherald.com), June 18, 2012, pp. 1–2. Retrieved May 18, 2013.

27. Emily Steel, "How to Handle 'I Hate Your Company.com'," *The Wall Street Journal*, September 5, 2008, p. B5; Angus Loten, "Web-Reputation Managers Get a Bad Rap," *The Wall Street Journal*, July 26, 2012, p. B5.

28. Gregory S. Babe, "The CEO of Bayer Corp. On Creating a Lean Growth Machine," *Harvard Business Review*, July–August 2011, pp. 41–45.

29. James and Wooten, "Leadership as (un)Usual," p. 142.

30. Jaques, "The Leadership Role in Crisis Prevention," p. 272.

31. Cited in Tamara Lytle, "Rising from the Rubble," *HR Magazine*, September 2011, p. 66.

32. John O. Whitney, "Turnaround Management Every Day," *Harvard Business Review*, September–October 1987, p. 52.

33. "Workplace Violence," www.osha.gov. Retrieved April 30, 2013.

34. Stephen J. Romano, Micòl E. Levi-Minzi, Eugene A. Rugala, and Vincent B. Vah Hasselt, "Workplace Violence Prevention: Readiness and Response," *FBI Law Enforcement Bulletin* (www.fbi.gov/stats), January 2011, pp. 1–5; Susan M. Heathfield, "Workplace Violence: Violence Can Happen; Recognizing the Potential for Workplace Violence," *About.com Human Resources.* 2009. Retrieved May 4, 2013.

10. Talent management and proactivity

Many of the activities traditionally included in human resource management are now referred to as "talent management" because the employees represent the talent the organization needs to function. An instructive definition of talent management is "a deliberate approach to attract, develop, and retain people with the aptitude and abilities to meet current and future organizational needs."[1] Considerable proactivity is required to accomplish these ends.

The relatively new practice of *employer branding* illustrates the type of proactivity involved in talent management. Some employees find that to recruit the best candidates, they need to exert the same effort they do to develop and market consumer brands. Employer brands target potential employees to project the image of the company as a desirable place to work. One of the factors prompting branding is that even when the unemployment rate is high, there is a limited supply of the most skilled candidates.

PepsiCo Inc. is one example of a company that has launched an employer-branding campaign in recent years. Paul Marchand, vice-president of global talent acquisition, was concerned that high-level candidates thought PepsiCo had positions available only for people with experience in the food and beverage industry. The company then launched a campaign including videos on its careers website and iPad app, plus posts on LinkedIn, Facebook, and Twitter to reflect the employer brand.[2] Although the impact of employer branding is difficult to measure, case history research suggests that the right brand for an employer can help in attracting and retaining talented workers.[3]

In this chapter we describe several aspects of talent management in which proactive thinking and behavior makes a contribution: talent management planning; enhancing employee wellness; offering attractive benefits; and succession planning.

TALENT MANAGEMENT PLANNING AND PROACTIVITY

Talent management planning, or workforce planning, is inherently proactive because such planning attempts to control the future. Talent management planning is the process of providing for the movement of people into, within, and out of an organization to support the firm's business strategy. The planner attempts to make things happen by having the right number, and right kinds, of people at the right time. Our intent here is not to present an overview of talent management planning, but to illustrate how proactivity contributes to its success in three areas: recruiting for future needs, diversity initiatives, and initiatives for employee retention.

Recruitment for Future Needs

Predicting the future needs of the organization depends both on the workforce that will be available and the needs of the organization for which the manager or human resource professional is making predictions. Another major factor is the business strategy of the organization, such as whether the company will have physical stores, online stores, or outsource manufacturing and customer support.

Workforce planning

Workforce planning is proactive because it forecasts not only the number and type of employees to meet future business needs, but the ratio of internal to external resources and the skills mix. Predicting the mix of skills that will be needed is difficult because the mix may change as the business moves forward. Another future factor to consider is anticipated spans of control: with wider spans fewer managers will be needed, and there are likely to be fewer layers of management.[4]

Scenario planning can be used to help human resource professionals visualize what types of workers their organization will need in the future. The same type of planning can suggest how to create the type of environment and organizational culture that will attract the needed workers. A germane example is Oticon, a hearing-aid manufacturer located in Copenhagen, Denmark. Faced with a shortage of engineers in the country, combined with a strong need for engineers, the director of human resources helped design a workplace to appeal to them. The workspace is open, with few walls and cubicles. The entire building is equipped with Wi-Fi and Internet access so the engineers can have impromptu brainstorming sessions.[5]

An example of a sophisticated approach to proactively recruiting for the future takes place at weapons maker Alliant Technosystems Inc. (ATK).

The company began a metrics approach to anticipating future recruiting needs, with the goal of improving the recruiting capability of one division. With success in one division as a starting point, the company continues to attain greater precision in anticipating its future demand and supply of technical workers. Based on an analysis of previous instances of involuntary turnover, a "flight-risk model" is used to calculate the probability of attrition for each employee. In one year, for example, ATK accurately projected high turnover in a key plant maintenance group.

A model such as that used at ATK can help a firm prepare for turnover and take proactive steps to reduce the problem. One approach is to develop targeted recognition programs to attempt to retain turnover risks. Furthermore, the company can step up recruiting when the turnover risks rise for difficult-to-replace talent.[6]

Initiatives for cultural and demographic diversity
Developing a diverse workforce is both a strategy and an informal practice in the majority of organizations. Proactivity is frequently required for an organization to recruit the culturally and demographically diverse talented workers it wants and needs. Several examples of this type of proactive thinking are described next.

1. Proactivity to appeal to a diverse customer base Many companies take some initiative to appeal to a culturally and demographically diverse customer base. Verizon Corporation, however, has taken unusually robust initiatives to cater to the language preferences of its Latino customers. A major reason for thinking proactively about how to have a targeted appeal to Latinos is that two-thirds of the U.S. Latino population is concentrated in four of Verizon's largest markets: New York, Florida, Texas, and California. Several hundred thousand Verizon customers received their bills in Spanish. New York-based Verizon developed a staff multicultural marketing team and works with advertising and marketing firms that specialize in targeting Hispanics and other minorities. The company stays visible in minority communities by supporting events such as the Latin Grammys.

An indirect Verizon initiative in terms of appealing to diverse customers is to have the workforce reflect the diversity of its customers. To meet that goal, 36 percent of the company's employees and 39 percent of its management team are minorities. Verizon has also taken the initiative to offer mentoring and development programs such as the Hispanic Professional Development Workshop. Furthermore, company leadership has for many years promoted cultural diversity among its suppliers. Verizon CEO Ivan Seidenberg says that, "These relationships contribute to customer loyalty, stimulate economic development and tap into the innovation and entre-preneurship we need to win in a competitive marketplace."[7]

2. A major corporation initiative to welcome LGBT employees   Officials from most companies, if asked, would say that they welcome gay, lesbian, bisexual, and transgender employees. Leadership at IBM has been proac-tive since 1995 in making members of the LGBT demographic group feel welcome, starting with a LGBT taskforce. Furthermore, IBM was one of the first companies to have diversity and inclusion policies that mention specifically the LGBT community. IBM continues to lead the way by creating an atmosphere where LGBT employees are not only valued, but encouraged to think freely and be themselves. A company spokesperson believes that the encouragement enables LGBT employees at IBM to fully contribute to the workplace and to clients.

Brad Salavich, a former LGBT diversity manager for IBM in Armonk, New York, points to the advantages that proactive LGBT policies can have on a company's reputation and applicants. He notes that employers who attract and support LGBT applicants and employees have an edge in gaining a fair share of talent. Salavich says, "They want the best employ-ees, and they want a reputation among applicants as having a culture that supports women, minorities, and LGBTs."[8]

3. A large-scale initiative to attract disabled workers   Several years ago Walgreens, a major player in pharmaceutical retailing, opened a state of the art distribution center in Windsor, Connecticut, designed specifically to employ people with disabilities. As with a previously opened distribu-tion center, the goal was to have people with disabilities hold at least one-third of the available positions. Approximately 50 percent of the Windsor distribution employees have disclosed physical or cognitive disabilities, including autism. Deb Russell, the Walgreens manager of outreach and employee services, noted when the center opened that the company had long recruited and hired workers with disabilities. However, the experi-ence of creating a disability-friendly environment in the distribution center was "the first time we have looked at the issue in a systemic, holistic way. It has been a transforming event."[9]

More than one dozen major U.S. companies have followed the Walgreens initiative of hiring disabled workers for distribution centers. Barbara Otto, a specialist in preparing disabled workers for full-time employment, observes that other initiatives employers can take to recruit disabled workers include job boards built around the disability commu-nity and job fairs designed to attract the disabled. Otto also encourages employers to look for ways to fill a larger number of higher-level positions with disabled workers, not just assembly line-type distribution center positions.[10]

4. A training program for minority vendors   Terry J. Lundgren, the chief executive officer at Macy's, has spearheaded an initiative to develop a close relationship with minority customers. He decided to seek out small retailers already serving minority customers and stock their products on the shelves of the many Macy's stores. This example is different from the three just presented because the aim is to attract culturally diverse suppliers and customers rather than employees. Yet, the presence of culturally diverse customers and suppliers may facilitate minority recruiting.

Recognizing that small-business firms often lack the resources to serve a major retailer, Macy's developed a training program to aide minority vendors. Participants receive information and guidance about large-scale retailing, and the most promising are awarded the opportunity to sell through Macy's. One winner makes dresses primarily for Hispanic women, another finalist designs cosmetics targeted at African-American women, and another makes plus size swimsuits. Top-level management at Macy's forecast that this cultural diversity initiative would result in sales of goods from minority-owned and women-owned businesses of $1 billion annually two years after the program had begun.[11]

Initiatives for employee retention

A major strategy of talent management is to retain valuable employees, and any aspect of talent management can contribute to retention. Being proactive about selecting employees who are a good fit for the organization will ultimately result in lower voluntary turnover, and therefore higher retention. Also, recruiting enough employees from one demographic group to form a critical mass will often result in less involuntary turnover among other members of the same demographic group. For example, an employee who uses a wheelchair is likely to feel more welcome working for an organization where there are other wheelchair users.

One particularly proactive aspect of enhancing retention is to look for indicators of possible turnover, and then intervene to prevent the turnover. (The flight-risk model at a weapons maker mentioned above incorporated this approach.) The proactive approach includes investing in retention in the present even if turnover is low, such as paying the expenses of key workers to attend professional conferences to make them feel valued. Using turnover data with other data to predict future worker turnover shifts such data analysis from the passive to the proactive mode.

According to human resources consultant Brian Wilkerson, four general attributes and behaviors that can affect turnover at any organization are

(a) the local economy, (b) the characteristics of the job, (c) the frequency rate of employee promotions, and (d) the pay increase frequency. The task of the proactive analyst is to figure which of these four factors might be significant at a given time in a given organization. A relevant example is that promotion statistics can be a harbinger for involuntary turnover among high-potential workers. More than three years in the same position can provoke turnover intentions. An economic factor associated with turnover is that when personal consumption increases, turnover increases 30 to 60 days later as the labor market expands to meet increased demand.

Changes in employee behavior can also be predictive of turnover intention. A major clue of attrition risk is when a worker becomes more quiet than is typical. The increase in quietness could be related to a personal problem, yet the intervention of the supervisor talking with the employee could be helpful in preventing unwanted turnover.[12] The conversation might reveal that the worker is unhappy with a work factor, or has a personal problem requiring attention. Referral to a company-sponsored counseling service could be the intervention of choice.

ENHANCING EMPLOYEE WELLNESS

A domain of human resource and talent management based heavily on prevention and proactivity is the promotion of employee wellness, or a state of good health rather than an absence of illness or injury. The importance of health-problem prevention was explained succinctly by Ralph de la Torre, CEO of Steward Health Care System, a group of community hospitals based in Massachusetts. He believes that many countries must change the fundamental way in which healthcare is managed.

In his analysis, the United States is a society that believes you lead life the way you want to, and then at the end, when health starts failing rapidly, you apply resources and get interventions from medical specialists to keep you alive longer and more healthily. De la Torre believes this approach is back ended, and an extremely expensive way of getting healthcare. A problem facing the country at the start of the Affordable Health Care Act was that it had never paid for wellness or prevention in the past. With the younger generation, it will be possible to focus more on wellness and prevention.[13]

An employee wellness program is a company-sponsored activity designed to support employees to learn and sustain behaviors that reduce health risk, improve quality of life, and enhance personal effectiveness. These programs are designed to prevent many problems that could result in employee illness and sometimes injury, absenteeism, work stress, and medical insurance claims. As employees avoid becoming emotionally and physically unhealthy, illness-related costs for the employer often decrease.[14] For these programs to work, the employee must be motivated to experience good physical and mental health.

The employee wellness movement in business, education, government, and non-profit organizations is a vast topic. Our primary concern is to indicate how wellness programs are highly proactive in the sense of anticipating potential problems, and taking action before the problems occur.

Table 10.1 summarizes the type of proactive interventions attempted in wellness programs. A basic initiative of an employee wellness program would be to ensure that employees had regular medical checkups to detect present or potential physical health problems. Equally basic would be to provide employees the opportunity for physical exercise to help prevent such health problems as morbid obesity, high blood pressure, and weak bones likely to fracture in a fall.

Another example of the proactivity of wellness programs is an attempt to prevent accidents among remote workers. Employers and employees often neglect workplace safety practices including ergonomics for remote workers, especially those who work from home. As a result the risk of health problems or injury to remote workers increases. Although paying attention to the proper ergonomics with remote workers is not ordinarily part of a wellness program, such attention can pay dividends in terms of employee well-being.

The Telework Learning Center in Fairfax, Virginia, collected data on the health and safety of teleworkers during a four-year period. Among the survey participants, 38 percent reported work-related discomfort, soreness, or pain. Problems occurred the most frequently in the back, wrist, neck, and shoulders. Those employees who telecommuted the most frequently were more likely to experience such pain. Preventive measures around such physical problems include the following:

1. *Select conscientious and responsible workers.* Some teleworkers predispose themselves to ergonomic injuries because they spend so much time in personal life using a keyboard, such as searching the Internet and accessing social media sites three hours per night. Because these several hours are added to the regular workload of keyboarding, injuries are likely to happen, such as carpal tunnel syndrome.
2. *Train on injury prevention.* The employer might offer a webinar on ergonomics safety at home, or launch a website about how to prevent injuries.[15]
3. *Inspect home offices, perhaps through self-evaluation.* Privacy issues limit employer inspections of the work area in the home used for telework. However, the employer might suggest that workers use an online self-evaluation process.

Table 10.1   Employee Wellness Program Initiatives and Some of the Problems they Attempt to Prevent

Medical Condition Oriented
- Giving employees financial incentives, usually in the form of lower health insurance premiums, for participating in wellness programs, including company-paid physical exams. Similarly, giving employees an opportunity to receive lifestyle coaching geared toward leading a healthy lifestyle.
- Providing financial incentives for keeping certain key health indicators, such as bad cholesterol level and weight, at acceptable levels. The financial incentive typically takes the form of lower health insurance premiums for being a non-smoker or having a body-mass index within the acceptable range.
- Periodic measurements of workers' weight, blood pressure, blood sugar, and cholesterol to identify warning signs of potential problems. For example, a worker whose blood pressure has risen might be encouraged to decrease the consumption of salt, lose weight, and participate in physical exercise with the goal of preventing a serious cardiac disease.
- Giving employees the opportunity to take an annual online health assessment and working on goals identified in the program (such as reducing stress levels), and reducing the cost of health insurance premiums for participating in the program.
- Offering free flu vaccines.
- Vision wellness program of offering prescription as well as non-prescription sunglasses to prevent retinal damage from ultraviolet rays.

Physical Activity Oriented
- Encouraging, including paying, employees to take a minimum of 7000 steps daily which reinforces the Center for Disease Control's recommendation of 30 minutes of daily physical activity in order to prevent a variety of chronic diseases. (Biometric instruments can be used to track participation, plus the use of a pedometer.)
- Pay-for-prevention model in which participants are rewarded for getting more physically active in ways that are pleasing to their lifestyle, including walking, dancing, swimming, yoga, or other physical activities.
- Encouraging employees to take a 10-minute recess during working hours in order to engage in physical activity such as jumping rope, playing tetherball, engaging in yoga, shooting a basketball, or riding a bicycle. (With this wellness initiative and similar programs, the company faces the challenge of providing on-premises showers, and encouraging employees to bring a change of clothing to the workplace.)
- Building an on-company-premises walking track and encouraging employees to use the track.
- Building an open central staircase with elevators tucked in a corner to promote the use of walking up and down stairs, thereby enhancing physical health through development of muscles and fewer problems of obesity.

- Participation in the Global Corporate Challenge to encourage employees to be less sedentary and participate in physical exercise. Participants are organized into teams, and receive a pedometer to count the steps they take, with a goal of 10,000 steps daily.
- The installation of walk-station devices that are low-speed treadmills with integrated desks and laptop hookups so employees can carry out tasks such as reading reports and making phone calls while physically exercising.
- The installation of standup desks would enable employees to be more physically active while working at the office.

Oriented Toward Providing Wellness Information
- Providing a modest financial incentive for attending a seminar on healthy eating, particularly for those employees whose current medical condition would make lowering blood pressure or weight reduction quite difficult.
- Disseminating wellness newsletters that contain information about staying healthy.
- Coaching employees about health issues either by telephone or a web-based program.

Source: The wellness initiatives above are based on information in the following sources: Susan J. Wells, "Get Moving: Give Employees Tools to Be Active, Even during the Workday," *HR Magazine*, September 12, 2012, pp. 30–36; Excess Scripts, "Behavior: The Decisive Factor for Better Health and Value," *Workforce Management*, April 2010, p. S6; Jeffrey Pfeffer, "Could We Manage Not to Damage People's Health?" *Harvard Business Review*, November 2011, p. 42; John Tuzzi, "The Doctor Will See You Now. And Now. And Now." *Bloomberg Businessweek*, May 20–May 26, 2013, pp. 27–28; Patricia Anstett, "Companies Push Employees to be Proactive About Health," *Detroit Free Press*, August 19, 2012.

TAKING THE INITIATIVE ON EMPLOYEE BENEFITS

Employee benefit programs are linked to talent management in the sense that benefits can be used to attract and retain employees. A recurring example is that the benefit of flexible working hours, including the opportunity to work remotely, is a major recruiting lure. An employee benefit initiative taken by Google Inc. illustrates how a proactive approach to an employee benefit can enhance employee satisfaction and productivity, and aid the physical environment at the same time.

Google owns and operates a fleet of 73 luxury double-decker buses, and also leases 26 others. On a daily basis, the fleet transports about 4500 employees, or about one-third of the employees at company headquarters, located in Mountain View, California. Although a major investment, the buses are an employee benefit that appears to save the company money.

The buses are equipped for computer use, including Internet access, that results in employees working an extra couple of hours commuting back and forth from work. Google also saves on real estate because underground parking spaces are expensive to construct. If Google had to build a parking space for each of the bus commuters, the cost would be about $400 million. Also, instead of parking spaces, more office space can be constructed at company headquarters.

Google has also made other investments in transportation to save on carbon emissions. During the day, if a Google employee needs to run an important errand, including picking up a sick child at school, the employee can use, at no cost, one of 52 electric and hybrid cars parked on campus. To encourage employees to drive electric-powered vehicles, Google management has installed 395 electric chargers.

Larry Page, CEO co-founder and CEO, is determined to find creative solutions to building a sustainable environment. He believes that the corporate world needs to operate in a way friendly to the environment, and is determined to build the first zero-carbon company in the United States. "Zero carbon" refers to being so energy efficient and using so much clean power that no greenhouse gas is emitted. Whether or not such a goal is possible is debatable. (For example, how much carbon-powered electricity is used throughout the world each day in searching Google?) In reference to Page's goal, Urs Hölzle, the senior vice-president who oversees the company's proactive approach to being green, says, "As we become a bigger users of energy, we wanted to make sure we were not part of the problem, but part of the solution."[16]

A smaller-scale example of proactivity in talent management (or at least human resource management) is for company management to deal proactively with the issue of restrooms for transgender employees. The reason that this subject calls for proactivity is that some employees believe that a person who has changed sex should not be permitted to use a company restroom designated for his or her new sex. (We use the term "sex" instead of "gender" because sex is a biological fact, whereas gender refers to a role – at least in technical terms.)

A report in *HR Magazine* notes that employers must be prepared to identify the restroom that transgender employees will use, and also to deal constructively with the concerns of coworkers. The issue is particularly emotionally intense after an employee announces his or her plan for gender reassignment surgery. The U.S. Occupational Safety and Health Administration regulations, as well as equivalent organizations in many other countries, stipulate that employers must follow federal sanitation standards by providing restrooms for all employees, regardless of their sexual expression or gender identity.

Taking proactive steps to foster an inclusive culture will aid employers in avoiding possible gender identity discrimination claims and possible lawsuits. The same report urges employers to ask sexually transitioning employees what restroom they are comfortable using and when. The employer can then discuss the transition period with other employees and enable coworkers to openly ask questions. One option is to suggest that the employee use the restroom reserved for his or her present gender. The transgender employee might be encouraged to use a single-user or unisex restroom. (Informal observation suggests that this works well in many workplaces.) However, the transgender employee cannot be forced to use the designated restroom because it might be interpreted as sex discrimination.

Another proactive step with respect to restrooms for transgender workers is for the employer to implement a policy of nondiscrimination and develop a training program that includes gender identity and gender expression to promote fair treatment of all employees.[17]

SUCCESSION PLANNING AND PROACTIVITY

In a well-managed organization, replacements for executives who quit, retire, or are dismissed are chosen through leadership succession, an orderly process of identifying and grooming people to replace managers. Succession planning is vital to the long-term health of an organization, and therefore an important responsibility of senior leadership. Instead of engaging in a flurry of activity after a key person leaves the organization, the planning is done in an orderly and proactive way over time. Succession planning anticipates a future in which one or more key people will no longer be with the organization, and takes constructive action about that possibility. A review of over 400 articles on the subject urged business firms to invest sufficient resources and attention toward succession planning to promote the long-term survival of the firm.[18]

According to Procter & Gamble CEO A. G. Lafley, planning for leadership succession is the most important activity of the company's board of directors. Nevertheless, boards and CEOs often neglect this major responsibility because other business matters seem more pressing at the time. When Lafley first took office as CEO of Procter & Gamble in 2000, the process of selecting and developing succession candidates began immediately.

In 2009, a company veteran, Robert A. McDonald, was appointed chief executive and president. When McDonald suddenly resigned in 2013, Lafley returned to the company as chairman and CEO.[19] (Although it seems like a twist in succession planning not to select an internal candidate, it shows that the board had a proven executive in mind to replace the current CEO should the need arise.) The goal was to develop a slate of strong internal CEO candidates, regularly. When the time therefore came to select one person for the CEO position, a group of plausible candidates would be available.

Here we glance at the problems often found in succession planning, then give a proactive and systematic method of improving leadership and management succession.

Problems with Succession Planning

A concern about succession planning is that it is often done poorly, which results in leaders who are a poor fit for their responsibilities. Ram Charan reports that two out of five CEOs fail in their first 18 months. The failure results from a variety of factors, such as making poor decisions about new products, demoralizing the organization, or engaging in highly unethical practices. One of the most important approaches to successful succession planning is to develop enough strong leaders within the company.[20]

Succession planning is also essential in family businesses, but often the process is avoided because it is so emotional. For example, it is difficult to tell someone that his or her sibling is better qualified to become CEO. Alexandra Solomon, who conducted a family business study, said that rather than being proactive, many family businesses treat the succession problem with denial. Solomon notes that a seamless succession is difficult with a plan, yet almost impossible without one.[21] Part of anticipating the future deals with how to deal with family members who are inactive in the business, yet might want to become active when a key family member leaves the business or dies.

Developing a Pool of Successors

Effective, proactive succession planning leaves the organization adequately prepared for expansion, the loss of a key employee, having a candidate available for a newly created position, and employee promotions. When succession planning is successful, it builds bench strength.[22] Developing a pool of successors is a key component of succession planning. The steps involved in developing a pool of successors (or succession management) follow:[23]

- Evaluate the extent of an organization's pending leadership shortage.
- Identify needed executive competences based on the firm's future business needs, values, and strategies.

- Identify high-potential individuals for possible inclusion in the pool, and assess these individuals to identify strengths and developmental needs to determine who will stay in the high-potential pool.
- Establish an individually tailored developmental program for each high-potential candidate that includes leadership development programs, job rotation, special assignments, and mentoring. Rising stars should be given the opportunity to change responsibilities every three to five years.
- Select and place people into senior jobs based on their performance, experience, and potential. While in these positions, the leaders should have access to board members, including making presentations. The managers develop a sense of what matters to directors, and directors get to see first hand the talent in the pipeline.
- Continuously monitor the program and give it top management support.

Developing a pool of candidates, therefore, combines evaluating potential with giving high-potential individuals the right type of developmental experiences. To the extent that these procedures are implemented, a leadership and management shortage in a given firm is less likely to take place.

To help preserve a strong pool of candidates for future assignments, financial services giant Aetna focuses on mentoring young managers with high potential. A specific program is that eight high-level Aetna managers, including chief executive Ronald Williams, meet one-on-one with eight target candidates for an hour each month for a year. To qualify, the protégés must have at least a decade of experience at the company and have received high performance evaluations.[24] IBM is another example of a company that has achieved positive results with its system of succession planning. When well-regarded CEO Sam Palmisano planned to retire at the end of 2011, three strong successors were available, with Virginia Rometty being chosen as CEO, beginning January 1, 2012. A highly placed executive recruiter, Dennis Carey, said that IBM had mastered the art of developing the next generation, and faced the problem of riches as opposed to the problem of poverty.[25]

SUGGESTIONS FOR APPLICATION

1. Talent management provides a wide opportunity for proactive thinking in order to enhance individual and organizational effectiveness in the many ways mentioned in this chapter. Another example is for an organization to take the initiative to establish rigorous and scientifically

based selection procedures. Effective selection procedures result in more employees who are a good fit for the organization and who perform well, thereby strengthening the organization.

2. A strongly proactive approach to recruiting is to keep searching to make contact with people who might have the talent the organization needs, even when a present recruiting need does not exist. In the words of Tom Bonney, the founder and managing director of financial consulting firm CMF Associates, a, "Even if I don't have a need, I am always looking."[26]

3. A bold, proactive approach to improving employee wellness is to prevent damaging employee health through negative management practices. According to Jeffrey Pfeffer, management's decisions contribute to mortality and morbidity as much as, if not more than, employees' own actions, such as not getting sufficient physical exercise. Among the negative practices he cites are:

- Layoffs have been shown to increase the risk of dying from cardiovascular accidents by 44 percent, and may also increase the risk of suicide.
- Long working hours may lead to accidents, high blood pressure, and many problems related to insufficient sleep.
- Failure to provide health insurance because many more of the uninsured are less likely to participate in preventive screenings, such as mammograms and cholesterol-level testing.
- Lack of control over one's job combined with high demands is a known contributor to job stress.[27]

The proactive step in relation to these problems would be for company leadership to minimize as many conditions and practices as possible that interfere with employee wellness.

SUMMARY

Proactivity is required to attain many of the goals of talent management. Employer branding represents the type of proactivity included in talent management. Employer brands target potential employees to project the image of the company as a desirable place to work.

Talent-management planning attempts to control the future. The planner attempts to make things happen by having the right number and right kinds of people at the right time. Workforce planning is proactive because it forecasts not only the number and type of employees to meet future business needs, but the ratio of internal to external resources and the skills mix. Scenario planning can be used to help human resource professionals visualize what types of workers their organization will need in the future. The same type of planning can suggest how to create the type of environment and organizational culture that will attract the needed workers.

Proactivity is frequently required for an organization to recruit the culturally and demographically diverse talented workers it wants and needs. These activities include (1) proactivity to appeal to a diverse customer base, (2) a corporate initiative to welcome LGBT employees, (3) a large-scale initiative to attract disabled workers, and (4) a training program for minority vendors.

A major strategy of talent management is to retain valuable employees, and any aspect of talent management can contribute to retention. One particularly proactive aspect of enhancing retention is to look for indicators of possible retention, and then intervene to prevent the turnover. One example is that an employee staying in the same position for more than three years can provoke turnover intentions. A major clue of attrition risk is when a worker becomes more quiet than usual.

A domain of human resource management based heavily on prevention and proactivity is the promotion of employee wellness. Focusing on wellness and prevention can lower healthcare costs. Table 10.1 summarizes the types of proactive interventions attempted in wellness programs. A basic initiative of an employee wellness program would be to ensure that employees had regular medical checkups to detect present or potential physical health problems. Another example of the proactivity of wellness programs is an attempt to prevent accidents among remote workers.

Employee benefit programs are linked to talent management in the sense that benefits, such as flexible working hours, can be used to attract and retain employees. The Google example of providing buses for transporting workers to and from work is an attractive benefit and also is geared toward environmental sustainability. A small example of proactivity in talent management is for company management to deal proactively with the issue of restrooms for transgender employees.

Succession planning is vital to the long-term health of an organization. Such planning anticipates a future in which one or more key people will no longer be with the organization, and takes constructive action about that possibility. A concern about succession planning is that it is often done poorly, which results in leaders who are a poor fit for their responsibilities. Effective, proactive succession planning leaves the organization adequately prepared for expansion, the loss of a key employee, and having a candidate available for a newly created position and employee promotion. Developing a pool of successors is a key component of succession planning.

Talent management provides a wide opportunity for proactive thinking to enhance individual and organization effectiveness in the many ways mentioned in this chapter. Rigorous selection methods are also important. A strongly proactive approach to recruiting is to keep searching to make contact with people who might have the talent the organization needs in the future. A bold, proactive approach to improving wellness is to prevent damaging employee health through negative management practices, such as layoffs and long working hours.

REFERENCES

1. Derek Stockley, "Talent Management Concept – Definition and Explanation," *www.derekstockely.com*. Retrieved May 29, 2013.
2. Joe Light, "Employer Branding," *The Wall Street Journal*, May 16, 2011, p. B9.
3. Sandeep K. Krishnan, "The Importance of 'Employer Branding'," *Deccan Herald* (www.deccdanherald.com), pp. 1–3. Retrieved May 28, 2013.
4. Fay Hansen, "Staffing Down to a Science," *Workforce Management*, April 21, 2008, p. 16.
5. Adrienne Fox, "At Work in 2020," *HR Magazine*, January 2010, p. 21.
6. Ed Frauheim, "Numbers Game," *Workforce Management*, March 2011, p. 20.
7. Quoted in Anna C. Davidson, "Verizon's Plan Scores," *Hispanic Business*, September 2010, p. 24.
8. Quoted and cited in Diane Cadrain, "Sexual Equity in the Workplace," *HR Magazine*, September 2008, p. 46; *Pride in Diversity IBM* (www.prideindiversity.com). Retrieved May 30, 2013.
9. Quoted in Susan J. Wells, "Counting on Workers with Disabilities," *HR Magazine*, April 2008, pp. 44–49. Quote is from p. 45.
10. Barbara Otto, "Walgreens Is Not Always the Answer," *HUFFPOST HOME* (www.huffingtonpost.com), January 12, 2013, pp. 1–2. Retrieved May 27, 2013.
11. Cotton Timberlake, "At Macys, the Many Colors of Cash," *Bloomberg Businessweek*, January 16–January 22, 2012, pp. 21–22.
12. Adrienne Fox, "Drive Turnover Down," *HR Magazine*, July 2012, pp. 22–27.
13. Cited in Geoff Colvin, "Health Care's New Maverick: Steward HealthCare Systems Is Building a Model for the Future," *Fortune*, April 13, 2012, p. 98.
14. Leonard Berry, Ann M. Mirabito, and William B. Baun, "What's the Hard Return on Employee Wellness Programs?" *Harvard Business Review*, December 2010, p. 106.
15. Ray Mauer, "Neglecting Ergonomics Safety for Teleworkers Can Be Costly," *HR Magazine*, September 2012, p. 12.
16. Quoted in Brian Dumaine, "Google's Zero-Carbon Quest," *Fortune*, July 23, 2012, pp. 75–76.

17. Patricia Graves, "How Should a Company Handle Issues Related to the Use of Workplace Restrooms for a Transgender Employee?" *HR Magazine*, August 2012, p. 28.

18. Ip Barry and Gabriel Jacobs, "Business Succession Planning: A Review of the Evidence," *Journal of Small Business and Enterprise Development*, Issue 3, 2006, pp. 326–350.

19. Michael J. de la Merced, "Abruptly, P& G Chief Ends Career of 33 Years," *The New York Times*, May 23, 2013 (www.nytimes.com), Retrieved May 23, 2013, pp. 1–2.

20. Ram Charan, "Ending the Succession Crisis," *Harvard Business Review*, February 2005, pp. 72–81; Ram Charan, *Leaders at All Levels* (San Francisco: Jossey-Bass, 2008).

21. Alexandra Solomon et al., "'Don't Lock Me Out': Life-Story Interviews of Family Business Owners Facing Succession," *Family Process*, No. 1, 2011, pp. 14–16; Alexander Macinnes, "Families Need Succession Plan Before It's too Late," *The Miami Herald* (www.miamiherald.com), June 19, 2011, pp. 1–2. Retrieved April 25, 2013.

22. Susan M. Heathfield, "Succession Planning," *About.com Human Resources* (http://humanresources.about.com), p. 1. Retrieved June 2, 2013.

23. William C. Byham, "Grooming Next-Millennium Leaders," *HR Magazine*, February 1999, pp. 46–50; Joseph Weber, "The Accidental CEO," *BusinessWeek*, April 23, 2007, p. 068.

24. Quoted in Victoria Barret, "Talent Search," *Forbes*, March 1, 2010, p. 26.

25. Katie Hoffman, "For Its 100th Birthday, Will IMB Get a New CEO?" *Bloomberg Businessweek*, June 13–June 19, 2011, pp. 22–23.

26. Cited in Chris Penttila, "Talent Scout," *Entrepreneur*, July 2008, p. 20.

27. Jeffrey Pfeffer, "Could We Manage Not to Damage People's Health?" *Harvard Business Review*, November 2011, p. 42.

11. Leadership influences on proactivity

A worker with a proactive personality is likely to engage in proactive behavior that enhances individual and organizational productivity. Yet the leader can also exert an important influence on the extent to which this proactivity emerges. Chapter 1 included a preliminary discussion of how the leader can enhance proactive behavior through such means as encouraging self-efficacy, providing workers with flexible work roles, granting empowerment and autonomy, and contributing to high-quality leader–member exchanges. A recent analysis of individual differences and leadership suggests that the leader has a role in developing proactivity among followers.[1]

Jenna Fagna, the president of Tequila Avión, illustrates how a leader can facilitate workers becoming more proactive. She says that as a younger manager she was too prescriptive by telling subordinates exactly what she wanted them to do. Gradually Fagna realized that workers achieve things in different ways. In her present leadership role, she attempts to step back and say, "Here's what we're going for. Just go and do it." Fagna has found that if she takes that approach, more times than not, the person will do much more than she expected. Equally important, the worker will be proactive enough to figure out a much better way to get the task done.[2]

In this final chapter of the book we describe how leaders influence worker proactivity from two broad perspectives: exerting charismatic and transformational leadership, and creating a climate for proactivity.

THE INFLUENCE OF CHARISMATIC AND TRANSFORMATIONAL LEADERSHIP

A charismatic leader has positive and compelling qualities that make others want to be led by that person. A transformational leader combines charisma with other qualities to bring about positive, major changes in the organization. As a result of these positive qualities, both charismatic and transformational leaders will often bring out the best in group members, including making it more likely that they will be proactive. Here we look at the possible links between charismatic and transformational leadership, and proactive behavior, separately.

Influence of Charismatic Leadership on the Proactive Personality and Behavior

As a starting point in thinking about how a leader's charisma might trigger proactivity in others, you are invited to personalize the meaning of charisma by responding to the checklist presented in Figure 11.1. To understand why charismatic leadership might facilitate proactivity among group members, it must be emphasized that charismatic leadership involves a relationship or interaction between the leader and the people being led. Furthermore, the people accepting the leadership must attribute charismatic qualities to the leader.[3]

The connection between leader vision and proactive performance

A major way in which a charismatic leader can trigger proactive behavior among subordinates is to express an exciting vision – the expression of an idealized image of the future based around organizational values.[4] Mark A. Griffin, Sharon K. Parker, and Claire M. Mason conducted a study that included how leader vision influences the change-oriented behavior of proactivity in the workplace. The study was conducted in a large public sector organization in Australia, responsible for providing scientific and technical services within the state's health sector. At the time, the organization was undergoing a transformational change in order to compete with private sector providers. Data of the study were conducted over two periods of time, with a final longitudinal sample of 102 employees.

Individual task proactivity was measured by asking study participants to describe how often they actively initiated change, such as "How often have you come up with ideas to improve the way in which your core tasks are done?" Responses ranged from 1 (*very little*) to 5 (*a great deal*). A key moderating variable in the study was role breadth self-efficacy, referring to employees' perceived capability of carrying out a broader set of work tasks. (This same factor was described in Chapter 1 as an influence on proactive behavior.) Employees rated how confident they would feel carrying out a range of interpersonal and integrative tasks beyond their technical job, such as contacting customers and suppliers to discuss problems, and designing new work procedures.

Leader vision was measured by asking respondents if the leader (a) "creates an exciting and attractive image of where the organization is going," (b) "has a clear understanding of where the organization is headed in the future," and (c) "expresses a clear direction for the future

Listed below are a variety of characteristics and behaviors often associated with leaders who are perceived to be charismatic, as well as with other people who are not in formal leadership roles. Indicate whether each characteristic or behavior appears to be representative of you. It may be helpful for another person who has observed you frequently, including coworkers, family members, and others in your network to rate you also. When agreement exists with your self-rating and the rating of another person it suggests that the rating might be accurate.

No.	Characteristic or behavior	My rating		Other person's rating	
		Yes	No	Yes	No
1.	Several people at least have told me that I am charismatic.	❏	❏	❏	❏
2.	I have a solid, firm handshake.	❏	❏	❏	❏
3.	I treat everyone as if he or she were very important.	❏	❏	❏	❏
4.	I give many sincere compliments to people.	❏	❏	❏	❏
5.	I have created a vision for at least one group to which I have belonged.	❏	❏	❏	❏
6.	I express my emotions freely to group members.	❏	❏	❏	❏
7.	I inspire trust and confidence in others.	❏	❏	❏	❏
8.	I make ample use of true stories in dealing with others.	❏	❏	❏	❏
9.	I am considered to be a candid person.	❏	❏	❏	❏
10.	I think big with respect to what my group can accomplish.	❏	❏	❏	❏
11.	I smile frequently even when I am not in a happy mood.	❏	❏	❏	❏
12.	I am willing to take personal risks.	❏	❏	❏	❏
13.	I demonstrate to others that I am passionate about what I want them to accomplish.	❏	❏	❏	❏
14.	I am quite an energetic person.	❏	❏	❏	❏
15.	I am usually successful in maintaining an optimistic attitude even when events are not going well.	❏	❏	❏	❏
16.	My posture is quite good when I am with another person or a group.	❏	❏	❏	❏
17.	I make frequent use of analogies and metaphors when I am with other people. (An example: "We are as strong and likable as a Panda bear.")	❏	❏	❏	❏
18.	I like to tell true stories to motivate others.	❏	❏	❏	❏
19.	I thank people frequently, even the members of my own group.	❏	❏	❏	❏
20.	I challenge other people intellectually.	❏	❏	❏	❏

Note: scoring and interpretation: if "yes" is the accurate response for 15 or more of these statements, you are probably perceived by many others to be charismatic.

Source: Statement 13 is based on John Antonakis, Markika Fenley, and Sue Liechti, "Learning Charisma," *Harvard Business Review*, June 2012, p. 129.

Figure 11.1   Checklist of charismatic behaviors

of the unit." Responses ranged from 1 (*strongly agree*) to 5 (*strongly disagree*).

A key result of the study relevant to our purposes here is that a strong leader vision, as well as role breadth self-efficacy for subordinates, led to later proactive worker behavior. The positive influence of role breadth self-efficacy only came about when the leader had a strong vision. An implication of the study offered by the team of researchers is that leaders can motivate more proactivity among subordinates by presenting a clear and compelling vision of the future that differs from what exists in the present. For the vision to have a strong impact, it is also necessary to assure that workers have high role breadth self-efficacy.[5]

To help focus on the nature of a compelling and discrepant (different from the present) vision, consider the following two examples that have had a major impact on the world of commerce:

- In 1992, a man named Jeff Bezos was a senior vice-president for the hedge fund D.E. Shaw. He developed a dream, or vision, of a company that would sell books on the Internet. His boss thought the idea was good, but better suited for someone who didn't have a good job. Within 48 hours, Bezos quit so he could carry out his vision of founding Amazon.com.
- In 1981, engineer Narayana Murthy had a vision of India competing with other countries in the industrial world by taking on the software development work that had long been the exclusive domain of the West. As one of six co-founders of Infosys and its CEO for 21 years, Murthy helped ignite the outsourcing revolution that has brought billions of dollars in wealth to India, and established the country as a player in the field of outsourcing internationally.[6]

The impact of charismatic leadership on followers' initiative taking
As described in Chapter 3, taking the initiative is a major component of proactive behavior. A study conducted with 543 physicians and nurses in German hospitals confirmed the idea that charismatic leadership is associated with initiative taking by subordinates. Charismatic leadership, as measured by questionnaires, was associated with initiative taking by members of the leaders' professional staff. As in other studies, it was also found that when leaders granted more autonomy to staff members, the link between leader charisma and initiative taking by subordinates was even stronger. An implication drawn from the study is that an effective way to bring about initiative taking by staff members would be to train leaders in behaving charismatically.[7] Although there is a strong personality component to charisma, many of its component behaviors (such as

those presented in Figure 11.1) can be developed. For example, a leader can learn to talk about a vision for the group, give more compliments, smile more frequently, and use positive, forceful nonverbal communication such as good posture.

The charismatic leader acting as a model of proactivity for group members
A major reason a leader is perceived to be charismatic is that he or she has a constellation of traits and behaviors that many people find to be positive and agreeable. As a result of being agreeable or well liked, constituents tend to regard the leader as a model to follow. The leader is therefore in a position to bring to the surface the proactive tendencies of workers who model the leader, providing that the leader is proactive. The leader becomes a model of proactive behavior by acting in ways such as the following:

- Frequently talking about new opportunities and challenges for the group.
- Pointing to events and equipment in the organizational unit that could profit from change.
- Reducing costs within the organizational unit before higher-level management mandates such reductions.
- Requesting that group members be on the alert for talented people that could become members of the unit in the future.
- Introducing a creative idea to the group.

The leader being a model of proactive thinking and behavior is likely to be influential because modeling has been long known to be an effective influence tactic. When a model is attractive, competent, and successful, the probability increases that the model's behavior will be imitated by others.[8]

The association between leader proactive personality and perceptions of charisma
Although the focus here is how charisma may facilitate proactive behavior in others, it completes the picture to recognize that a leader who is more proactive is more likely to be perceived as charismatic. J. Michael Crant and Thomas S. Bateman conducted a study with 156 dyads of managers and their immediate managers at a Puerto Rican financial services organization to examine the link between a proactive personality and perceived charisma. As part of the study, the 156 managers completed a test of proactive personality, whereas the managers' immediate supervisors rated their charismatic leadership and in-role behavior (expected job performance). The results suggested that self-reported proactive personality is positively associated with independent ratings by supervisors of charis-

matic leadership. The results also showed that charismatic leadership was associated with job performance.[9]

Influence of Transformational Leadership on Proactive Personality and Behavior

The transformational leader is characterized by a focus on bringing about positive, major changes by moving constituents beyond their self-interests and toward the good of the group, the organization, or society. The essence of transformational leadership is developing and transforming people.[10] It is therefore within the scope of a transformational leader's influence to foster proactivity among group members.

Two studies reported together, Deanne N. Den Hartog and Frank D. Belshack sought to explore how transformational leadership, along with role breadth self-efficacy and job autonomy, enhances employee proactive behavior. The studies were conducted in the Netherlands, with 69 companies participating in one study and 59 in the other. The participants had a variety of professional backgrounds and worked in industries such as retail, government, finance, and consultancy.

Ratings of work behavior were made by both colleagues and supervisors. Altogether 308 employee–supervisor or employee pairs participated in the study. In both studies transformational leader behavior, job autonomy, and role breadth self-efficacy were measured by questionnaires, and proactive behavior was measured by self-ratings, peer ratings, and supervisor ratings. Transformational leadership was measured in terms of perceptions by a subordinate, not self-ratings by the leader.

The study focused on proactive behavior rather than proactive personality. However, a proactive personality is often the driver of proactive behavior. In Study 1, proactive behavior was measured in terms of initiative. In Study 2, proactive behavior was measured in terms of prosocial proactive behavior. A sample item measuring prosocial proactivity was, "At work, this employee takes the initiative to share knowledge with colleagues."

In line with previous research, the authors of the study found a positive relationship between transformational leadership and proactive behavior. It was also found that employees were more proactive when they experienced a higher degree of job autonomy. The specific finding was that in situations of high autonomy, transformational leadership is associated positively with proactive behavior for those individuals who have high role breadth self-efficacy. (The researchers categorize this complex finding as a three-way interaction among the variables of transformational leadership, autonomy, and self-efficacy.)

The results therefore emphasize the importance of transformational leadership for bringing about proactive worker behavior. Yet, job autonomy and role breadth self-efficacy are also contributors to proactive behavior.[11] Perhaps a transformational leader has the insight to grant more leeway to group members to help encourage their proactivity.

CREATING A CLIMATE FOR PROACTIVITY

The thesis of this book and the writing of many scholars and businesspeople that employee proactivity enhances individual and organization productivity, suggest that leaders should work toward establishing a climate for proactivity. Several leadership initiatives already mentioned in Chapter 1, such as granting more job autonomy and establishing a climate for creativity, help create an organizational climate that fosters proactive behavior. In general, a satisfying work environment will foster a willingness in many employees to look to prevent problems and find new ways to improve performance. The checklist presented in Figure 11.2 provides a sampling of characteristics of a satisfying work environment.

Read the following characteristics of a satisfying work environment. Respond "Yes" or "No" as to whether the characteristic generally applies to your present or most recent place of work.

No.	Statement	Yes	No
1.	Company leadership acts like they believe human resources are their most valuable asset.	❑	❑
2.	Most employees seem to trust top-level management.	❑	❑
3.	Most employees seem to trust each other.	❑	❑
4.	Workers appear to be satisfied with their employee benefits.	❑	❑
5.	Pay and other forms of compensation appear to be fair.	❑	❑
6.	Employees generally feel that they are part of a team.	❑	❑
7.	Employees are encouraged to offer suggestions and complaints.	❑	❑
8.	Employees can generally get the information they need to do their job.	❑	❑
9.	Employees can generally get the information they need to satisfy their curiosity about possible developments in the company.	❑	❑
10.	There are plenty of opportunities for promotion from within.		
11.	Employees who are not part of top-level management are not made to feel as if they are second-class citizens.	❑	❑
12.	Managers accept the fact that sometimes family and personal life responsibilities take priority over work responsibilities.	❑	❑
13.	There are good opportunities for skill development and other forms of new learning.	❑	❑
14.	Employees in all roles receive ample appreciation and recognition.	❑	❑
15.	Positive feedback occurs regularly.	❑	❑
16.	As you walk around the company, you see a lot of people smiling.	❑	❑

17.	Employees do not rely exclusively on e-mail, texting, and company websites, but sometimes talk with each other in person or by phone.	❏ ❏
18.	When you have a problem with your work, there is almost always somebody to go to for help.	❏ ❏
19.	Low-performing employees are given a chance to improve. However, if they do not improve, they are likely to lose their job.	❏ ❏
20.	We have opportunities for advancement for talented and ambitious employees.	❏ ❏
21.	Most employees appear to take pride in their work.	❏ ❏
22.	Most employees I meet take pride in working for this organization.	❏ ❏
23.	It is fairly typical for employees in the company to recruit their friends to work here.	❏ ❏
24.	Turnover seems quite low in comparison with other companies.	❏ ❏
25.	A lot of employees consider their job to be exciting.	❏ ❏
26.	Management does not make excessive use of favoritism.	❏ ❏
27.	You don't see much backstabbing in our organization.	❏ ❏
28.	The workforce is culturally diverse, including higher-level positions.	❏ ❏
29.	Job loss is not much of a worry in this company.	❏ ❏
30.	Cost cutting appears to be done only when absolutely necessary.	❏ ❏

Note: interpretation: if you responded "yes" to 25 or more of the above statements, you work, or did work, in a rewarding, satisfying environment in which large numbers of problems are prevented. Also, this type of environment will encourage many workers to be proactive. Responding "yes" to between 11 and 24 statements suggests that your work environment is typical with respect to being satisfying. If you responded "yes" to 10 or fewer statements, you have an unsatisfying work environment in which not enough problems are prevented, and many workers will feel hesitant to be proactive.

Keep one caution in mind in interpreting these scores. If you are highly optimistic or highly pessimistic (and a chronic complainer), your perception might be too biased to allow an accurate analysis of this type.

Figure 11.2   A checklist for characteristics of a satisfying work environment

In this section we describe four key strategies and tactics that contribute to a climate for proactivity: the hiring of high-asset, proactive employees the encouragement of worker initiative; the encouragement of whistleblowing; and the facilitation of employee engagement.

The Hiring of High-Asset, Proactive Employees

As emphasized by Adam M. Grant and Susan J. Ashford, proactive employees act in advance of problems, and they intend to change things and have a positive impact.[12] If the organization contains enough of these proactive workers, the climate of the organization is likely to become one that fosters proactivity. An analogy is that if you have a critical mass of serious and intelligent students in a school, the climate for learning will be enhanced. A key leadership strategy for creating a climate that favors pro-activity would therefore be to hire employees with proactive personalities and a past record of proactive behavior. Evidence of having demonstrated proactivity would therefore be a useful selection factor. An employment test measuring tendencies toward having a proactive personality might also be included in the selection methods, providing the test had been properly validated.

An example of a specific method of employee selection that is likely to find proactive employees is the hiring of *asset employees*, as described by Matthew Beecher.[13] An "asset employee" refers to a person who is likely to improve the organization – a primary characteristic of the proactive worker. The hiring manager would focus on the strengths and skills of the applicant that may enhance a specific department. Beecher emphasizes that average employees typically meet job requirements but choose not to exceed them. Although they may have strengths that could propel them toward superior performance, they lack the motivation to capitalize on these strengths.

In contrast, the best employees are assets because they exceed their pay grade in value and contributions. Being proactive, asset employees continually improve the organization. These employees use their talents to correct inefficiencies and reduce expenses. At the same time they strengthen the corporate climate and culture by fostering teamwork and a respect for a strong work ethic. In summary, asset employees who are selected into the organization will often accomplish the following:

- Enhance organizational productivity.
- Use nearly all work time, including downtime, to advance the company, such as attempting to bring past customers back or looking for a few cost savings.
- Advance the company's culture, such as finding ways to appropriately encourage and compliment coworkers.
- Give the best effort to complete work assignments.

During the hiring process, asset employees can provide specific examples of how they improved a previous organization or organizational unit. Sample interview questions for helping to determine consistent use of strengths, and proactivity, are as follows: (1) At your previous job, how important was your role in helping the company make a profit? (2) How have your personal strengths directly improved your prior places of employment? (3) What are two problems you worked on in the past without the prompting of your boss? Please describe your action steps in those situations.

The interviewer observations should be supplemented with discussions with prior managers and coworkers about the candidate's use of strength and initiative taking. Quite often such information is difficult to attain because of privacy issues, and the concerns that many people have about the legal implications of saying something negative about a past employee. In many cases these concerns about legal issues are unfounded but that does not overcome the hesitancy of many people to comment negatively about the characteristics and behaviors of a former worker at any job level.

The Encouragement of Worker Initiative

In Chapter 1, it was explained how employee initiative can be fostered when a worker has control over the job, including a feeling of job autonomy, a climate of risk taking, and participative leadership. Earlier in this chapter a study was described suggesting that charismatic leadership facilitates initiative. Here the focus is on how the organizational climate can encourage the initiative aspect of proactive behavior, thereby enhancing organizational productivity. Leaders play a key role in establishing the organizational climate.

Climate for initiative

As the concept is advanced by Markus Baer and Michael Frese, the climate for initiative refers to formal and informal practices and procedures that support a proactive and self-starting approach to work that is sustained through persistence. Worker initiative is closely related to taking-charge behavior. Research suggests that top-level management support for an overall climate of initiative contributes substantially to workers taking the initiative.

The analysis of Baer and Frese indicates that the climate for initiative is positively related to organizational performance. For example, initiative taking by a large number of employees might result in new product ideas, the improvement of work processes, and cost savings. Specific mechanisms for bringing about personal initiative include (1) company leadership and coworkers allowing and encouraging personal initiative of individuals and groups; (2) individuals and groups feeling responsible for their work; (3) workers exercising more discretion in how they perform their jobs; and (4) employees working on their ideas longer and more intensely in order to convert them into useful suggestions.

The payoff to the organization from more initiative taking includes new ideas, smoother processes for production and services, better implementation of innovations, and, ultimately, better performance. To attain such ends it is helpful for managers to state and show by deeds that mistakes for having tried will be tolerated. For example, at a sports clothing manufacturer, a swimsuit designer convinced top management that a unisex swimsuit, much like the swimsuits of 60 years ago, would have a large market today because of the interest in androgynous clothing and appearance. The line met with almost no demand in the market. The CEO explained to the designer, "Shrug it off. Mishits are inevitable in the fashion world."

In a climate favoring initiative, actions are taken to prevent problems and errors that lead to serious disruptions in production. Also, actions and ideas that enhance production are self-started even if nobody is around to provide assistance or give orders. The same type of climate encourages tackling problems and difficulties with persistence. For these reasons, a climate that enhances initiative would increase organizational performance.

Another argument in favor of a climate for initiative is that the climate might function as a contingency variable that supports process innovations to their full potential. (An organizational process innovation is a deliberate and novel attempt to change a product or process.) Initiative taking is important because when a new process is introduced unexpected problems may arise, calling for initiative to fix the problem. A leadership tactic in reference to establishing the right climate for fixing unanticipated problems would be to tell workers in advance they have a key role to play in dealing with unanticipated problems. For example, a distributor of DVDs introduced a complicated, automated telephone-ordering system whereby a customer could order DVDs by number or title without speaking to a person. The supervisor alerted the workers in advance to please spot any problems and recommend a solution. One of the supervisor's comments was, "The IT people cannot work out all the glitches by themselves. We need your help."

Baer and Frese backed up the above analysis with a study of 47 mid-sized German companies. Initiative was measured by a questionnaire, with a sample item being, "People in our company usually do more than they are asked to do." The performance measures used were achievement of company goals and return on assets. Company goal achievement included the company achieving its own goals and in comparison with direct competitors. The results showed that the climate for initiative was related to both goal achievement and improvement in return on assets over time.[14]

The initiative-freeing organizational form to encourage initiative

Isaac Getz conducted intensive interviews with leaders at 18 American and European companies that encourage initiative to the extreme. The specific type of organization studied was labeled the *F-form* – an organizational form in which employees have complete freedom and responsibility to take action they, not their managers, decide is best. Examples of these organizations include W.L. Gore & Associates, USAA, IDEO, SAS Institute, and Oticon. Across the business firms studied, successful F-form adoption yielded financial performance that placed the companies at the top or near the top of their industry.

For the F-form organization to be adopted, a liberating style of leadership had to be implemented by the head of the company. Five leadership practices found in the F-form organization are listed next:

1. *Liberating leaders create an environment for intrinsic equality.* Listening to employees rather than telling them what to do is a major driver of equality. Intrinsic equality is also attained by removing certain work practices that did not satisfy workers' needs for equality, such as time-recording devices, locked supply closets, private offices for executives, hierarchical organizational charts, and titles or ranks.
2. *Liberating leaders share their world-class vision of the company so employees will feel ownership of the vision.* Widespread dissemination of the vision helps employees know what is in the best interests of the company so they can direct their initiative in the right direction. For example, if the company wants to be a leader in on-time delivery, employees will know that they should take the initiative to prevent problems that could create late deliveries.
3. *Liberating leaders create an environment that satisfies people's need to grow.* Creating an environment for personal growth, such as paying for employees to take classes outside of work, helps them feel intrinsically equal. As a result, employees are more willing to take the initiative to serve customers in the same fashion they would like to be served.
4. *Liberating leaders create an environment that satisfies people's need to self-direct.* Satisfying the need to self-direct increases work motivation, including a willingness to find problems and resolve them. For example, at the financial services firm USAA, the environment that facilitates self-direction includes the authority to spend whatever time service representatives think is necessary to solve a customer's problem, whether it is business or personal. Employees respond with self-motivated actions for the benefit of the customer, leading to more success for USAA.
5. *Liberating leaders become the culture keepers.* A key role for the liberating leader is to maintain a culture in which employees direct themselves and take the initiative to solve problems. An example of culture maintenance would be for company leaders to regularly ask employees what they need to do their jobs better.[15]

The Encouragement of Whistleblowing

An extremely proactive step for an employee to take is to bring to higher-level management's attention wrongdoing within the organization. Whistleblowing is particularly useful to higher-level management if the whistleblower reports the wrongdoing to company leadership rather than to an outside agency. In this way higher-level management might be able to resolve the problem before it becomes a crisis because the problem is reported to the outside world. The major step organizational leadership can take to encourage whistleblowing is to be supportive of employees who report legitimate instances of wrongdoing, such as price fixing, sexual harassment, theft, and accepting bribes from contractors.

An analysis of many studies of whistleblowing by social scientists and legal scholars led Marcia P. Miceli, Janet P. Near, and Terry Morehead Dworkin to several conclusions about effective methods for encouraging employees to report wrongdoing:

1. *Conduct training.* Companies should teach managers and employees how to deal with concerns about wrongdoing without fear of retaliation. A useful model is the widespread company training about preventing sexual harassment.
2. *Establish formal mechanisms for reporting wrongdoing.* Establishing ethics hotlines or having an organizational culture that welcomes employee feedback demonstrates to employees that it is acceptable and safe to bring forth concerns.
3. *Offer financial incentives.* Reward systems that provide incentives for accurate whistleblowing would not only reduce employee concerns about retaliation, but boost proactivity by making it financially rewarding. An example of an appropriate financial incentive would be a percentage of savings recovered through whistleblowing, such as the company recovering embezzled funds.

To prevent indiscriminate whistleblowing, all reports of wrongdoing should be investigated fully and fairly.[16] One complaint of wrongdoing should not be regarded as a conviction.

The Facilitation of Employee Engagement

As mentioned in Chapter 4, engaged workers are more likely to direct their proactivity toward high performance. Here we look at a fundamental way in which leaders can facilitate worker engagement that results in proactive behavior that benefits the organization. The leadership approach to facilitating engagement is to interact directly with managers at lower levels in the organization or directly with employees. The frontline managers include manufacturing supervisors, heads of research and development, sales managers, and customer service managers. According to experienced turnaround manager, Fred Hassan, CEOs and other executives should conduct face-to-face conversations with small groups of frontline managers on a regular basis. These conversations provide company leadership with timely, unfiltered information about what is happening in the business. The same information can be useful for quickly spotting problems and opportunities.

When the people directly responsible for supervising the vast majority of a company's employees are engaged, the result is a charged-up organization with frontline managers being proactive about making suggestions for improvement and spotting problems. An example is that the sales manager at a Russian division of Schering Plough reported the problem of how long it took to get corporate approval to assign a company car to a sales representative. As a consequence, sales force productivity suffered as sales reps took trains and buses to visit customers, and some joined competitors who promised immediate use of a company vehicle.[17]

LifeGift is a not-for-profit company that recovers organs and tissues. Proactivity by employees to search diligently for donors is essential to carrying out the company's mission. To enhance employee engagement, company managers initiate quarterly one-on-one discussions with each of their employees about any subject of interest to the workers. As measured by a survey tool from LeadershipIQ, worker engagement has increased through these discussions. It appears that worker persistence in terms of searching for donors was also enhanced.[18]

SUGGESTIONS FOR APPLICATION

1. Many different approaches to developing charisma have been proposed. One of the more effective, easy-to-implement techniques to develop charisma is to maintain eye contact. A person who maintains eye contact with another person without crossing over into staring will create a positive impression. Maintaining steady eye contact suggests a healthy self-image. Steady eye contact also projects self-confidence, which is important because charismatic people are typically self-confident. A person who can look you directly in the eye and keep the conversation running smoothly appears to be open and not attempting to shade the truth.

Begin practicing good eye contact in a non-threatening environment such as with family and friends. Later you can develop your skill further by maintaining eye contact with people who do not know you well, including those encountered at networking events, and store associates.[19]

2. Creating an appealing vision can facilitate the proactive behavior of constituents. It is therefore worth a leader's effort to develop an appealing and compelling vision. Information from sources such as the following is useful in crafting a vision.

- Your own intuition about developments in your field, the market you serve, and the preferences of your constituents.
- A group discussion of what it takes to delight the people your group serves.
- Websites, annual reports, management books, and business magazines to find the type of vision statements formulated by others.
- For a vision of the organizational unit, support the organization's visions so you can match the vision of your unit to that created by organizational leadership.[20]

3. Research evidence suggests that the most effective leadership approach to facilitating proactive behavior among subordinates is for the leader to be laid back and introverted rather than emphasizing his or her outgoing and extraverted qualities. The authors of the study in question, Adam M. Grant, Francesca Gino, and David A. Hofmann, sent questionnaires to managers and their employees at 130 franchises of a U.S. pizza delivery company. Managers were asked to rate their own extent of extraversion. Employees were asked to estimate how often they and their coworkers "try to bring about improved procedures," among other proactive behaviors. Data were also collected on store profitability, yet controlling for location such as being close to a college campus. (A laboratory study was also conducted about extraverted leaders and proactive employees, finding comparable results.) Among the findings in the pizza franchise study that provide clues to the best leadership approach to proactive employees were the following:

- In stores where employees were below average in proactive personality, extraverted leadership was associated with 16 percent higher profits than average.
- In stores where employees offered ideas, extraverted leadership was associated with 14 percent lower profits.

A key conclusion drawn from the study is that when employees are proactive, extraverted leadership is associated with lower performance. The problem is that extraverted leaders may attempt to come up with most of the ideas for improvement themselves, rather than listening carefully to employee suggestions. Furthermore, with proactive employees leaders need to be receptive to suggestions from the group. When employees are not proactive, extraverted leadership was associated with higher group performance. The implication is that with less proactive group members, the leader needs to act more demonstratively and set a clear direction.[21]

SUMMARY

The leader can exert an important influence on the extent to which worker proactivity emerges.

Both charismatic and transformational leaders will often bring out the best in group members, including proactivity. One reason is that charismatic leadership involves a relationship or interaction between the leader and group members.

A major way in which a charismatic leader can trigger proactive behavior among subordinates is to express an exciting vision. A study showed that a strong leader vision, as well as role breadth self-efficacy for subordinates, led to later proactive worker behavior. However, the positive influence of role breadth self-efficacy only came about when the leader had a strong vision.

A study conducted in German hospitals confirmed the idea that charismatic leadership is associated with initiative taking by subordinates. When leaders granted more autonomy to staff members, the link between leader charisma and initiative taking by subordinates was even stronger.

The leader is in a position to bring to the surface the proactive tendencies of workers who model the behavior of a proactive leader. The leader becomes a model of proactive behavior by acting in ways such as frequently talking about opportunities and challenges for the group, and introducing a creative idea to the group. A leader who is more proactive is more likely to be perceived as charismatic. A study showed that self-perceived proactive personality is positively associated with independent ratings of charismatic leadership by supervisors.

It is within the scope of a transformational leader's influence to foster proactivity among group members. A study found a positive relationship between transformational leadership and proactive behavior, and that employees were more proactive when they experienced a higher degree of autonomy. Specifically, in situations of high autonomy, transformational leadership is associated positively with proactive behavior for workers with high role breadth self-efficacy.

Four key strategies and tactics that contribute to a climate for proactivity are (a) the hiring of high asset, proactive employees, (b) the encouragement of worker initiative, (c) the encouragement of whistleblowing, and (d) the facilitation of worker engagement. The encouragement of worker initiative includes establishing a climate for initiative, and using the initiative-freeing organizational form. A fundamental leadership approach to facilitating engagement is to interact directly with managers at organizational levels, as well as with employees.

One of the most effective, easy-to-implement techniques of developing charisma is to maintain eye contact. Creating an appealing vision can facilitate the proactive behavior of constituents. Research evidence suggests that the most effective leadership approach to facilitating proactive behavior among subordinates is for the leader to be laid back and introverted rather than emphasizing outgoing and extraverted qualities.

REFERENCES

1. John Antonakis, David D. Day, and Birgit Schyns, "Leadership and Individual Differences: At the Cusp of a Renaissance," *Leadership Quarterly*, August 2012, p. 645.
2. Cited in Adam Bryant, "Here's My Vision, and Here's Yours. Let's Make It Work," *The New York Times* (www.nytimes.com), June 1, 2013, p. 2. Retrieved June 6, 2013.
3. Andrew J. DuBrin, *Leadership: Research Findings, Practice, and Skills*, 8th edition (Mason, OH: South-Western/Cengage Learning, 2013), p. 74.
4. Alannah E. Rafferty and Mark A. Griffin, "Dimensions of Transformational Leadership: Conceptual and Empirical Extensions," *Leadership Quarterly*, June 2004, p. 332.
5. Mark A. Griffin, Sharon K. Parker, and Claire M. Mason, "Leader Vision and the Development of Adaptive and Proactive Performance: A Longitudinal Study," *Journal of Applied Psychology*, January 2010, pp. 174–182.
6. John A. Byrne, "Great Ideas Are Hard to Come By," *Fortune*, August 8, 2012, pp. 69, 84.
7. Sabine Boerner and Elisabeth Dütschke, "The Impact of Charismatic Leadership on Followers' Initiative-Oriented Behavior: A Study in German Hospitals," *Health Care Management Review*, Issue 4, October/December 2008, pp. 332–340.
8. Charles C. Manz and Henry P. Sims, Jr., "Vicarious Learning: The Influence of Modeling on Organizational Behavior," *Academy of Management Review*, January 1981, pp. 105–113.
9. J. Michael Crant and Thomas S. Bateman, "Charismatic Leadership Viewed from Above: The Impact of Proactive Personality," *Journal of Organizational Behavior*, February 2000, pp. 63–75.
10. Marshal Sashkin and Molly G. Sashkin, *Leadership that Matters: The Critical Factors for Making a Difference in People's Lives and Organizations' Success* (San Francisco: Berrett-Koehler, 2003).

11. Deanne N. Den Hartog and Frank D. Belschak, "When Does Transformational Leadership Enhance Employee Behavior? The Role of Autonomy and Role Breadth Self-Efficacy," *Journal of Applied Psychology*, January 2012, pp. 194–202.
12. Adam M. Grant and Susan J. Ashford, "The Dynamics of Proactivity at Work," *Research in Organizational Behavior*, Volume 28, pp. 3–34.
13. Matthew Beecher, "Only Assets Need Apply," *HR Magazine*, November 2011, pp. 84–85.
14. Markus Baer and Michael Frese, "Innovation is Not Enough: Climates for Initiative and Psychological Safety, Process Innovations, and Firm Performance," *Journal of Organizational Behavior*, Volume 24, Number 1, 2003, pp. 45–68. The analysis follows closely from Baer and Frese, but the examples are original.
15. Isaac Getz, "Liberating Leadership: How the Initiative-Freeing Radical Organization Form Has Been Successfully Adopted," *California Management Review*, Summer 2009, pp. 32–58.
16. Marcia P. Miceli, Janet P. Near, and Terry Morehead Dworkin, "A Word to the Wise: How Managers and Policy-Makers Can Encourage Employees to Report Wrongdoing," *Journal of Business Ethics*, Volume 86, 2009, pp. 379–396.
17. Fred Hassan, "The Frontline Advantage," *Harvard Business Review*, May 2011, pp. 106–114.
18. Garry Kranz, "Losing Lifeblood," *Workforce Management*, July 2011, pp. 24–25.
19. Chukwuma Asala, "How to Develop Charisma," *Gaebler Resources for Entrepreneurs* (www.gaebler.com), p. 2. Retrieved June 5, 2013.
20. A couple of ideas in this list are based on "Nailing Down Your Vision: 8 Steps," *Executive Leadership*, September 2007, p. 2.
21. Adam M. Grant, Francesca Gino, and David A. Hofmann, "The Hidden Advantages of Quiet Bosses," *Harvard Business Review*, December 2010, p. 28; Carmen Nobel, "Introverts: The Best Leaders for Proactive Employees," *Harvard Business School Working Knowledge* (http://hbs.edu), October 4, 2010, pp. 1–3; Adam M. Grant, Francesca Gino, and David A. Hofmann, "Reversing the Extraverted Leadership Advantage: The Role of Employee Proactivity," *Academy of Management Journal*, June 2011, pp. 528–550. Retrieved May 23, 2013.

Name index

Subject index